HANDS ON C++ (UNIX/GNU C++ VERSION)

Joel Adams
Department of Mathematics and Computer Science
Calvin College

Laboratory Manual

C++: AN INTRODUCTION TO COMPUTING

Joel Adams
Sanford Leestma
Larry Nyhoff

Prentice Hall, Englewood Cliffs, New Jersey 07632

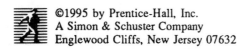 ©1995 by Prentice-Hall, Inc.
A Simon & Schuster Company
Englewood Cliffs, New Jersey 07632

Printed in the United States of America

10 9 8 7 6 5 4 3

ISBN   0-13-359456-4

Prentice-Hall International (UK) Limited, London
Prentice-Hall of Australia Pty. Limited, Sydney
Prentice-Hall Canada Inc., Toronto
Prentice-Hall Hispanoamericana, S.A., Mexico
Prentice-Hall of India Private Limited, New Delhi
Prentice-Hall of Japan, Inc., Tokyo
Simon & Schuster Asia Pte. Ltd., Singapore
Editora Prentice-Hall do Brasil, Ltda., Rio de Janeiro

Table of Contents

Preface

There is an old Chinese proverb that reads:

> *I hear and I forget,*
> *I see and I remember,*
> *I do and I understand.*

The proverb points out that human learning (or understanding) is best accomplished as an active, hands-on process involving a variety of our senses. In recognition of this, computing has increasingly become a laboratory discipline, in which dry, abstract lectures are being replaced by hands-on laboratory experiences. By doing so, the passive listeners of a lecture are replaced by active participants in a laboratory experiment. Learning occurs by *doing*.

This book provides a set of exercises for a laboratory course in which students are introduced to computer programming using the language C++. Unlike most books on C++, no previous programming experience is assumed. The particular implementation of C++ used in this book is **GNU C++**, a high-quality software product available for free from *The Free Software Foundation* that is available on many computers running the **UNIX** operating system.

Organization.

As a programming language, C++ is a *hybrid* of imperative and object-oriented features, meaning that it provides features of both. The book is organized to exploit this hybrid nature, with the early exercises in this book introducing the fundamentals of imperative programming. Once these basics have been mastered, object-oriented ideas are gradually incorporated until the later exercises concentrate almost exclusively on object-oriented topics.

Each exercise consists of three parts:

1. *The laboratory exercise*. This portion of the exercise is to be done in a closed lab, with instructor and/or TA available for help if the student becomes stuck.

2. *A pre-lab question list*. The laboratory exercises average approximately 12 pages in length. If a student arrives at a closed lab session unfamiliar with the day's material, then s/he will waste a significant amount of time becoming familiar with that material. To prevent this from occurring, the back of the title page for each exercise consists of five simple questions, whose answers can be found in the lab exercise. By requiring their students to answer (and turn in) these questions in order to be admitted to a lab session, instructors can ensure that students have read the exercise before-hand.

3. *Programming projects*. Four programming projects (of varying difficulty levels) are provided with each lab. An instructor can assign a project of the appropriate difficulty level to be completed outside of the closed laboratory session. A project grade sheet is provided with suggested point values, to simplify project evaluation.

The laboratory exercises can be done individually or collaboratively (though each student should get hands-on experience). The pre-lab exercises and projects were designed to be done as individual work.

Pedagogical Issues.

In keeping with recommendations made at the 1994 SIG/CSE workshop on *Implementing Closed Labs*, the exercises incorporate a number of pedagogical features. These include:

- the statement of objectives for each exercise,
- the inclusion of group projects to provide students with experience working in groups,
- the inclusion of experiments and experimentation to help students learn to apply the scientific method to their computing activities, and
- the extensive use of modeling to introduce new topics.

A total of seventeen exercises have been provided. Schools operating on the semester calendar can choose from among these exercises, selecting those appropriate for their course. Schools operating on a quarterly calendar have the option of dividing the exercises across two quarters.

We would be remiss if we neglected to mention that C++ is a *huge* language. As a simple measure of its size, consider that its parent language C has 32 keywords, while C++ has 48 keywords — a 50% increase! The exercises in this book are intended to introduce novice programmers to C++, not explore the language exhaustively. By the time a student completes the exercises in this book, s/he should be capable of reading and understanding any of the many books that provide comprehensive coverage of the C++ language. Advanced topics such as exception handling, pure virtual functions and abstract base classes are not covered in this book, and are left for the student to explore once they have firmly grasped the fundamentals.

Code Distribution.

In addition to being distributed on disk from the publisher, the C++ files for these exercises are also available in UNIX format via anonymous ftp from `ursa.calvin.edu` (remember to set ftp to *binary* mode). They are stored in the directory `pub/HandsOnC++` in the two files `labs.tar.gz` and `MyLib.tar.gz` . Once transferred, these files can be unpacked with the (GNU and UNIX) `gunzip` and `tar` commands (e.g., using `gunzip labs.tar.gz` will uncompress `labs.tar`; using `tar -xf labs.tar` will then "unarchive" the `labs` directory).

Feedback.

Because everyone is human, feedback is encouraged on those exercises (or parts of exercises) that are particularly effective, and those that need modification. Positive and negative comments can be directed to the author at the following U.S. mail address:

Department of Mathematics and Computer Science
Calvin College
Grand Rapids, MI 49546

or to `adams@calvin.edu` via the Internet.

Acknowledgments.

Thanks to Larry Nyhoff and Shawn Menninga for their proofreading and corrections. Special thanks go to my wife Barbara whose faith, hope and love keep me going. Finally, thanks to God the Father, Son and Holy Spirit who sustains me daily.

Lab 1

The Programming Environment

Note to the Instructor:

Your students will need to be informed about the following issues:

1. How is a computing session initiated at your particular institution?
   (e.g., do they have to turn the machine on, log on,
      give a password, change their password, etc.)

2. What environment-specific details do they need to know about your institution?
   (e.g., are they using dumb terminals, X-windows, etc.)

3. Must students do anything special to print hard copies at your particular institution?
   (e.g., name the printer, pick up hard copies at a different location, etc.)

4. How is a computing session terminated at your particular institution?
   (e.g. must they log out, turn the machine off or leave it running, etc.)

5. Which of the four projects do you wish them to perform when they have completed the lab?

The exercise assumes that GNU C++ (g++) and emacs are installed on your system.

Objectives.

1. To introduce the laboratory computing environment;
2. To introduce the editing, compiling, and execution of a program; and
3. To introduce simple file manipulation commands.

Prelab Questions:

1. What kind of computing environment is provided by UNIX?

2. A program can be stored on a disk in a container called a _____?

3. A container in which related files can be kept is called a _____?

4. Translating a high-level program into a machine-language program involves two steps: _____ and _____ that program.

5. A file may be referred to by either its _____ name or its _____ name.

Introduction.

The main purpose of this lab is to introduce you to the computing environment of your laboratory. Much of the material in this lab is fundamental to the remainder of the course, and you should make every effort to understand not only what, but why you are doing each step.

Before we can begin our session, your instructor must inform you how one begins a session with the computer at your particular institution. The way this is done differs from school to school, according to the kind of computer being used, whether they are networked or stand-alone, whether a security system is in place, and so on. Among the things your instructor will tell you will be the answers to the following questions:

1. Should the computer be turned on at the beginning of the exercise and off at the end of the exercise, or does it remain on all of the time ?

2. Do users of the computer have personal accounts (requiring one to login to begin an exercise), or can anyone use the computer ?

3. If users have personal accounts:

  a. How do I find out my *username* (the name by which I am known to the computer) ?
  b. How do I find out my *password* (the secret word that allows access to my account) ?
  c. Is it necessary to *change my password* (and if so, how is it done) ?

4. If a windowing environment (X-windows, OpenWindows, etc.) is to be used:

  a. Must I do something special to enter that environment?
  b. What role does the mouse play in that environment?
  c. How do I exit that environment?

5. What must I do to quit a session using the computer ?

About this Manual.

In this (and every other) exercise, instructions will be printed in the Times font (the one you are reading). To help you distinguish the instructions from what appears on the monitor screen, text that the computer displays on the screen will be shown in `Courier Bold` font. Text that you are to type or enter will be shown in the `Courier Plain` font. The distinction between *typing* something and *entering* something is as follows:

• to *type* the letter y, simply press the keyboard key marked y.
• to *enter* the letter y, press the keyboard key marked y, and then the key marked `Return`

  (it may be marked `Carriage Return`, `CR`, `⏎`, or perhaps `Enter` on your particular machine).

Getting Started with UNIX.

Follow your instructor's instructions for beginning a session. When you see something like

%

then the computer is ready for your session to begin. What you see is called the system prompt — the computer's operating system (UNIX) is waiting for you to enter your first command. In the space below, write the system prompt on your computer:

Interacting with the Computer.

Next, we will learn to interact with your computer. A UNIX interaction has three steps:

1. The computer displays a prompt and waits for you to enter a command.
2. You enter a command.
3. The computer executes (performs) that command (if it is able to), and when it is finished, displays another prompt.

At that point you're at step 1 again. The commands we'll ask the computer to perform take different amounts of time to complete. Some will take a fraction of a second. Others may take a long time. Others will continue to execute indefinitely, until we specifically ask them to stop.

The way in which you interact with a computer depends upon the *computing environment* of its operating system. For example, an environment in which you repeatedly:

> (i) are prompted for a command,
> (ii) enter a command, and
> (iii) the machine displays the result of the command

is called a *command-line environment* — an environment in which you interact with the machine by entering commands following the system prompt. The UNIX environment is case-sensitive, and UNIX commands use lower-case letters, so your *caps-lock key* should be *off*.

Another common UNIX environment is *X-windows* — an environment in which you use the mouse to interact with on-screen windows, menus and icons; in addition to the typed commands of the UNIX command-line environment. Since these commands are fundamental to both command-line UNIX and X-windows, we will concentrate on them in this exercise.

In order to use a command-line environment, you must learn those commands that the environment understands. Let's see what happens if you type something other than a command the environment recognizes. Enter

```
% qwerty
```

How does the system respond ?

If you try more nonsense words, you'll find that the system responds in the same way. It's thus safe to make mistakes and mistype commands - you won't harm the computer.

Directories and Files.

Very soon, we'll be entering and running a simple program. But when we are done, we'd like to be able to save that program somewhere safe — somewhere that, if the power goes off, your program can still be retrieved. To save your program safely, the computer stores it on magnetic media (usually a *hard disk*) in a container called a **file**.

Over the course of the semester, we'll create dozens of files, and so some means of organizing them is needed. Just as the documents in a filing cabinet are often kept in manila folders, we can create a container in which to keep related files, called a *directory*. Let's do it! Enter

```
% mkdir projects
```

The `mkdir` command is the UNIX command to <u>m</u>ake-a-<u>dir</u>ectory. By giving the word `projects` after the `mkdir` command, we tell the system that we want to make-a-directory named projects. Practice by using the `mkdir` command to make three directories: one named `practice`, one named `labs` and one named `mylib`.

Viewing the Contents of a Directory.

Next, let's learn how to look at what's inside of a directory. Enter

```
% ls
```

The `ls` command stands for <u>l</u>i<u>s</u>t the contents of a directory. If all is well, you should see four things listed there:

`labs`	is one of the directories you just made;
`mylib`	is another of the directories you just made;
`practice`	is another of the directories you just made; and
`projects`	is the other directory you just made.

The `ls` command can also be used to find out what's in a particular directory. Try entering:

```
% ls labs
```

If you follow the `ls` command with the name of a directory, it displays what's in that directory. Each of your directories are new (i.e., empty) and so there is nothing for `ls` to display.

To get a more detailed listing of the current directory, enter

```
% ls -l
```

The `-l` is called a *switch* that causes the `ls` command to generate a <u>l</u>ong (i.e., detailed) listing.

Detailed information is available about each UNIX command (like `ls`) in the *on-line manual*. For example, if you enter

```
% man ls
```

the <u>man</u>ual entry for `ls` will be displayed that provides exhaustive information about that command, including all of its switches, and the meaning of the long listing information.

Removing a Directory.

Since we made `practice` just for practice, let's get rid of it. Enter

    % rmdir practice

The `rmdir` command is the re̲move di̲rectory command. Whatever directory you specify following the command will be removed from the current directory, provided that it is empty. To remove a non-empty directory named *DirectoryName*, the command

    % rm -r DirectoryName

can be used (but should only be used when *DirectoryName* contains nothing important).

Use the `ls` command to verify that `practice` no longer exists.

Identifying the Working Directory.

When you begin a computing session, UNIX always starts you out in the same place — a special directory called your *home directory*. The directory in which you are working at any given time is called your *working directory*. (Your home directory never changes, but your working directory can.) Here is what happens when I find the name of the working directory:

    % pwd
    /homex/adams

`pwd` which stands for p̲ath to the w̲orking d̲irectory. Try it and record what is displayed:

UNIX systems utilize what is called a *hierarchical directory system*, meaning that the directories in the system are organized in a *tree* structure. At the base of the tree is a directory named / that is the *root* of the directory system. Within / are a number of *subdirectories*, including `usr`, `sys`, `include`, and so on, each of which contains other directories and/or files. On my UNIX system, the users' home directories are stored within one of these subdirectories whose name is `homex`. Within `homex`, the name of my home directory is `adams`.

Now, if you compare this to my output from `pwd`, you can see that `pwd` displays / (the root directory) followed by `homex`, followed by a slash (to separate directory names) followed by `adams`. That is, `pwd` lists the sequence of directories between the root directory and my working directory, with slashes between the directory names. Since my working directory is currently my home directory, the last name that `pwd` displayed is my home directory!

Now, apply this to the output from your `pwd` command. What is the name of your home directory?

A last word on the home directory: UNIX treats the tilde character (~) as an abbreviation for your home directory, which can save you a lot of typing if the path to your home directory has lots of characters. We will make use of this abbreviation at the end of the lab.

Changing to a Different Directory.

If we created all of our files in our home directory, it would soon become cluttered. By grouping related files within a directory, one's files can be kept more organized. Thus, we created `labs` in which we'll store the files for our lab exercises, and `projects` in which you can store your programming projects files (we'll discuss `mylib` in a later lab exercise.)

Since we are working on a lab, let's change the working directory to directory `labs`. Enter

```
% cd labs
```

The `cd` command is the <u>c</u>hange <u>d</u>irectory command that changes the working directory to the directory whose name follows the command.

Next, use the `pwd` command and record its output:

Compare this output to that generated the first time you entered `pwd`. Explain the difference:

To see *everything* in a directory, enter

```
% ls -a
```

The `-a` switch tells `ls` to list <u>a</u>ll of the contents of a directory. You will notice two odd items:

> `.` – another name for the working directory (whatever directory you are in); and
> `..` – another name for the *parent directory* of the working directory.

Now consider: We created `labs` within the directory where we began. The `cd labs` command took us from that directory "down" into `labs`. How do we get from `labs` back "up" to the directory where we began? Enter the command:

```
% cd ..
```

This command moves the working directory "up" one directory because `..` is always a synonym for the parent of the working directory, regardless of its actual name. (Since that directory is our home directory, we could also have used `cd ~` in this case.)

Use `pwd` to verify that you are currently "in" your home directory, recording its output:

To wrap up this section, do the following:

1. Change directory back "down" into `labs`;
2. Make a new directory (inside `labs`) named `lab1`; and
3. Change directory from `labs` "down" into `lab1`.

Your First Program.

Once you are "in" the directory lab1, you are ready to write your first C++ program. Writing a program consists of two steps:

1. Writing a *source program* in a high-level language (i.e., C++) and storing that program in a file; and
2. Translating that source program into a machine-language program (i.e., a *binary executable*).

The first step can be accomplished using a tool that allows you to create and edit files containing text (i.e., characters) and is thus called a *text editor*. The text editor used throughout this manual is named **emacs**, a product of the Free Software Foundation that is available for free from a variety of Internet sites.

Once we have created a file containing our source program, the second step can be accomplished through the use of a C++ *compiler* — a program that translates C++ programs into machine language. Graphically the process can be pictured as follows:

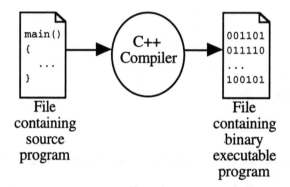

| File containing source program | C++ Compiler | File containing binary executable program |

As we shall see in Lab 4, this is a bit of a simplification, but it is sufficiently accurate to give you an idea of what is occuring.

The C++ compiler used throughout this manual is named **g++** and it (like emacs) is a product of the Free Software Foundation and is available for free from a variety of Internet sites.

Editing a File.

Our first program will input a base-10 integer and display it in base-8 (octal) and base-16 (hexadecimal). We will thus name the binary program bases, and name the source program bases.cc (GNU C++ source programs end in .cc, by convention.) We can use emacs to create the source program by entering:

```
% emacs bases.cc
```

Since the file bases.cc does not exist in the working directory, emacs will create a new, blank *editing buffer* named **bases.cc** into which you can type a program. If a file named bases.cc existed in the working directory, then emacs would open that file and read it into the editing buffer).

Within the **bases.cc** buffer, enter and personalize following C++ source program:

```
/*-------------------------------------------------------------------
Program bases demonstrates basic I/O in C++.

        Written by: John Doe, MM DD, YYYY.
        Written for: CS I, at University College.

Specification:
        Input(keyboard): an integer;
        Output(screen): the base 8 and base 16 representations
                        of the input integer.
--------------------------------------------------------------------*/

#include <iostream.h>

int main(void)
{
        int
                Value;          // a container to hold the input integer

        // 0. print a message explaining the purpose of the program.
        cout << "\nThis program inputs a base-10 integer"
             << "\n\tand displays its value in bases 8 and 16\n";

        // 1. ask the user to enter an integer.
        cout << "\nPlease enter an integer: ";

        // 2. input an integer, storing it in variable Value.
        cin >> Value;

        // 3. output the base-8 and base-16 representations of Value.
        cout << "\n\nThe base-8 representation of " << Value << " is "
             << oct << Value
             << ",\n\tand the base-16 representation is "
             << hex << Value
             << "\n\n";

        return 0;
}
```

Regardless of whether you are working in a X-windows or on a terminal, you can use the arrow keys on your keyboard to reposition the cursor within the editing buffer. If you mistype something, it can be removed using the *delete* (or *backspace*) key. The emacs C-d command (typing the Control and d keys simultaneously) can be used to delete the character beneath the cursor, and C-k can be used to delete from the cursor to the end of the line.

You can always undo the effects of an emacs command using the *undo* command: C-x u (type Control and x simultaneously, then type the u key by itself).

If you are working in the X-windows environment, then you can reposition the cursor by 1) pointing the mouse where you want the cursor to appear and 2) clicking the left mouse button. A block of text can be selected by *dragging* (depressing the left mouse button while moving the mouse) though the selected text does not remain highlighted. Operations for cutting and pasting text can be selected from the **Edit** menu.

Saving Your Work.

When you have finished typing, enter the emacs command `C-x s` (hold down the `Control` and x keys simultaneously. Then type the s key separately.) `Emacs` will respond with a *confirmation query* (in the mini-buffer at the bottom of the window):

```
Save file .../labs/lab1/bases.cc? (y, n, !, ., q, C-r or C-h)
```

To save the contents of the buffer in a file named `bases.cc`, respond with

```
Save file .../labs/lab1/bases.cc? (y, n, !, ., q, C-r or C-h) y
```

If you are using X-windows, then the **Save Buffer** choice can be selected from the **File** to save what you have written, without the confirmation query.

Translating Your Program.

When your source program is entered and saved, it is time to translate it into the computer's machine language. This is done using the emacs *compile* command: `M-x compile` (type the `Meta`, `Escape`, or `Edit` key, then the x key, and then the word `compile`.) Emacs will respond with a query:

```
Compile command: make -k
```

For simple programs like this one, the easiest way to translate the program is to replace the `make -k` with an explicit call to the GNU C++ compiler `g++`:

```
Compile command: g++ bases.cc -o bases
```

This invokes `g++` and tells it that the source program is in the file `bases.cc`. The `-o` switch tells `g++` that its output (the binary executable program) is to be placed in a file named `bases`.

When you enter this command, emacs splits its window in two, displaying the **bases.cc** buffer (containing your source program) in one half and displaying a new ***compilation*** buffer (containing the information produced by your compile command) in the other half. If you have typed **bases.cc** correctly, then a message like:

```
Compilation finished at Mon Sep 5 9:12:44
```

will be displayed in the ***compilation*** buffer. If you instead see an error listing:

```
bases.cc: In function `int main()':
...
Compilation exited abnormally with code 1 at Mon Sep 5 9:12:44
```

then you have made typing errors in entering the program. The emacs *next-error* command: `C-x ` (`Control` and x, followed by left-quote) will move the cursor to the line in your source program where it discovered the error (but the error may be on a previous line). Compare the program above with what you have written and then change what you have written to fix the error. Then use the compile command again to see if you fixed the mistake. (Note that we need not retype the "`g++ bases.cc -o`" bases because emacs "remembers" it from before.) Repeat this *edit-compile cycle* as many times as needed for your program to compile correctly.

Running Your Program from the Command-Line.

Running program bases is the same as any other program — we must enter its name following an operating system prompt. However, getting from emacs to the operating system prompt differs in the command-line and X-windows environments.

If you are using a terminal and the UNIX command-line environment, use the emacs *suspend* command: C-z. The operating system will then suspend emacs and display the operating system prompt, indicating it is ready to accept a command.

If you are using X-windows, there is no need to suspend emacs — it is just one of many windows. Instead, locate a different window called an **xterm** in which the system prompt is displayed. (If there is no xterm present, try clicking the left mouse button while pointing at the background of your screen. On many systems, this displays a menu from which you can choose xterm to create a new xterm window.) Simply move the mouse into this window and it is ready to accept your command.

Once you are at the operating system prompt, use pwd to check that your working directory is lab1. (If not, change directory to make it so.) Then use ls to display the contents of lab1, to make sure that both bases.cc and bases are there. At that point, you can enter

```
% bases
```

and your program should execute successfully. If it does not, ask your instructor for help.

Returning to emacs from the Command-Line.

If you are using a command-line environment (i.e., you suspended emacs using C-z), then you can return to emacs by entering

```
% fg
```

which changes the state of emacs from being suspended, making it the foreground process. If you are using the X-windows environment, then simply move the mouse from the **xterm** window back into the **emacs** window.

Printing a Hard Copy.

A paper copy of electronic information is called a *hard copy*. It is often useful to have a hard copy of one's source program, which is in the file bases.cc. To print a hard copy of bases.cc, enter

```
% lpr bases.cc
```

The lpr command is the line printer command that prints a hard copy of the file whose name is given. If your laboratory has multiple printers, it may be necessary to enter

```
% lpr -PPrinterName bases.cc
```

Your instructor will inform you of the name of the printers if necessary.

Applying the Scientific Method.

An important part of any science, including the science of computing, is to be able to build your inferences into hypotheses, and then design and carry out experiments to test your hypotheses. The next part of this exercise involves applying the scientific method to infer (from the statements within bases.cc) how the C++ output system works.

Hypothesis.

Construct a hypothesis on how output text can be made to begin on a new line.

Experiment.

In the space below, design an experiment using bases.cc that tests your hypothesis.

Observations.

Perform your experiment, re-translating bases.cc into machine language, and detail the results in the space below:

If your hypothesis were rejected, construct a new hypothesis based on what you observed. Then design and perform new experiments to test those hypotheses. Repeat this process (on separate paper, if need be) until your hypothesis is not rejected.

Note that although your hypothesis was not rejected, this does not prove that it is correct. The scientific method can only prove that a hypothesis is *false*, it can never prove it to be *true*.

Quitting emacs.

To quit emacs (as opposed to suspending emacs), the emacs *quit* command: `C-x C-c` (Cntrl and `x`, then `Cntrl` and `c`) can be used. Users of X-windows have the option of selecting **Exit Emacs** from the **File** menu.

Copying a File.

It is sometimes useful to be able to make a copy of a file, to avoid having to retype it. For example, to make a copy of `bases.cc` in a different file named `bases.2`, enter:

    % cp bases.cc bases.2

The `cp` command makes a copy of the file with the first name, and names the copy the second name. Use the `ls` command to check that both the original and the copy are listed.

It's more often the case that we need to make a copy of a file in a directory different from the one in which the file currently resides. How are we to do this ? The key is to learn a bit about how files and directories are named. Both of the names `bases.cc` and `bases.2` are the *relative names* of these files — to use them, we must be in the same directory as they are.

However, every file/directory also has an *absolute name*: a name that starts with the base directory, and lists each directory between there and the file name, just as in the output from `pwd`. For example, the absolute name of `bases.cc` on my machine is as follows: `/homex/adams/C++/labs/lab1/bases.cc`, or more briefly `~/C++/labs/lab1/bases.cc`.

To use an absolute name, you need not be in the same directory as that file or directory! For example, try entering:

    % mkdir ~/projects/proj1

What did we just do ? We used the `mkdir` command to make a new directory, but where did we make it ? Recall that earlier in the exercise, we made two directories: `labs` and `projects`. We just made a new directory inside `projects`, called `proj1`, using an absolute path name!

Almost all of the UNIX file manipulation commands can use either relative or absolute file names. You thus don't need to be "in" a directory to see its contents: Enter

    % ls ~/projects

and you should see the directory you just made.

Similarly, to put a copy of `bases.cc` in that new directory, you can enter:

    % cp bases.cc ~/projects/proj1

and a copy of `bases.cc` will be stored in that directory. The `cp` command thus behaves differently depending on whether you specify a file or a directory as the second name: if you specify a *file* as the second name, then the `cp` command will store the copy in a file with that name. If you specify a *directory* as the second name, then `cp` will place the copy in that directory using the name of the original. Use `ls` to verify that the copy is in `proj1`.

Renaming a File.

Sometimes we decide after the fact that a file would be better off with a different name. To change the name of bases.2 to bases.old, enter:

```
% mv bases.2 bases.old
```

The mv command changes the name of (or mo_ve_s) the first file-name to the second file-name. It can be used with both relative and absolute file names, and can be used to rename directories.

Creating and Printing a Hard Copy of an Execution.

Besides a hard copy of one's program, it is often useful to have a hard copy of the output from one's program. To do this, we must (1) record the output of the program in a file; and (2) print that file using lpr. To record the output of bases in a file, enter

```
% script
```

The script command runs a program that records everything that appears on the screen of a terminal (or everything that appears within an xterm window). Thus, if you subsequently execute bases, then its output will be recorded by script. Once bases has terminated, enter

```
% exit
```

to terminate script, which informs you that its recording is in a file named typescript. A hard copy of the file typescript can then be printed using lpr, as described previously.

Cleaning Up Your Directory.

The various files you have created take up valuable disk space, and so we will remove all of the files from lab1 except for our source program, bases.cc (the others can always be easily re-generated from your source program.) To remove bases.old, enter

```
% rm bases.old
```

The rm command stands for re_move_, and will delete whatever file you specify after it. Earlier we saw that the -r switch tells rm to _r_ecursively remove a directory and its contents.

Use the rm command to remove the files typescript, bases.cc~ (a back-up file created by emacs) and bases. Then use the ls command to verify that all of the files except bases.cc are gone. If there are others remaining, use the rm command to remove them, as well.

Then end your session with the computer, following your instructor's instructions.

Note: The last page of this manual is a Quick-Reference summarizing some of the UNIX and emacs commands, provided so that you can find it quickly when necessary ...

Phrases you should now understand:

Environment, Command-Line, Directory, File, Editor, Compiler, Hard Copy, Printer.

Objectives:

1. Gain further experience using the text editor and compiler;
2. Gain experience with sequential programming.

Introduction.

Using the program `bases.cc` as a model, solve one of the problems below (your instructor will tell you which one to do).

Projects.

1.1. Write `flies.cc` — a program that produces the following output:

```
                like
        flies               an
    Time                        arrow ...

    Fruit           like
            flies           bananas.
```

1.2. Write `recipe.cc` — a program that produces the following output:

```
    Pop  1  cup  of  popcorn
    Melt  1  stick  of  butter
    Combine  popcorn  and  butter
    Salt  to  taste
```

1.3. Write `direct.cc` — a program that produces detailed directions to your house, such as:

```
    Take  I-96  to  U.S.  131
    Take  131  3  miles  south  to  Hall  St.
    Take  Hall  1  mile  east  to  Madison  Ave.
    Take  Madison  3  blocks  north  to  Sherman  St.
    Take  Sherman  2  blocks  east  to  1000  Sherman  St.
```

1.4. Write `describe.cc` — a program that produces output describing yourself, such as:

```
    Name:    Jane  Doe
    Gender:  Female
    Year:    Freshman
    Phone:   555-9876
    Other:   No  further  information  available
```

Be certain that you use `rm` to clean up your directory when you are all finished.

Project 1 Due Date _____

Turn in this grade sheet, attached to a hard copy of

a. your source program; and
b. the output from an execution of your binary executable program.

Name _____

Category	Points Possible	Points Received
Complete Documentation.................................	10	_____
Source Program..	20	_____
Correct Execution...	20	_____
T o t a l..	**5 0**	_____

Lab 2

Program Development

Note to the Instructor:

Preparation for this lab includes the following steps:

1. Create a *class directory*, such that every student in the class can read its contents.

2. Copy the contents of the distribution disk into this directory.

3. Review (with the students) absolute and relative file names, and how to copy files from one directory to another.

4. Inform the students of the absolute name of the file they need to copy for today's exercise (`hypot.cc`).

The exercise assumes that the GNU debugger (`gdb`) has been correctly installed on your system for use in conjunction with GNU emacs. If it has not, then you should instruct your students to skip those parts of the exercise that deal with the debugger.

Objectives:

1. Practice using the computing environment.
2. Gain experience with the five stages of program development.
3. Introduce the use of the symbolic debugger.

Prelab Questions:

1. What is the name of the file in which `cin`, `cout`, the `<<` operator and the `>>` operator are declared?

2. What is the name of the file in which the `sqrt()` function is declared?

3. Updating and modifying a program over the course of its lifetime is called _____ that program.

4. Finding and eliminating the errors in a program is called _____ that program.

5. The process of executing a program with sample data, to try to find logical errors is called _____ that program.

Preparing Your Workspace.

Create and change directory into labs/lab2 (Use your UNIX Quick Reference at the end of this manual, if you've forgotten the commands since last time). Then copy the file hypot.cc from your class directory into lab2 (your instructor will tell you the name of the class directory). Verify that the copy was made. Then invoke emacs to begin today's exercise:

```
% emacs hypot.cc
```

The Problem.

Our problem today is to write a program, such that a user can enter the lengths of the two legs of a right triangle, and the program will display the length of its hypotenuse.

The process of developing a program to solve a problem involves five stages:

1. The precise specification of the problem,
2. The design of an algorithm to solve the problem,
3. The step-wise coding of that algorithm in a programming language,
4. The testing, and debugging of the program, until it can be deemed correct, and
5. Performing any maintenance (or alteration) required over the lifetime of the program.

Today's exercise is to use these stages to develop a program that solves our problem.

Problem Specification:

A precise **specification** of a problem involves identifying two basic aspects of that problem:

1. In the space below, list those values that *must be provided to the computation* in order for it to begin solving the problem (These are the values that must be input from the keyboard.)

2. In the space below, list those values that *the computation must produce* in order for the problem to have been solved (These are the values that must be output to the screen.)

Use this information to complete the specification of your source program. Then personalize its opening documentation before continuing.

Design.

Once the problem is clearly specified, the next stage in developing a program is the **design** stage, in which:

    A. The *objects* involved in solving the problem are identified.
    B. The *operations* to be applied to those objects are identified.
    C. An *algorithm* is constructed that specifies the order in which the operations are applied to the objects, in order to solve the problem.

For example, in our problem, we can identify the following objects:

    • *Leg1*, the length of one of the legs of the right triangle
    • *Leg2*, the length of the other leg of the right triangle
    • *Hypotenuse*, the length of the hypotenuse of the right triangle

The relationship between these objects is given by the Pythagorean Theorem:

$$Hypotenuse^2 = Leg1^2 + Leg2^2$$

or

$$Hypotenuse = \sqrt{Leg1^2 + Leg2^2}$$

We can thus identify the following operations that are needed to solve our problem:

    • Input two real values from the keyboard and store them in variables (*Leg1* and *Leg2*).
    • Square two real values (*Leg1* and *Leg2*).
    • Add two real values ($Leg1^2 + Leg2^2$).
    • Take the square root of a real value ($\sqrt{Leg1^2 + Leg2^2}$).
    • Store a real value in a real variable (the preceding square root in *Hypotenuse*).
    • Output a real value (*Hypotenuse*).

Once our objects and operations are identified, an algorithm can be constructed that specifies the order in which the operations are to be applied to the objects. Step 0 of a program algorithm should always be to display a message that explains the program. Step 1 often involves performing the input operation suggested by our specification. The last step is usually performing the output operation suggested by our specification. That leaves the middle step(s): taking the input and using it to produce the output. In this case, this is quite easy, thanks to Pythagoras and his formula.

We can write these steps (in pseudo-code) as an algorithm as follows:

    0. Display a message on the screen explaining the purpose of the program;

    1. Prompt the user for, and input the leg lengths from the keyboard, storing them in the variables *Leg1* and *Leg2*;

    2. Using *Leg1* and *Leg2*, calculate the hypotenuse length using the Pythagorean Theorem, storing the result in the variable *Hypotenuse*;

    3. Display a descriptive message and the value of *Hypotenuse* on the screen.

Coding, Testing and Debugging.

Once we have designed an algorithm to solve our problem, we must **encode** that algorithm in the notation of a high level programming language (i.e., C++). We can begin this process by constructing a minimal C++ program, consisting of

```
int main(void)
{
    return 0;
}
```

Add these lines to your source program, after its opening documentation. We can then **test** the correctness of what we have written by compiling it. Enter M-x compile and then:

Compile command: g++ -g hypot.cc -o hypot -lm

The -g switch tells g++ to save the information needed by the GNU debugger (discussed below) and must be given if the debugger is to be used. The -lm switch must appear last, and tells g++ to link in the math library, as we will be using the square root function (see below).

If your program does not compile correctly, then what you have entered contains *syntax errors* or **bugs** (i.e. your program is not a "grammatically correct C++ sentence"). In order for your program to compile, you must return to the editor and correct these errors, which is called **debugging** your program.

Once we have the minimal C++ program constructed, we are ready to encode our algorithm. To do so, we want to take each step of the algorithm and write one or more C++ statements that perform that step. **Step-wise translation** is the process of translating an algorithm into a program, one step at a time. We therefore begin with the first step:

Step: 0. Display a message on the screen explaining the purpose of the program;

Coding: This step can be performed using a C++ **output statement** — to display a sequence of values $Value_1 \ldots Value_n$ on the screen, we can use the form:

```
cout << Value1 << Value2 << ... << Valuen;
```

Add an output statement to your source program to display the following message, using \n to print blank lines before and after the message, so that it is easy to read:

```
Given  two  right  triangle  leg  lengths,
    this  program  computes  the  hypotenuse  length.
```

When you have added the commands to your source program, re-compile it. The compiler should generate an error message like the following:

```
hypot.cc:  In  function  int  main()
hypot.cc:  'cout'  undeclared...
```

The problem is that the meanings of the symbols cout and << are declared in a system file named iostream.h, not in your program. To access these declarations from that file, we can insert iostream.h, by adding an **include directive** just before the int main(void) line:

```
#include <iostream.h>
```

This `#include` directive must appear in any program that performs output using `cout` and `<<`. The `#` symbol must be the first column, in order for it be processed correctly. The `<>` around the file name tell the compiler to look in a special system "include" directory for `iostream.h`, rather than in your current directory. Try to remember the error message (or make a note of it) so that if you see that message again, you will know how to "debug" that error.

Now, recompile your program to check that what you have written is free of *syntax errors*. If not, you can infer that the error(s) lies in the text you have added since your last correct compilation. Find your error(s) within those lines and use the editor to correct them.

When your source program compiles correctly, execute `hypot` to test that it displays the intended message. If not, the statements you have added contain *logical errors*. Compare your source program statements against the output produced by `hypot`, modifying them as needed.

When your program is error-free, proceed to the next step of our algorithm, which is:

Step: 1. Prompt the user for, and input the leg lengths from the keyboard,
             storing them in the variables *Leg1* and *Leg2*;

This step is performing multiple actions, so let's **refine** it (break it down into *substeps*).

Step 1 Refinement. We can break step 1 into two substeps:

Substep: 1a. Prompt the user for the two leg lengths with a screen message;

Coding: Encode substep 1a as you did step 0. Verify its correctness before proceeding.

Substep: 1b. Input two real values, storing them in variables *Leg1* and *Leg2*;

Coding: We can encode this step in C++ using an **input statement**, whose general form is:

```
cin >> Var1 >> Var2 >> ... >> Varn
```

This statement reads a sequence of values from the keyboard, and stores them in the variables $Var_1 \ldots Var_n$ provided that the system file `iostream.h` has been included (as we did earlier).

Add an input statement to your source program to perform step 1b. Then compile your source program again. Similar (but different) errors should be generated, but this time it is *our variables* that are undefined. C++ requires that objects be declared before they are used, using a declaration of the form:

```
Type   Var1,      // a comment describing this variable
       Var2,      // a comment describing this variable
       ...
       Varn;      // a comment describing this variable
```

where `Type` is the type of object being defined, and $Var_1 \ldots Var_n$ are the variables' names.

In C++ the type `double` is used to define real values. One of the nice features of C++ is that declarations are statements (and can thus appear wherever a statement is permitted, unlike most languages), so insert a declaration for `Leg1` and `Leg2` just before your input statement. Then recompile and correct any other syntax errors before proceeding.

Checking the Value of a Variable.

While the compiler will inform us of any syntax errors our program contains, it cannot detect logical errors. The simplest way to check for logical errors is to examine the values of the variables in our program as the program executes, and verify that they are what they are supposed to be. GNU emacs provides a simple way to check variable values, using an associated GNU product named **gdb** (which stands for gnu debugger).

The most convenient way to use the debugger is to split your emacs window into two buffers. This has probably already been done for you by the emacs *compile* command. If not, use either of the emacs *split screen* commands: C-x 2 or C-x 3 (C-x 1 can be used to make emacs display a single buffer). Then use the emacs *other buffer* command: C-x o to move the cursor from the **hypot.cc** buffer to the ***compilation*** buffer (this can be done with a simple mouse-click if you are using X-windows). There, enter the emacs *gdb* command: M-x gdb to invoke gdb. Emacs will respond with a query:

```
Run gdb (like this): gdb
```

after which you should enter the name of the executable program you wish to run:

```
Run gdb (like this): gdb hypot
```

Emacs then creates a new buffer named ***gud-driver*** in which it displays an introductory message, followed by the *gdb prompt*:

```
(gdb)
```

gdb uses a command-line environment, in which you interact through entering commands. For example, enter the gdb *run* command:

```
(gdb) r
```

Your program will then execute from start to finish within gdb. This is not what we want — we'd rather be able to execute our program one line at a time so that we can inspect the values of variables used on that line.

To accomplish this, we must *set a break point*, which is sort of like placing a "stop sign" at a statement so that execution will halt when it reaches that point. Move the cursor from the ***gud-driver*** buffer back into the **hypot.cc** buffer. Position the cursor on the line containing the output statement for step 0 of our algorithm. Then enter C-x SPC (SPC is the spacebar) and a message like the following should appear in the ***gud-driver*** buffer:

```
Breakpoint 1 at 0x22a: file hypot.cc line 16
```

Now, we have a "stop sign" in place, we can run **hypot** in a controlled manner. Move the cursor back to the ***gud-driver*** window and enter

```
(gdb) run
```

After an introductory message, gdb will tell you that it is stopping at breakpoint 1, and re-display its prompt. If you look in the **hypot.cc** buffer, you will notice that gdb has displayed an "arrow" indicator (=>) on the line where we set the breakpoint. This arrow always points to the statement that will be executed next.

Now, we can use gdb commands to execute each statement in turn. For example, enter

```
(gdb) n
```

which tells gdb to execute the next statement. You should see the arrow indicator advance to the next statement. Continue to do so until the input statement in hypot.cc is reached. At that point, you can use the gdb *print* command:

```
(gdb) p Leg1
```

and gdb will display

```
$1 =
```

followed by the value of Leg1. Use the print command to find the values of Leg1 and Leg2:

If the values of Leg1 and Leg2 are strange real values, then you can infer that these values are probably just whatever bit patterns were left over in their memory space (i.e., they were not *initialized*); however if the values of Leg1 and Leg2 are zeros, then you can infer that they probably were initialized for us.

Use the next command to execute the input statement, and gdb will pause while you enter values for Leg1 and Leg2. What values did you enter?

Use the gdb print command to display the values of Leg1 and Leg2. What values are displayed?

Use the gdb print command to display the value Leg1+Leg2. What value is displayed?

You can thus use the debugger to display the current value of a variable *or expression* at any point in your program (following its declaration). The key points to remember are

1. You must compile using the -g switch;
2. Split the emacs window into two buffers, one for gdb and one for your source program;
3. In the non-source program buffer, enter M-x gdb to invoke gdb ;
4. In the source program buffer, use C-x SPC to set a breakpoint;
5. In the gdb buffer, use r to run a program, c to continue execution to the next breakpoint,
   n to execute the next statement, p to print the value of an expression, and q to quit.

When you are done experimenting, you can quit gdb by entering its quit command:

```
(gdb) q
```

The debugger will display a termination message and then quit. If you want, move the cursor back into the **hypot.cc** buffer and use C-x 1 to make emacs display a single buffer.

We are now ready to resume translating, with the next step of our algorithm.

Step: 2. Calculate the hypotenuse length using *Leg1*, *Leg2*, and the Pythagorean Theorem, storing the result in the variable *Hypotenuse*;

Coding: We can encode this step using the **assignment statement**, whose general form is:

```
VariableName = Expression ;
```

where `VariableName` is the name of the variable in which we are storing the result (`Hypotenuse`), and `Expression` is a sequence of operands and operators that produce a value.

To perform step 2, our assignment statement must encode the Pythagorean Theorem formula:

$$Hypotenuse = \sqrt{Leg1^2 + Leg2^2}$$

and so our expression will need to take the square root of the subexpression: $Leg1^2 + Leg2^2$

While C++ has no exponentiation operator, this subexpression can be encoded using the C++ addition and multiplication operators (+ and *). To take the square root of this subexpression, we can use the function `sqrt()`, whose form is:

```
sqrt( Expression )
```

The system file `math.h` must be included to use `sqrt()`, as that is where `sqrt()` is declared. Modify your program as necessary to store the square root of $Leg1^2 + Leg2^2$ into *Hypotenuse*: Then use the compiler to check that what you have written is free of syntactic errors. When it is, find out what error message is generated if your source program is compiled without linking in the math library (i.e., without the `-lm` switch). Record it below:

Then recompile with the `-lm` switch and practice using gdb by executing `hypot` in a controlled fashion. Enter 1 and 1 for `Leg1` and `Leg2`, and check that the correct result (1.414214) is being stored in `Hypotenuse`.

We then continue to the next step of our algorithm:

Step: 3. Print a descriptive message and the value of *Hypotenuse* to the screen.

This step involves more than 1 action, and so we might be tempted to refine it into two steps as we did for step1. However, the C++ output statement

```
cout << Val1 << Val2 << ... << Valn;
```

allows us to output a sequence of values $Val_1...Val_n$ (just as >> allowed us to chain together the input variables in step 1.) In your program, construct an output statement, such that if the value of `Hypotenuse` is 1.414214, then the message

```
--> The hypotenuse length is: 1.414214...
```

is displayed with blank lines above and below it (to make the result stand out). Retranslate your program, and when it is free of syntax errors, continue in the exercise.

Testing.

The fourth phase of program development is a thorough **testing**, in which we execute our program using sample data, to try and find any logical errors in the program. Execute hypot with the following easy-to-check values, to see if you get the correct answers. If you do not, use the debugger to find and fix the logical error in your program.

Leg1	Leg2	Theoretical	Hypotenuse	Observed
1.0	1.0	1.414214		_____
3.0	4.0	5.000000		_____
5.0	12.0	13.00000		_____

When you have a reasonable degree of confidence that your program is correct, it is complete. Make sure that your source program has been saved, and quit emacs.

Program Maintenance.

Unlike programs that are written by students, "real world" programs may be used for many years. It is often the case that such programs must be modified several times over the course of their lifetimes, a task which is called program **maintenance** . Maintenance is thus the final stage of program development. Some studies have shown that the cost of maintaining a program can account for as much as 80% of its total cost! One of the goals of Object-Oriented Programming is to try to reduce this maintenance cost, by writing code that is reusable.

To simulate program maintenance, suppose that hypot must display only three decimal digits instead of the usual number. To do so, its source program must be altered, so restart emacs.

The number of decimal digits in a real number is called the *precision* of that number. To show only three decimal digits, we must alter the default precision. This can be done with an I/O manipulator called setprecision() (declared in the file <iomanip.h>) whose general form is:

```
setprecision( IntegerExpression )
```

If <iomanip.h> is included and setprecision() is placed in an output statement:

```
cout << Val_1 << setprecision(i) << Val_2 <<   ... << Val_n ;
```

then real values before it (i.e., Val_1) will be displayed with the default precision, but real values following it (i.e., Val_2 ... Val_n) will be displayed with precision i. Modify your source program so that Hypotenuse is displayed with precision 3. Don't forget the #include directive before the int main(void) line! Then test the correctness of your modification.

Phrases You Should Now Understand.

Problem Specification, Design, Pseudo-code Algorithm, Coding, Testing, Debugging, Stepwise Translation, Step Refinement, Source Program, Executable Program, Assignment Statement, Expression, Subexpression, Input Statement, Output Statement, I/O Manipulator.

Objectives.

1. Practice specifying a problem;
2. Practice constructing an algorithm; and
3. Practice translation of an algorithm into C++; and
4. Practice testing an executable program.

Introduction.

Your instructor will assign you one of the following problems. To solve your problem, write a program that inputs the necessary information to compute and output the indicated values, as efficiently as possible. Following the pattern in the lab exercise, begin by specifying the problem, construct an algorithm to solve the problem, and then employ stepwise translation to encode your algorithm in C++. Then test your program thoroughly, using the facilities at your disposal.

Projects.

2.1. Write a program to find the circumference and area of any <u>circle</u>, as follows:

$Circumference = 2 \times \pi \times Radius$, and
$Area = \pi \times Radius^2$.

2.2. Write a program to find the surface area and volume of any <u>regular cylinder</u>, as follows:

$SideSurfaceArea = 2 \times \pi \times Radius \times Height$, and
$Volume = \pi \times Radius^2 \times Height$.

2.3. Write a program to find the circumference and area of any <u>ellipse</u>, computed as follows:

$Circumference = 2 \times \pi \times$ the square root of $(((Height/2)^2 + (Width/2)^2) / 2)$, and
$Area = \pi \times \dfrac{Height}{2} \times \dfrac{Width.}{2}$

2.4. Write a program to find the surface area and volume of any <u>sphere</u>, computed as follows:

$SurfaceArea = 4 \times \pi \times Radius^2$, and
$Volume = 4 \times \pi \times Radius^3 / 3$.

Project 2 Due Date _____

Turn in the project grade sheet, attached to a hard copy of:

(i) your source program, and
(ii) an execution of your source program using 3 different sets of data.

Be sure to delete all excess files from your directory when you are finished.

Name _____

Category	Points Possible	Points Received
Correctness and Efficiency	50	_____
Complete Documentation	35	
- Who, What, Where, etc	10	_____
- Specification	10	_____
- In-Program Comments	5	_____
- Meaningful Identifiers	5	_____
- White Space	5	_____
User-Friendliness	15	
- Opening Message	5	_____
- Descriptive Input Prompts	5	_____
- Labeled Output	5	_____
Total	**100**	_____

Lab 3

Expressions

Note to the Instructor:

Lab 3 contains a series of experiments that explore the rich set of operations provided by C++. Some can be done with "pencil and paper," or in the student's heads, while others will require them to modify, translate and execute a program. Each of these has been designed to enhance the student's understanding of the expressions and operators supported by C++.

You should review each experiment. If you do not want your students to perform all of the experiments (e.g., to conserve time), you should inform your students of this at the beginning of the lab period.

Special note: The source program in this exercise is named `expr.cc`. On most UNIX systems:

1. `expr` is the name of a system utility for evaluating expressions; and
2. when executing a program, the system directory where expr resides is searched first, before one's working directory.

These two points mean that if your students should give their executable program the name `expr`, and then try and run their program by typing `expr`, the system utility (which sits and waits for the user to type an expression) will be executed instead of the students' executable. This problem can be avoided with either of two approaches:

1. students can either give their executable a name distinct from `expr` (e.g., `Expr`) using the `-o` switch to `g++`; or
2. they can execute their program by typing `./expr`, which tells UNIX that they wish to execute the version of `expr` that is in the working directory.

Either way, this provides a "teachable moment" for students to learn more about the UNIX operating system.

Objectives.

1. Explore the C++ fundamental types.
2. Explore the assignment and related expressions.
3. Explore input and output expressions.

Prelab Questions:

1. What are the five C++ arithmetic operators?

2. The order in which an expression's operators are applied is usually determined by the _____, and the _____ of those operators.

3. Commonly used functions are stored in _____, so that they can be accessed by any program that wants to use them.

4. The symbols ++ and -- perform the _____ and _____ operations.

5. A sequence of one or more operands and zero or more operators, that combine to generate a value is called a(n) _____.

Introduction.

Today's exercise involves a series of experiments, each investigating a different aspect of a concept that is fundamental in C++ and other programming languages: the **expression**. The term expression can be defined as follows:

> *An **expression** is a sequence of one or more **operands**, and zero or more **operators**, that when combined, produce a **value**.*

For example, the sequence

```
12
```

fits the definition of an expression, since it consists of one operand (12) and zero operators that combine to produce a value (12). More familiarly, the sequence

```
2 + 3
```

fits the definition of an expression, since it consists of two operands (2 and 3) and one operator (+) that combine to produce a value (5). Operands need not be constants — the sequence

```
2.5 * x - 1.0
```

fits the definition of an expression, since it consists of three operands (2.5, x and 1.0) and two operators (*, -) that combine to produce a value (1 less than the product of 2.5 and x).

These last two examples have been *arithmetic expressions*, that is, expressions whose operators are familiar arithmetic operators. As we shall see in today's exercise, C++ provides a rich set of arithmetic operators, as well as many non-arithmetic operators that allow C++ programmers to construct non-arithmetic expressions.

The Experimental Laboratory.

Begin by creating and changing directory to labs/lab3, and then copy the lab3 files from the class directory. Take a moment to view the file(s). Then use emacs to edit the file expr.cc.

The form of the iostream interactive output statement can be given as follows:

```
cout << Expression1 << Expression2 << ... << ExpressionN;
```

When execution reaches an output statement, Expression1 is evaluated and displayed, after which Expression2 is evaluated and displayed, after which ..., after which ExpressionN is evaluated and displayed. An output statement thus provides a simple "laboratory" in which we can "experiment" with expressions, and practice their construction.

Experiment 1: Simple Expressions.

Study the source program `expr.cc`, particularly the lines

```
cout << endl << i << '+' << j << " = " << i + j
     << endl << x << '+' << y << " = " << x + y
     << "\n\n";
```

In the space below, write what you think will appear on the screen when this program is executed (don't worry, wrong guesses are not penalized).

Use the compile command to translate `expr.cc`. Then execute `expr`. What is displayed?

If what was displayed was what you anticipated, give a detailed explanation of why you said what you did. If what was displayed differs from what you anticipated, explain what was wrong with your thinking.

From this, we can see that the effect of the `iostream` interactive output statement is to display on the screen the value of each *Expression¡* in the statement. We can also see that the word `endl` (declared in `iostream.h`) produces the same value as the newline character (`'\n'`).

Simple Expressions.

An expression that has a single operand and no operators is called a **simple expression**. Two of the expressions in the output statement in `expr.cc` are not simple expressions. Which of the expressions are not simple expressions?

Note that the value of a simple expression may consist of multiple characters when displayed. That is, while a simple expression is made up of a single operand, a single operand is not synonymous with a single character.

Experiment 2: Characters and Character Strings.

One of the simple expressions in the output statement is `'+'` and another is `" = "`.

A. In the space below, form a hypothesis that explains when characters should be surrounded with single-quotes (`'`) and when they should be surrounded with double-quotes (`"`). Don't worry about your hypothesis being wrong — it's finding out *why* it is wrong that is important.

B. Next, in the space below, design an experiment to test your hypothesis. This part you *should* worry about — if your hypothesis is wrong, then your experiment must tell you so.

C. Then carry out your experiment, and report its results in the space below:

D. If your hypothesis was shown to be incorrect, repeat steps A through C, until your hypothesis and experimental results agree.

Experiment 3: Arithmetic Expressions.

While simple expressions are sometimes useful, the process of *computation* involves the application of operators to operands. C++ provides a number of arithmetic operators that can be applied to numeric operands, including:

+   *addition*, computes the sum of two (integer or real) operands
−   *subtraction*, computes the difference of two (integer or real) operands
*   *multiplication*, computes the product of two (integer or real) operands
/   *division*, computes the quotient of the division two (integer or real) operands
%   *modulus*, computes the remainder of the division of two integer operands

While addition, subtraction and multiplication are similar for integers and reals, division and modulus are quite different, so let's spend some time exploring them.

1. Modify the output statement in the source program, to enable you to complete the following table, for `int` variables i and j, and `double` variables x and y (Hint: Add an input statement that allows you to enter values from the keyboard):

i	j	x	y	i / j	i % j	x / y
4	1	4.0	1.0	_____	_____	_____
4	2	4.0	2.0	_____	_____	_____
4	3	4.0	3.0	_____	_____	_____
4	4	4.0	4.0	_____	_____	_____
4	5	4.0	5.0	_____	_____	_____
4	6	4.0	6.0	_____	_____	_____
4	7	4.0	7.0	_____	_____	_____
4	8	4.0	8.0	_____	_____	_____
4	9	4.0	9.0	_____	_____	_____

2. Now, suppose that ABCD are the 4 digits of an arbitrary integer value. With or without the computer, give the values of the following expressions in terms of A, B, C and D:

```
ABCD / 1    = _____          ABCD % 1    = _____
ABCD / 10   = _____          ABCD % 10   = _____
ABCD / 100  = _____          ABCD % 100  = _____
ABCD / 1000 = _____          ABCD % 1000 = _____
```

Integer division and remaindering can thus be used to "tear apart" integer values.

3. How can integer remaindering tell us if an integer i is evenly divisible by an integer j?

4. How can integer remaindering tell us if an integer i is even? If i is odd?

Experiment 4: Operator Precedence.

The arithmetic operations of addition, subtraction, multiplication and division are familiar ones. However, when these operations are *mixed* within an expression, some mechanism must be used to determine which operation is to be performed first. This is important because the value of the expression can change, based on the order in which operators are applied.

To illustrate, consider the expression:

```
16 + 8 / 4
```

If the operations are simply performed from left-to-right (+, then /), the expression evaluates to

```
(16 + 8) / 4 = 24 / 4 = 6
```

but if the division operation for some reason is treated as "more important" and performed before the addition operation, then the expression evaluates to

```
16 + (8 / 4) = 16 + 2 = 18
```

The result of an expression thus depends on the order in which operators are applied. Using your source program, find out which operator is applied first in the preceding expression, and report it below, before continuing:

The order in which operators are applied is determined by a characteristic called **operator precedence**. Each C++ operator is given a precedence or priority level, and operators with higher priority levels are applied before those with lower priority levels. In C++, the precedence of the arithmetic operators are as follows:

High:	+ (positive), – (negative)
Medium:	*, /, %
Low:	+ (addition), – (subtraction)

Parentheses can be used to change the order in which operators are evaluated, with the operator in the inner-most parentheses being applied first. For example, in the expression

```
((9-1) * (1+1))
```

the subtraction is performed first, then the addition, and finally the multiplication.

Using "pencil and paper," find the value of the following expression:

```
1 / 2 * (3 - 4) * 5 + (6 % 7 - (8 - 9) / 8)
```


Then use your source program to check your answer.

Experiment 5: Operator Associativity.

You may have wondered what happens when the next operator to be applied could be either of two operators that have the same precedence level. For example, in the expression:

```
8 - 4 - 2
```

if the left-most subtraction is performed first, then the expression evaluates to

```
(8 - 4) - 2 = 4 - 2 = 2
```

while if the right-most subtraction is performed first, then the expression evaluates to

```
8 - (4 - 2) = 8 - 2 = 6
```

Thus, we see again that *the order in which operators are applied determines the value of the expression*. However, some characteristic other than precedence must be used in such situations, because each of the operators in question have the same precedence level.

This new characteristic is called **operator associativity**. More precisely, in an expression

$$x \; \Delta_1 \; y \; \Delta_2 \; z$$

where Δ_1 and Δ_2 are two operators with the same precedence level, if Δ_1 is applied before Δ_2, then Δ_1 and Δ_2 are described as **left-associative**, but if Δ_2 is applied before Δ_1, then they are described as **right-associative**. That is, the expression

```
8 - 4 - 2
```

will evaluate to 2 if - is left-associative, but will evaluate to 6 if - is right-associative. Use your sample program to find out the associativity of the - operator and report it below:

What is the associativity of the division operator / ?

The associativity of the addition and multiplication operators are more difficult to determine, because the **associativity property** holds for these operators, namely:

```
(x + y) + z
```
produces the same value as `x + (y + z)`
and
```
(x * y) * z
```
produces the same value as `x * (y * z)`

So we'll just tell you what you might have guessed: each of the C++ arithmetic operators +, -, *, / and % are left-associative, as are the majority of the operators in the language. However, not all of them are, as we shall see before the end of today's exercise.

To see a complete list of C++ operators, their precedence levels and their associativities, see Appendix C of *C++: An Introduction To Computing* (the textbook accompanying this manual.)

Experiment 6: Expressions Containing Functions.

In the last exercise, we saw that the square root operation can be performed through the use of a **function** named `sqrt()`, which is provided by the `math` library. While C++ provides the basic arithmetic operations through operators, additional operations are provided through such functions, which are usually stored in **libraries** so that they are readily accessible to any program that needs them. For example, the math library provides the following functions, most of which should be familiar to students who have had a course in trigonometry:

Function	Description
`sin(x)`	Sine of x (in radians)
`cos(x)`	Cosine of x (in radians)
`tan(x)`	Tangent of x (in radians)
`asin(x)`	Inverse sine of x (in radians)
`acos(x)`	Inverse cosine of x (in radians)
`atan(x)`	Inverse tangent of x (in radians)
`sinh(x)`	Hyperbolic sine of x (in radians)
`cosh(x)`	Hyperbolic cosine of x (in radians)
`tanh(x)`	Hyperbolic tangent of x (in radians)
`log10(x)`	Base 10 logarithm of x
`log(x)`	Base e (natural) logarithm of x
`pow(x,y)`	x raised to power y
`exp(x)`	e raised to the power x
`sqrt(x)`	Square root of x
`ceil(x)`	Smallest integer not less than x
`floor(x)`	Largest integer not greater than x
`fabs(x)`	absolute value of x

In each of these functions, the argument x is a real (`double`) value.

These functions are declared in the system file `math.h`, and so it is necessary to place the line

```
#include <math.h>
```

before the beginning of one's main program. The definitions of these functions are stored in the math library (`libm.a`), which is *not* automatically searched by most UNIX system compilers. To use one of these functions, you must therefore compile with the `-lm` switch:

Compile command: `g++ expr.cc -o expr -lm`

Modify your program as needed to find the following values (Hint: do them simultaneously, to reduce the time spent recompiling):

_____ the base-10 log of 1000.0   _____ 10.0 raised to the power 3.0

_____ the sine of π (3.14159) radians   _____ the cosine of π (3.14159) radians

_____ the inverse sine of 0.0   _____ the inverse cosine of 1.0

_____ the ceiling of 9.9   _____ the ceiling of 9.1

_____ the angle whose sine is 1   _____ the angle whose cosine is 1

Experiment 7: Declarations.

Given the ability to construct expressions, it becomes useful to be able to store the value of an expression. That is, if we have an expression whose value is needed several times, it is most time-efficient to evaluate the expression once, store its value, and then access the stored value, rather than spending time reevaluating the expression.

To illustrate, suppose that our problem involves two constant data objects: π and 2π. In the first approach, we might use π and recompute 2π each time it is needed:

```
// use 3.14159 and recompute 2.0 * 3.14159 each time it is needed
```

By contrast, the second approach is to store π and 2π with a statement called a **declaration**:

```
double
      Pi = 3.14159,
      TwoPi = 2.0 * Pi;
```

and then use these names each time their values are needed:

```
// use Pi and TwoPi each time they are needed
```

Take a moment and place this declaration in your source program and then modify the output statement to display the values of `Pi` and `TwoPi`, to check the value that has been stored.

A simplified general form of a declaration is

```
Type IdentifierList ;
```

where: *IdentifierList* is a list of one or more identifiers (separated by commas), each of may optionally be given an initial value with an initializer:

```
= ConstantExpression
```

and *Type* indicates the type of value we expect to store in the identifiers.

When execution reaches such a statement, storage is reserved for each identifier in *IdentifierList*, and each initializer is evaluated and its value placed in the storage associated with its identifier. An uninitialized identifier is described as **undefined**.

In the space to the right, construct error-free declarations for the identifiers:

• `Sum`, containing the integer value zero:

• `Letter`, containing the question-mark character:

• `Answer`, able to hold a character but left uninitialized:

Use your source program to test their correctness, if necessary.

Experiment 8: Constant Declarations.

The only problem with our declarations of `Pi` and `TwoPi` is that their values are *constants* (that should not change as the program executes), and their declaration declares their names as *variables* — objects whose values can vary as the program executes.

To illustrate, place the following assignment statement somewhere following the declaration statement and recompile:

```
Pi = -1.1;
```

No error will be generated, because we are simply changing the value of a variable, which is perfectly valid.

Next, alter the declaration statement as follows:

```
const double
        Pi = 3.14159,
        TwoPi = 2.0 * Pi;
```

and recompile. Record the error message generated in the space below:

By preceding a declaration with the keyword `const`, we allow the compiler to generate an error if we should mistakenly try to change the value of the object being declared. This should always be done for identifiers whose values should remain constant during program execution.

Construct error-free constant declarations for the identifiers:

• `SpeedOfLight`, containing the value 3.0×10^8:

• `MinScore` and `MaxScore`, containing the integer values 0 and 100, respectively:

• `MiddleInitial`, containing the appropriate character for your middle initial:

The type of an expression is the type of value it produces when evaluated. When declaring variables or constants, the type used to declare the identifier should always be the same as the type of value being stored in that identifier's storage.

Experiment 9: Assignment Statements.

Once we are able to declare variables, the next useful operation is to be able to change the value of those variables. This is most commonly done with an assignment statement:

```
Variable = Expression ;
```

Here, `Expression` is any valid C++ statement and `Variable` is an identifier that has been declared as a variable, whose type matches that of `Expression`. When execution reaches this statement:

1. `Expression` is evaluated; and
2. Its value is stored in the memory associated with `Variable`.

Unlike other languages, the assignment symbol (=) is an actual *operator that returns a value*. This means that the sequence of symbols

```
Variable = Expression
```

is itself an expression. We might determine what value is produced by this operator by performing an experiment that uses an output statement to display that value:

```
cout << ( Variable = Expression ) << endl;
```

(Note that the parentheses are necessary, because = has lower precedence than <<).

Using an experiment like this, determine what value is produced by the assignment operator. Report your findings in the space below:

Experiment 10: Assignment Associatitivy.

Because the assignment symbol (=) is an actual operator that returns a value, the sequence of symbols

```
Variable = Expression
```

is itself an expression that can appear to the right of an assignment operator, so that a statement with the form

```
w = x = y = z;
```

is a valid assignment, a phenomenon sometimes called **assignment chaining**.

The question is, what happens when execution reaches this statement?

The answer depends on the associativity of the assignment operator (=). That is, if assignment is left associative, then the expression is evaluated as

```
(((w = x) = y) = z)
```

but if assignment is right associative, then the expression is evaluated as

```
(w = (x = (y = z)))
```

We can determine the answer with an experiment. If we initialize w, x, y and z to different values, perform this assignment, and then display their values, the values that appear should provide us with enough information to determine whether assignment is left or right associative.

Conduct this experiment and record your conclusions in the space below:

Experiment 11: Assignment Shortcuts and Expressions.

There are some assignment operations that are performed so commonly, C++ provides special operators for them. For example, instead of writing

```
Sum = Sum + Count;
```

C++ provides the += operator that allows us to write the equivalent statement:

```
Sum += Count;
```

which saves us from having to retype the same identifier twice. This "shortcut" is provided for each of the arithmetic operators: if Δ is an arithmetic operator, then an expression of the form:

```
Varable1 = Variable1 Δ Expression
```

can be written as

```
Variable1 Δ= Expression
```

Each of these "shortcut" operators can be chained in the same manner as a normal assignment. For example, using pencil and paper, determine the values of w, x, y, and z after the following statements execute:

```
int   w = 8,
      x = 4,
      y = 2,
      z = 1;

w -= x /= y *= z += 1;
```

In what order are the operators applied?

Verify the correctness of your findings using your source program, recording any discrepancies in the space below.

Experiment 12: Increment and Decrement Expressions.

There are other assignments that occur so commonly, C++ provides special operators for them, too. For example, if x and y are integer variables, then in place of having to write

      x = x + 1;   and   y = y - 1;

C++ allows us to write

      x++;   and   y--;

The operators ++ and -- are called the **increment** and **decrement** operators, respectively. Each has two forms: the *prefix* form and the *postfix* form. When used as a statement:

      ++x;

or

      x++

the prefix and postfix forms are equivalent. Their difference is in the value returned by the operator. We can design an experiment to determine this difference:

```
int    x1,
       x2,
       Prefix,
       Postfix;

cin >> x1;              // input a value
x2 = x1;                // make a copy
Prefix = ++x1;          // save result of prefix form
Postfix = x2++;         // save result of postfix form
                        // display results
cout << endl << " x1: " << x1 << " x2: " << x2
     << "prefix: " << Prefix << " postfix: " << Postfix << endl;
```

Using several executions of your source program with a variety of input values, perform this experiment, and report your findings below:

Experiment 13: I/O Expressions.

Unlike most languages, C++ performs I/O through the use of expressions. To illustrate, the general form of an output expression is

```
Ostream << Expression
```

where *Ostream* is the name of an ostream (a type defined in the iostream library), << is the output or extraction operator, and *Expression* is any valid C++ expression.

When execution reaches such an expression, *Expression* is evaluated and its value is inserted onto *Ostream*. For example, in the output statement

```
cout << 2 + 3 ;
```

cout is the name of an ostream object defined in the iostream library that connects an executing program to an interactive output device (e.g., a computer monitor). The expression 2 + 3 is evaluated and the value 5 inserted onto cout, causing it to appear on your screen.

Does this indicate that the << operator is higher or lower in precedence then the + operator?

We have also seen that output expressions can be **chained** together, as follows:

```
cout << 1 << 3 << 5 << endl;
```

What is displayed? (Use your source program, if necessary.)

Does this indicate that the << operator is left, or right associative?

Now, if we combine the output expression general form given above with our knowledge of the associativity of the << operator, it should be evident that the values produced by the << operator is its left operand (the *Ostream*), to permit the chaining of output expressions.

The input operator has the same precedence and associativity as the output operator, and the value it produces is its left operand (an *Istream*), to permit the chaining of input expressions.

Phrases You Should Now Understand.

Expression, Simple Expression, Operand, Operator, Operator Precedence, Operator Associativity, Integer Division, Library Function, Variable Declaration, Constant Declaration, Operator Chaining, Increment Operator, Decrement Operator, Output Operator, Input Operator.

Objectives.

1. Gain further experience constructing expressions.
2. Gain further experience writing programs.

Introduction.

Each of the following projects involves the construction of expressions of various types, in solving a particular problem, and so will give you practice building expressions. Your instructor will tell you which project to do.

Projects.

3.1. Write a program that finds the resistance of an electronic circuit with three parallel resistors *R1*, *R2* and *R3*. The resistance can be computed using the following formula:

$$Resistance = \frac{1}{\frac{1}{R1} + \frac{1}{R2} + \frac{1}{R3}}$$

3.2. Write a program that, given the amount of a purchase and the amount received in payment, computes the change in dollars, half-dollars, quarters, dimes, nickels and pennies.

3.3. A point in a two-dimensional coordinate system can be designated in either or two ways:

- A *rectangular coordinate* is a pair (x, y), where x is the horizontal distance along the x-axis, and y is the vertical distance along the y-axis.

- A *polar coordinate* is a pair (r, θ), where r is the distance from the origin, and θ is the angular displacement from the horizontal axis.

Polar coordinates can be converted to rectangular coordinates, using the formulas:

    x = r × the cosine of θ; and
    y = r × the sine of θ.

Write a program that can be used to convert polar coordinates to rectangular coordinates.

3.4. The two solutions of a quadratic equation $y = ax^2 + bx + c$ (assuming that $a \neq 0$) can be found using the **quadratic formula**:

$$x = \frac{-b \pm \sqrt{b^2 - 4ac}}{2a}$$

Write a program that finds both solutions of a quadratic equation, assuming that $a \neq 0$.

Project 3 Due Date _____

Turn in this grade sheet, attached to a hard copy of

a. your source program; and
b. three executions of your source program using sample data.

Name _____

Category	Points Possible	Points Received
Correctness and Efficiency	50	_____
Complete Documentation	35	
- Who, What, Where, etc	10	_____
- Specification	10	_____
- In-Program Comments	5	_____
- Meaningful Identifiers	5	_____
- White Space	5	_____
User-Friendliness	15	
- Opening Message	5	_____
- Descriptive Input Prompts	5	_____
- Labeled Output	5	_____
Total	**100**	_____

Lab 4

Functions and Libraries

Note to the Instructor:

This lab exercise deals with the construction of a separately compiled library. Separate compilation makes translation a 2-step process: each source file is *compiled* to create an object file (ending in `.o`). The object files are then *linked* to create a binary executable program.

To coordinate separate compilation, UNIX systems provide the `make` facility. To use this facility, a programmer prepares a special file called a `Makefile` (beginning with capital-M by convention, not necessity). The `Makefile` consists of a series of pairs lines of the form:

```
TargetFile: ComponentFile1 ComponentFile2 ... ComponentFileN
      Command
```

where `Command` is a UNIX command that makes `TargetFile` from the N `ComponentFile`s. For example, our binary executable program `driver` is made by linking the object files `driver.o` and `Metric.o`, and so the first pair in the `Makefile` is roughly as follows:

```
driver: driver.o Metric.o
      g++ driver.o Metric.o -o driver
```

Similarly, `driver.o` is made by compiling `driver.cc`, which includes (and thus depends upon) `Metric.h`, and so the second pair in the `Makefile` is roughly as follows:

```
driver.o: driver.cc Metric.h
      g++ -c driver.cc
```

The `-c` switch tells g++ to just compile `driver.cc` to create an object file, instead of compiling and linking to create a binary executable (which is the default action used in the previous labs). A similar rule specifies the making of `Metric.o`.

A partial `Makefile` is provided in the `lab4` directory on the distribution diskette, and the section **Creating a Makefile** teaches the student its structure and has them complete it.

Objectives.

1. Gain experience declaring simple functions.
2. Gain experience defining simple functions.
3. Gain experience creating separately compiled function libraries.

Prelab Questions:

1. A library is stored in two separate files: the _____ file and the _____ file.

2. A minimal function definition is called a function _____.

3. A value that is passed to a function when that function is called is an _____ to that function.

4. An object in a function in which a function argument is (automatically) stored is called a _____.

5. A program used solely to "test-drive" the functions in a library is called a _____ program.

Introduction.

As you likely found out when you purchased your textbooks this semester, books can be quite expensive. One way that this expense can be reduced is the idea of *sharing*: If you are unable to afford the full price for a book, and can find another person with the same problem, then you might purchase the book together, and share it. By having one person use the book and then another person *re-use* the book, the individual cost of using the book is cut in half.

The idea of a *library* is a generalization on this idea of sharing. If a community of people pools their resources, then they can buy and share a centralized collection of books. By doing so, each person has access to a greater set of books than he or she could afford individually.

The ideas of sharing, libraries and re-use are very important in C++, and we have already (unwittingly) used them extensively. For example, in the previous lab exercises, we wrote

```
#include <iostream.h>
```

Recall that the effect of this directive is to insert the contents of the file <iostream.h> (in which cin, cout, << and >> are declared) into our source program. Recall also that each of the programs we have written has re-used this same set of declarations. The file <iostream.h> is thus similar to a library of books, in that it contains a set of declarations that can be shared and re-used by any program that needs them. In fact, <iostream.h> is a part of the *iostream library* — a software library of I/O related functions.

Software libraries are particularly useful, because they reduce the cost of programming. For example, in a previous lab exercise, we used the sqrt() function from the *math library*, and so avoided the extra "cost" of having to write our own square root function. Libraries thus provide a place where groups of related functions can be stored, so that we (or even other programmers) can access them and thus avoid "re-inventing the wheel."

While C++ provides a number of ready-made libraries for us, C++ permits programmers to construct their own libraries. Constructing such a library is the subject of today's exercise.

Planning Ahead.

One issue that we must resolve before beginning is where we wish to store the libraries that we create. This is important because if we wish to use a programmer-defined library in a program, then we must tell the compiler where to find that library when we translate our program.

The common approach is to designate one directory as a special *library directory* in which we will store all of the libraries that we define. However, following this approach greatly complicates the exercise and obfuscates its objectives: functions, libraries and separate compilation. To keep our presentation simple, we will construct our library in ~/labs/lab4.

Planning a Library.

The library we will create today will provide us with a set of functions to convert English-system measurements into their metric-system counterparts. We will call our library `Metric`.

The first thing that we must decide is what measurement conversions we wish our library to provide. For example, the following are just a few of the useful conversions:

English Unit	Metric Unit	Conversion Formula
Inches	Centimeters	1 inch = 2.54 cm
Feet	Centimeters	1 foot = 30.48 cm
Feet	Meters	1 foot = 0.3048 m
Yards	Meters	1 yard = 0.9144 m
Miles	Kilometers	1 mile = 1.609344 km
Ounces	Grams	1 ounce = 28.349523 g
Pounds	Kilograms	1 pound = 0.3732417 kg
Tons	Kilograms	1 ton = 907.18474 kg
Pints	Liters	1 pint = 0.473163 l
Quarts	Liters	1 quart = 0.946326 l
Gallons	Liters	1 gallon = 3.785306 l

Our exercise today is to write a *subprogram* (more precisely, a *function*) to convert feet into meters. By storing this function in library `Metric`, it can be shared by any and all programs that need to convert feet into meters, allowing them to avoid "redefining the wheel."

Library Structure.

A library consists two separate files: the library's **header file** in which you *declare* all names that are to be accessible outside of the library; and the library's **implementation file** in which you *define* each of the names declared in the header file. One way to think of these files is that the header file provides an *interface* to the library, by providing just enough information for a program to use the names, without specifying their details. The implementation file contains all of the details about how those names are defined.

Why this separation ? The reason has to do with program maintenance. If we are writing a library, then we expect that a number of programs will make use of it. It is often the case that even a well-designed library may need to be updated (i.e., maintained), if a better way is discovered to perform one of its operations. If we have designed our operations carefully, then updating a library operation should simply involve altering its definition (in the implementation file), not its declaration (in the header file).

Now suppose that a program somehow made use of the definition details of a library operation. If it did, then updating that operation might change those details, and necessitate an update to the program as well. That is what we want to avoid at all costs — *updating a library operation should not require any updating of a program that uses that operation.*

This goal is the reason for separating a library operation's declaration from its definition. A program that uses an operation can "see" its declaration (by including the header file), but cannot "see" its definition (since the implementation file is not included).

Building the Header File.

Begin by creating and changing directory to `labs/lab4`. Then copy all of the files from the `lab4` class directory into your `lab4` directory. Invoke emacs to edit the file `Metric.h` (the name of the library's header file always ends in `.h`) and personalize its opening documentation. A simplified general form of a library header file is as follows:

```
OpeningDocumentation
DeclarationList
```

where `OpeningDocumentation` is a comment describing the library, its operations, and how to use them; and `DeclarationList` is any sequence of valid C++ declarations.

Declaring A Function (Specification).

While the specification for a program typically identifies the values that the program must (i) input and (ii) output, the specification of a subprogram typically identifies what values that subprogram must (i) *receive from the caller of the subprogram*, and (ii) *return to its caller*, as well as any values that it must input or output. For example, in order for a subprogram to convert feet to meters, we might specify:

```
/*--- FeetToMeters converts Feet to the equivalent number of Meters.

   Specification:
      receive: the number of feet to be converted, a real value;
      return:  the equivalent number of meters, also a real value.
-------------------------------------------------------------*/
```

Add this comment to `Metric.h`, following its opening documentation.

The declaration of a function has the following simplified general form:

```
ReturnType FunctionName ( ParameterDecList ) ;
```

where `ReturnType` is the type of value returned by the function, `FunctionName` is the name of the function, and `ParameterDecList` is a list of declarations of **parameters** — objects that will store values passed to the function when it is called. That is, *a parameter must be declared for each value that a function receives from its caller.*

A precise function specification tells us how to build the function declaration. To illustrate:

1. Its specification tells us that `FeetToMeters()` must return a real value to its caller, and so the `ReturnType` of `FeetToMeters()` should be `double`.

2. Its specification also tells us that `FeetToMeters()` must receive one real value from its caller (the number of feet to be converted), and so `FeetToMeters()` should have one `double` parameter, which we might call `Feet`.

We can thus complete our header file with this declaration of function `FeetToMeters()`:

```
double FeetToMeters(double Feet);
```

Building the Implementation File.

As stated previously, the definitions of library functions should appear in the library's implementation file, so use the emacs *find-file* command: C-x C-f to open the file Metric.cc. The general form of an implementation file is as follows:

```
OpeningDocumentation

#include "LibraryName.h"

DefinitionList
```

Take a moment to personalize the opening documenation, and add a #include directive that inserts our Metric library's header file. (Note that *quotes*, not <>, surround the file name.)

Defining A Function (Design).

The general form of a function *definition* is

```
ReturnType FunctionName ( ParameterDefList )
{
        StatementList
}
```

where ReturnType and FunctionName are the same as in a function declaration, and ParameterDefList is a list of parameter *definitions* (i.e., the parameter names must be supplied), and StatementList is a sequence of valid C++ statements.

A **function stub** is a minimal function definition — like a function declaration followed by a pair of empty braces, instead of a semicolon. For example, we might define the following stub for FeetToMeters():

```
double FeetToMeters (double Feet)
{

}
```

Insert this stub at the end of the implementation file and then compile it using the command:

Compile command: g++ -c Metric.cc

If all is well, then the function stub in Metric.cc should compile without generating any error messages. If you see error messages, then your function declaration (in the header file) likely does not match its definition (in this file). Such errors can usually be found by comparing the two against one another. Find and correct your error(s), before continuing.

Take a moment and consider what we just did. We just compiled a file that contains no main program and the compiler didn't generate an error. How can this be?

The answer is the idea of **separate compilation**. Translation is actually a two-step process: (1) *compiling* the source file creates an object file, and (2) *linking* the object file to any libraries it uses creates a binary executable. The -c switch tells g++ to stop after compiling, producing the object file Metric.o. What happens if you compile Metric.cc without the -c switch?

Designing Function `FeetToMeters()`.

Just as the form of a function's declaration and stub are determined by its problem specification, the *StatementList* of a function definition is determined by the design of the algorithm that solves its problem. We might start by identifying the following objects:

- *Feet*, the number of feet to be converted.
- the number of meters equivalent to *Feet*.

The relationship between these two objects is given in our table of metric conversions, where we see that there is a third (constant) object:

- The conversion factor 0.3048

Now that we have identified all of the objects needed to perform the conversion, we must identify the operations that are needed. The following operations seem necessary:

- Receive a real value in parameter `Feet` from the caller.
- Multiply `Feet` by the conversion factor.
- Return the result of the preceding multiplication to the caller.

The first operation is taken care of for us by the C++ function-call mechanism. When the caller evaluates an expression that calls our function, such as:

```
FeetToMeters(2.5);
```

then a copy of the argument `2.5` will automatically be stored in parameter `Feet` in our function. Thus, when our function begins execution, the value of `Feet` will be the value of the argument with which the function was called (`2.5`, in our example).

In the space below, construct a valid C++ expression that performs the second operation:

The third operation can be performed using the C++ `return` statement, whose general form is:

```
return Expression ;
```

where *Expression* is any valid C++ expression. In the space below and in the stub of `FeetToMeters()`, write a `return` statement that accomplishes the third operation:

Then recompile the implementation file of `Metric` to verify that what you have written is free of syntax errors. If it contains errors, they must lie in your return statement, so compare what you have written with the discussion above to find the error.

When the syntax errors have been corrected, our `FeetToMeters()` operation is ready to be tested by a program. The header file `Metric.h` provides an interface to the operation, by declaring function `FeetToMeters()`; and the implementation file `Metric.cc` provides the details of how function `FeetToMeters()` is implemented.

Writing a Program to Utilize the Library.

Next, use the find-file command to open `driver.cc` and personalize its documentation. In this file we will create a program whose sole purpose is to test `FeetToMeters()`. Such programs are called *driver programs*, because all they do is "test-drive" a library.

The Driver Program.

Specification. Since the purpose of a driver program is simply to test a library's operations, the specification of the problem a driver program must solve is straightforward:

Input(keyboard): A real value, stored in a variable *Feet*.
Output(screen): The number of meters equivalent to *Feet*.

Design. For such a program, the objects named in the specification are the only objects required to solve our problem. We can thus define the following algorithm:

A. Prompt for, and input a real value, storing it in *InValue*.
B. Output the value produced by calling `FeetToMeters(`*InValue*`)`.

Coding. Personalize the opening documentation in the driver program. Then use the preceding specification to complete its opening documentation.

Recall: An **argument** is a value that is passed to a function when the function is called.

For example, *InValue* is an argument to function `FeetToMeters()` in the expression:

`FeetToMeters(`*InValue*`)`

There are two important rules to remember when calling a function:

1. The number of arguments in a function call must equal the number of parameters in its declaration and definition.

2. The types of the first argument and first parameter, the second argument and second parameter, the third argument and third parameter, etc. must be the same.

The preceding algorithm can be encoded by starting with the minimal C++ program and then adding valid C++ statements that encode our algorithm. Be sure to use `#include` directives to insert the header files of both the `iostream` library and our `Metric` library.

Translation.

Since our program involves two files (`driver.cc` and `Metric.cc`), translating it becomes slightly more complicated. When a program consists of multiple files, the easiest way to translate them is with a special UNIX utility named **make** (where have you seen that before?). To use make, we must prepare a special file called a `Makefile`. As we shall see, this file coordinates the compilation of the source files and the linking of the object files. A partial `Makefile` is provided with this lab, and the next section involves completing it.

Makefile Structure.

Use the find-file command to open the file named Makefile. A simple Makefile consists of a series of pairs of lines, in which the first line of the pair names the file being made (called the *target*), followed by a colon (:), followed by the files from which it is made (called the *components*). The second line of the pair consists of a TAB, followed by a command that makes the target from the components. A carriage return *must* be present at the end of the second line. For example, our binary executable program driver is made by linking together the object files driver.o and Metric.o, so the first pair in our Makefile is as follows:

```
driver: driver.o Metric.o
    g++ driver.o Metric.o -o driver
```

In the same fashion, our driver program's object file driver.o is made from driver.cc, along with Metric.h (which driver.cc includes). Since driver.o is made by having g++ compile driver.cc with the -c switch, this pair appears as follows:

```
driver.o: driver.cc Metric.h
    g++ -c driver.cc
```

A similar pair is used to specify the way that Metric.o is made from Metric.cc and Metric.h. In the space below and at the end of your Makefile, construct such a pair. Don't forget the return at the end of the line — this is the most common Makefile error.

To test your Makefile, first remove Metric.o from your lab4 directory (you can issue a UNIX command like rm from within emacs through the emacs *shell* command M-x shell). Then use the emacs *compile* command M-x compile, but with the following command:

Compile command: make

This will invoke make, which reads your Makefile and begins by trying to make the first target it encounters (driver). However, make cannot create driver until both driver.o and Metric.o exist, and so it must make each of them in turn. Since driver.o is listed first, make jumps to the pair that tells it how to make driver.o. Since driver.o depends on driver.cc and Metric.h, and both of these exist, make executes the second line in this pair:

```
    g++ -c driver.cc
```

which creates driver.o, if driver.cc contains no syntax errors.

Once driver.o exists, make jumps to the pair that tells it how to make Metric.o (i.e., the pair of lines you just wrote). If you wrote the pair correctly, then you should observe the second line of that pair execute, creating Metric.o.

Once driver.o and Metric.o exist, everything needed to build the target driver is available, and so make returns to the first pair and executes its second line:

```
    g++ driver.o Metric.o -o driver
```

This produces the binary executable driver, finishing the translation.

Testing.

Once `driver` has been successfully translated, we are ready to test what we have written, to see if we can discover any logical errors. Execute `driver`, using the following sample data, to test the correctness of `FeetToMeters()`:

Feet	(Theoretical) Meters	(Observed) Meters
1.0	0.3048	_____
3.3	1.00584	_____

Since `FeetToMeters()` is a linear function, two appropriately chosen test values are sufficient to verify its correctness. Be sure to note and correct any discrepancies. When `driver` executes correctly, our driver program is complete!

More About make.

Before we quit, let's learn a bit more about how make works. Remember, when we translated `driver`, three steps occurred:

1. `driver.cc` was compiled, producing `driver.o`;
2. `Metric.cc` was compiled, producing `Metric.o`; and
3. `driver.o` and `Metric.o` were linked, producing `driver`.

Using emacs, alter `driver.cc` in some trivial way (i.e., add a blank line at the beginning of the file). Then use `M-x compile` to invoke make again. Do all three steps occur again? If not, which step is omitted?

UNIX systems associate a "last modification" date with each file. To avoid recompiling a file needlessly, the make program uses these dates to determine what files need to be recompiled. That is, `Metric.cc` had not been modified since `Metric.o` was created. The date on `Metric.o` was thus newer than that on `Metric.cc`. The make program noted this and concluded that `Metric.o` was up to date, and so did not waste time recompiling `Metric.cc`.

By contrast, when we made our trivial modification to `driver.cc` and then saved it, the file `driver.cc` became newer than the file `driver.o`. The make program noted this, concluded that `driver.o` was outdated, and so re-made `driver.o`.

This in turn made `driver.o` newer than `driver`, and so the make program reperformed the command to make `driver`, which relinked (the new) `driver.o` and (the old) `Metric.o`.

In general, make will only re-make a target if any of that target's components are out of date. To see this, make `driver` one last time (with no modification) and record the ouput below:

Phrases You Should Now Understand.

Library, Function, Parameter, Argument, Driver Program.

Objectives.

1. Gain further experience defining functions.
2. Gain further experience using libraries.
3. Gain experience working in groups.

Introduction.

This week's project is to expand the operations provided by library Metric, as a 4-person group project. Each group member is responsible for three different conversion functions.

Projects.

Each of the following projects is to be performed by a different member of your group, by adding the necessary function declarations and definitions to their own copy of library Metric.

4.1. Lengths.
A. Inches to Centimeters (1 inch = 2.54 cm);
B. Yards to Meters (1 yard = 0.9144 m); and
C. Miles to Kilometers (1 mile = 1.609344 km).

4.2. Weights
D. Ounces to Grams (1 ounce = 28.349523 g);
E. Pounds to Kilograms (1 pound = 0.3732417 kg); and
F. Tons to Kilograms 1 ton = 907.18474 kg).

4.3. Volumes
G. Pints to Liters (1 pint = 0.473163 l);
H. Quarts to Liters (1 quart = 0.946326 l); and
I. Gallons to Liters (1 gallon = 3.785306 l).

4.4. Areas.
J. Square Inches to Square Millimeters (1 sq. in. = 645.16 sq. mm);
K. Square Feet to Square Meters (1 sq. foot = 0.09290304 sq. m); and
L. Acres to Square Meters (1 Acre = 4.04686×10^3 sq. m).

Each group member is to write the functions for which they are responsible <u>on their own</u>, without consulting anyone else. The group should then meet together to define a master header file and implementation file, a copy of which can then be given to each group member. Then as a group, modify the driver program so that it performs the following steps:

> Print an explanatory message;
> Prompt for, and input a real value, storing it in *InVal*;
> Output the result of calling function A with *InVal* as an argument;
> Output the result of calling function B with *InVal* as an argument;
>   ...
> Output the result of calling function L with *InVal* as an argument.

Your driver program should thus test each function in the library.

The opening documentation of Metric should indicate which group member was responsible for which functions. Only that group member will be penalized for any errors in that set of functions.

Project 4 Due Date _____

As a group, turn in each group member's grade sheet, plus a hard copy of the following files:

a. `driver.cc`;
b. `Metric.h`;
c. `Metric.cc`;
d. 3 executions of `driver`, entering the values: 3.666667, 16.5, and 256.0.

Name _____

Category	Points Possible	Points Received
Driver Program........................	30	
Correctness........................	20	_____
Specifications.....................	5	_____
Style/Readability..................	5	_____
Header File........................	28	
Opening Documentation.............	10	_____
Specifications ($\times$ 3)................	9	_____
Function Declarations ($\times$ 3)...........	9	_____
Implementation File....................	42	
Function Definitions ($\times$ 3)...........	30	_____
Meaningful Identifiers...............	3	_____
Style/Readability..................	9	_____
Total............................	**100**	_____

Lab 5

Selective Execution

Objectives.

1. Introduce the construction of conditions;
2. Introduce the use of the selective control structures; and
3. Practice constructing subprograms.

Prelab Questions:

1. What are the six C++ relational operators?

2. What are the three C++ logical operators?

3. Name one of the C++ statements for performing selective execution.

4. Name the other C++ statement for performing selective execution.

5. The function `cin.good()` is an example of a special kind of function called a
_____ function.

Introduction.

One of the easiest ways to make a complex program user-friendly is to make it *menu-driven*. That is, rather than prompting the user in some vague sort of way, we present them with a menu of the choices available to them at each stage. Then all the user has to do is look at the menu and choose one of the choices. Since the menu always tells the user what their options are, the user needs no special knowledge, making such a program easy to use.

For example, a simple 4-function calculator program might prompt the user as follows:

```
Please enter:
    + to add two numbers;
    - to subtract two numbers;
    * to multiple two numbers; or
    / to divide two numbers.
-->
```

Thanks to the menu, a user knows exactly what they are to enter, rather than having to guess.

Today's exercise involves completing such a program, and learning about the C++ *control structures* (statements that control the flow of execution through your program) along the way.

Getting Started.

Create and change directory to `labs/lab5`. Copy the file `calc.cc` from the `lab5` class directory and then personalize its opening documentation. Then take a few moments to study its structure.

Specification.

The problem to be solved by a four-function calculator might be specified as follows:

```
/*------------------------------------------------------------------
...

Specification:
    input(keyboard): a char, stored in variable Operation;
                     two reals, stored in variables Op1 and Op2;
    output(screen): the result of the expression (Op1 Operation Op2).
-------------------------------------------------------------------*/
```

Today's exercise is to complete `calc.cc` so that it solves this problem.

Design.

From the preceding discussion and our specification, we can identify the following objects:

- *Menu*, a menu of the operations supported by the calculator.
- *Operation*, a character that indicates what operation the user wants to perform.
- *Op1*, the left operand in the expression being computed.
- *Op2*, the right operand in the expression being computed.
- *Result*, the result of the expression *Op1 Operation Op2*.

Since our function is to be a four-function calculator, we need the following operations:

- Output a menu of choices.
- Input a character value.
- Input two real values (after displaying an appropriate prompt).
- Do any <u>one</u> of the following, based on *Operation*:
    Add two real values,
    Subtract two real values,
    Multiply two real values, or
    Divide two real values.
- Store a real value in a real variable.
- Output a real value.

A menu is simply a (long) character string, so that displaying a menu can be accomplished with an output statement. Similarly, we can input character and real values using the input statement. The next-to-last operation can be accomplished with an assignment statement, and the final operation can be done with another output statement.

However, the fourth operation is unusual. How do we selectively perform *one* of the four arithmetic operations while *not performing the other three*?

The key to the question lies in the word *selectively*. That is, if the value *Operation* is ' + ', then we need to select the assignment statement:

```
Result = Op1 + Op2;
```

but if the value of *Operation* is ' - ', then we need to select a different assignment:

```
Result = Op1 - Op2;
```

whereas if the value of *Operation* is ' * ', then we need to select another assignment:

```
Result = Op1 * Op2;
```

while the value of *Operation* being ' / ' means that we need to select yet another assignment:

```
Result = Op1 / Op2;
```

Since we want to take different actions based on the value of *Operation*, it must clearly be used to somehow select the appropriate assignment statement.

Conditions.

In order to determine which assignment statement to perform, we need some means of determining the relationship between *Operation* and the various menu choice characters. This relationship can be determined with a new kind of operation called a *relational operator*. There are six of these operators (==, <, >, !=, <=, and >=) which behave as follows:

Expression	Evaluates to	Expression	Evaluates to
$x == y$	1, if x is equal to y; 0, otherwise.	$x \mathrel{!=} y$	1, if x is not equal to y; 0, otherwise.
$x < y$	1, if x is less than y; 0, otherwise.	$x >= y$	1, if x is greater than or equal to y; 0, otherwise.
$x > y$	1, if x is greater than y; 0, otherwise.	$x <= y$	1 if x is less than or equal to y; 0, otherwise.

Note that C++ uses the integer value **1** to represent the logical value *true*, and the value **0** to represent the logical value *false*. Expressions that evaluate to true (1) or false (0) are sometimes called **conditions**.

Use these operators to construct a condition that evaluates to true (1) if:

LetterGrade is equal to the char 'A':

Age is less than the integer 21:

GradePoint is greater than 2.5:

Score is less than or equal to *Average*:

The relational operators thus provide us with the means of comparing two values and returning true or false, based on their values.

The first step in selecting the appropriate assignment statement in our calculator problem is to build the appropriate conditions. In the space below, construct four conditions that can be used to relate *Operation* and a menu choice:

1. *Operation* is equal to '+':

2. *Operation* is equal to '-':

3. *Operation* is equal to '*':

4. *Operation* is equal to '/':

Selective Execution 1: The `if` Statement.

Once we have a means of determining the relationship between *Operation* and a given menu choice, we need to be able to select the appropriate assignment statement, based on the truth or falsehood of our set of conditions.

For executing statements selectively, C++ provides the `if` statement, whose general form is:

```
if ( Condition ) Statement1 [ else Statement2 ]
```

Here, `if` and `else` are C++ keywords, `Condition` is a C++ expression that evaluates to true (1) or false (0), and $Statement_1$ and $Statement_2$ are either individual or compound C++ statements (including other `if` statements). The brackets (`[` and `]`) are used to indicate that the `else` $Statement_2$ can be omitted.

When execution reaches an if statement, its `Condition` is evaluated. If it evaluates to true, then $Statement_1$ is executed, while $Statement_2$ (if present) is skipped. If it evaluates to false, then $Statement_1$ is skipped, while $Statement_2$ (if present) is executed.

In the absence of an `else` $Statement_2$ portion:

```
if ( Condition )
      Statement
```

an `if` statement is sometimes called a *single-branch* construct, since it allows the selective execution of a single section of code.

By contrast, an `if` statement with an `else` $Statement_2$ portion:

```
if ( Condition )
      Statement1
else
      Statement2
```

is sometimes called a *two-branch* (or *dual-branch*) construct, since it allows the selective execution of either of two sections of code.

A third form of the statement occurs when $Statement_2$ is another `if` statement:

```
if ( Condition1 )
      Statement1
else if ( Condition2 )
      .Statement2
...
else if ( Conditionn )
      Statementn
else
      Statementn+1
```

This form is called a *multi-branch* construct, since it allows the selection of any of n+1 different sections of code.

In the space below and in your source program, write a series of four if statements that encode the following multi-branching logic:

> If *Operator* is equal to '+', then set *Result* to the sum of *Op1* and *Op2*.
> Otherwise, if *Operator* is equal to '-', then set *Result* to the difference of *Op1* and *Op2*.
> Otherwise, if *Operator* is equal to '*', then set *Result* to the product of *Op1* and *Op2*.
> Otherwise, if *Operator* is equal to '/', then set *Result* to the quotient of *Op1* and *Op2*.
> Otherwise, display an "invalid menu choice" message.
> End if.

Use the emacs save as command: C-x C-w to save your source program under the name calc1.cc, translate it, and test the correctness of what you have written. Use the space below to record any difficulties you encounter, and how they were corrected.

When what you have written has been thoroughly tested, print a hard copy of calc1.cc.

Selective Execution 2: The `switch` Statement.

If we examine the multi-branch `if` statement that we just wrote, we see that it is functionally correct, in that it solves the problem. However, it suffers from a drawback: to perform the addition operation, one condition (`Operation == '+'`) is evaluated; to perform subtraction, two conditions (`Operation == '+'` followed by `Operation == '-'`) are evaluated; to perform multiplication, three conditions (`Operation == '+'` followed by `Operation == '-'` followed by `Operation == '*'`) must be evaluated, and so on. In general, selecting $Statement_i$ using a multi-branch `if` statement requires the evaluation of i conditions. Since evaluation of each condition consumes time, statements that occur later in the multi-branch `if` statement incur a *performance penalty* when compared with statements that occur earlier.

In certain situations, this penalty can be avoided by using the **`switch` statement**, an alternative selective execution statement whose simplified general form is:

```
switch ( ConstantExpression )
{
        CaseList1
                                StatementList1
        CaseList2
                                StatementList2
        ...
        CaseListn
                                StatementListn
        default :
                                StatementListn+1
}
```

where   `ConstantExpression` is any C++ expression that evaluates to a constant;
each $StatementList_i$ is a sequence of valid C++ statements, and
each $CaseList_i$ is one or more *Cases* of the form:

```
        case ConstantExpression :
```

When execution reaches a `switch` statement, the following actions occur:

1. The `switch` statement's `ConstantExpression` is evaluated.

2. If the value of `ConstantExpression` is present in $CaseList_i$, then execution begins in $StatementList_i$ and proceeds, until a `break` statement, a `return` statement, or the end of the `switch` statement is encountered.

3. If the value of `ConstantExpression` is not present in any $CaseList_i$, then the (optional) default $StatementList_{n+1}$ is executed, if present.

Note that a given value for `ConstantExpression` can appear in only 1 $CaseList_i$.

Note also that a `break` statement is usually used at the end of each $StatementList_i$, to force execution to leave the `switch` statement. If a `break` is not present, the C++ `switch` statement has an interesting *drop-through effect*, so that upon reaching the end of $StatementList_i$, execution proceeds to $StatementList_{i+1}$. This can be quite surprising, if you forget about it, or are used to using the similar case statements of other languages.

An important question is: Under what circumstances should a `switch` statement be used, instead of an `if` statement ?

The answer is that if an algorithm requires selective execution using multi-branch logic like the following:

> If (*Variable* is equal to *Value$_1$*) then
> > *StatementList$_1$*
>
> Else if (*Variable* is equal to *Value$_2$*) then
> > *StatementList$_2$*
>
> ...
>
> Else if (*Variable* is equal to *Value$_n$*) then
> > *StatementList$_n$*
>
> Else
> > *StatementList$_{n+1}$*
>
> End if

then the algorithm could be encoded using a multi-branch `if` statement:

```
if (Variable == Value1)
{
        StatementList1
}
else if (Variable == Value2)
{
        StatementList2
}
...
else if (Variable == Valuen)
{
        StatementListn
}
else
{
        StatementListn+1
}
```

but it is usually more efficient to use a `switch` statement with the form:

```
switch (Variable)
{
        case Value1:
                        StatementList1
                        break;
        case Value2:
                        StatementList2
                        break;
        ...
        case Valuen:
                        StatementListn
                        break;
        default:
                        StatementListn+1
}
```

The reason the `switch` statement solution is more efficient than the multi-branch `if` statement in such situations is that where execution of *StatementList_i* in a multi-branch `if` requires the evaluation of i conditions, a `switch` statement can select *StatementList_i* with the evaluation of a single condition. The `switch` statement thus eliminates the performance penalty of the multi-branch `if` statement.

In the space below and in your source program, replace the multi-branch `if` statement with a `switch` statement.

Then save your source program under the name `calc2.cc`, translate it and test the correctness of what you have written. Use the space below to record any difficulties you encounter.

When what you have written has been thoroughly tested, continue to the next section.

Defensive Programming.

At this point, the algorithm used by our source program can be described as follows:

0. Display an introductory message;
1. Display a menu of operations, and input a char,
    storing it in *Operation*;
2. Prompt for and input two real values, storing them in *Op1* and *Op2*;
3. If *Operation* is equal to '+', then
            Set *Result* to the sum of *Op1* and *Op2*;
    Else if *Operation* is equal to '-', then
            Set *Result* to the difference of *Op1* and *Op2*;
    Else if *Operation* is equal to '*', then
            Set *Result* to the product of *Op1* and *Op2*;
    Else if *Operation* is equal to '/', then
            Set *Result* to the quotient of *Op1* and *Op2*;
    Else
            Display an "invalid menu choice message";
    End if.
4. Display the value of *Result*.

Let's begin to think defensively. What mistakes might the user make? How would such mistakes affect the execution of our program?

Our program requires two actions of its users. The first is when they input a character for *Operation*, and the second is when they input the real values for *Op1* and *Op2*. It should be evident that errors could occur on either of these actions:

1. The user might enter a character other than +, -, *, or / for *Operation*; and
2. The user might enter a non-real value (e.g., any non-numeric value such as a letter).
3. For division, the user might enter a zero denominator (e.g., a divide-by-zero error).

To check for the first error, we might adjust our algorithm as follows:

0. Display an introductory message;
1. Display a menu of operations, and input a char,
    storing it in *Operation*;
**2. If *Operation* is '+', or *Operation* is '-',
    or *Operation* is '*', or *Operation* is '/', then**
        A. Prompt for and input two real values, storing them in *Op1* and *Op2*;
        B. If *Operation* is equal to '+', then
            Set *Result* to the sum of *Op1* and *Op2*;
        Else if *Operation* is equal to '-', then
                Set *Result* to the difference of *Op1* and *Op2*;
        Else if *Operation* is equal to '*', then
                Set *Result* to the product of *Op1* and *Op2*;
        Else (*Operation* must be equal to '/')
                Set *Result* to the quotient of *Op1* and *Op2*;
        End if.
        C. Display the value of *Result*.
    Else
        Display an "invalid menu choice message";
    End if.

That is, if we nest steps 2, 3, and 4 of our original algorithm within an appropriately designed selective execution statement, then they will executed only if the user enters a valid menu choice. But how do we construct a condition that reflects the "valid-menu-choice" logic:

> If *Operation* is '+', or *Operation* is '-', or *Operation* is '*', or *Operation* is '/', then
> ...

One way to do this is to use a `switch` statement with multiple cases in one case-list:

```
switch (Operation)
{
        case '+': case '-':
        case '*': case '/':
                // ... do steps 2A, 2B, and 2C

        default:
                cout << InvalidMenuChoiceMessage;
}
```

Then, steps 2A, 2B and 2C will only be performed if the value of *Operation* is a valid menu choice. However, instead of using the `switch`, let's take this opportunity to learn more about building conditions.

For situations where a complex condition must be built by combining simpler conditions, C++ provides three **logical operators**: `&&` (AND), `||` (OR), and `!` (NOT), whose effects can be described by the following truth table:

x	y	x && y	x || y	!x
0	0	0	0	1
0	1	0	1	1
1	0	0	1	0
1	1	1	1	0

In the space below and in your source program, construct a valid C++ `if` statement that encodes the logic:

> If *Operation* is '+', or *Operation* is '-', or *Operation* is '*', or *Operation* is '/', then
> ...

Then translate and test the correctness of what you have written, noting any difficulties you encounter in the space below:

Continue when you have thoroughly tested the correctness of your `if` statement.

Our next task is to take a remedial action if the user makes the second error:

 2. The user might enter a non-real value (e.g., any non-numeric value such as a letter).

To check for this error, we might adjust our algorithm as follows:

 0. Display an introductory message;
 1. Display a menu of operations, and input a char,
  storing it in *Operation*;
 2. If *Operation* is '+', or *Operation* is '-', or *Operation* is '*', or *Operation* is '/', then
   A. Prompt for and input two real values, storing them in *Op1* and *Op2*;
   B. If the user entered valid real values, then
    1. If *Operation* is equal to '+', then
     Set *Result* to the sum of *Op1* and *Op2*;
    Else if *Operation* is equal to '-', then
     Set *Result* to the difference of *Op1* and *Op2*;
    Else if *Operation* is equal to '*', then
     Set *Result* to the product of *Op1* and *Op2*;
    Else (*Operation* must be equal to '/')
     Set *Result* to the quotient of *Op1* and *Op2*;
    End if.
    2. Display the value of *Result*.
   Else
    Display a "non-real operand entered" message;
   End if;
  Else
   Display an "invalid menu choice" message;
  End if.

That is, we only want to compute and display *Result* if the user has entered real values. The question is, how do we encode the logic of the step:

 If the user entered valid real values, then ...

We have performed keyboard input using the `iostream` object named `cin`. Objects like `cin` have associated with them a number of **member functions**, that are called as follows:

```
cin.MemberFunction()
```

One of these member functions is the `good()` member function, whose behavior is defined as follows:

$$\text{cin.good()} = \begin{cases} 1 & \text{if the last read from cin was successful} \\ 0 & \text{otherwise} \end{cases}$$

Thus, if we call the `good()` member function of `cin` immediately after reading in the values for *Op1* and *Op2*, then the function will return true (1) if the values entered by the user are valid real values, but will return false (0) otherwise. We can therefore use a call to this function as a condition in an `if` statement, and so detect the input of non-real values.

Use the `good()` member function to modify your source program so that it behaves as specified by the previous algorithm. Then translate and test your program, using the space below to note any difficulties you encounter:

Your final task is to take an appropriate remedial action if the user commits the third error:

3. For division, the user might enter a zero denominator (e.g., a divide-by-zero error).

In the space provided below, introduce new logic that prevents division-by zero errors by displaying an appropriate message if the user enters zero for *Op2*:

0. Display an introductory message;
1. Display a menu of operations, and input a char,
    storing it in *Operation*;
2. If *Operation* is '+', or *Operation* is '-', or *Operation* is '*', or *Operation* is '/', then
    A. Prompt for and input two real values, storing them in *Op1* and *Op2*;
    B. If the user entered valid real values, then
        1. If *Operation* is equal to '+', then
            Set *Result* to the sum of *Op1* and *Op2*;
        Else if *Operation* is equal to '-', then
            Set *Result* to the difference of *Op1* and *Op2*;
        Else if *Operation* is equal to '*', then
            Set *Result* to the product of *Op1* and *Op2*;
        Else (*Operation* must be equal to '/')

        End if.
      2. Display the value of *Result*.
    Else
        Display a "non-real operand entered" message;
    End if;
Else
    Display an "invalid menu choice" message;
End if.

Then modify your source program to incorporate this logic, and test the correctness of your solution.

When you have thoroughly tested what you have written, print a hard copy of `calc2.cc` and then end your session with the computer.

Phrases You Should Now Understand.

Condition, Boolean Expression, Relational Operator, Logical Operator, Selective Execution, If Statement, Switch Statement.

Objectives.

1. Practice using selective execution.
2. Practice constructing conditions.
3. Practice program maintenance.

Introduction.

This week's project is to construct a practical, fool-proof metric conversion program, as specified by one of the project descriptions below (your instructor will tell you which one). Using the `Metric` library that we constructed last week, you are to write a program that provides its user with a menu of conversion operations and performs whichever conversion they choose.

Your program should be fool-proof, guarding against errors caused by the user entering an incorrect menu choice or non-numeric data.

Projects.

5.1. Write a program `Lengths` that allows the user to choose from the conversions:

> A. Inches to Centimeters,
> B. Yards to Meters, or
> C. Miles to Kilometers.

5.2. Write a program `Weights` that allows the user to choose from the conversions:

> A. Ounces to Grams,
> B. Pounds to Kilograms, or
> C. Tons to Kilograms.

5.3. Write a program `Volumes` that allows the user to choose from the conversions:

> A. Pints to Liters,
> B. Quarts to Liters, or
> C. Gallons to Liters.

5.4. Write a program `Areas` that allows the user to choose from the conversions:

> A. Sq. Inches to Sq. Millimeters,
> B. Sq. Feet to Sq. Meters, or
> C. Acres to Sq. Meters.

Project 5 Due Date _____

Turn in this grade sheet, attached to a hard copy of

1. your source program; and
2. an execution of your program, showing its behavior when the user:
      a. utilizes each of the legal menu choices A, B, and C;
      b. enters an illegal menu choice; and
      c. enters non-numeric data.

Name _____

Category	Points Possible	Points Received
Correctness	50	_____
Readability	45	
Documentation	25	_____
Meaningful Identifiers	10	_____
Use of White Space	10	_____
User-Friendliness	25	
Opening Message	5	_____
Menu Clarity	10	_____
Labeled Output	10	_____
Total	**120**	_____

Lab 6

Repetitive Execution

Objectives.

1. Practice the construction of conditions; and
2. Introduce the use of the repetitive control structures.

Prelab Questions:

1. Which of the C++ loops is a pretest loop?

2. Which of the C++ loops is a posttest loop?

3. Which of the C++ loops can provide both zero and one-trip behavior?

4. Which of the C++ loops is designed primarily for counting through ranges of numbers?

5. An `if-break` combination *must* be used if one wishes to exit which C++ loop?

Introduction.

In the last exercise, we saw that the `if` and `switch` statements utilize a *condition* (an expression that evaluates to true or false) to permit a program to execute statements selectively. For example, the code fragment:

```
if (Op2 != 0)
      return (Op1 / Op2);
else
{
      cout << "\nError: Divide by zero attempted !\n";
      return 0;
}
```

uses the condition `Op2 != 0` to control the execution of the indented statements, so that if `Op2` is equal to zero, the compound statement following the else is executed, while if `Op2` is not equal to zero, then the statement before the `else` is executed.

However, most modern programming languages also utilize conditions to permit statements to be executed *repeatedly*. These **repetitive execution statements** typically permit a set of statements to be executed over and over, so long as some condition evaluates to true.

As an example use of this capability, suppose that we have ten lengths that we need to convert from English- to metric-system measurements. Using the program we wrote last week (which uses only selection) the conversion program must be executed ten separate times. However, by adding a repetitive execution statement to that program, a single execution of the program could be used to solve all ten problems (or one or two or one hundred).

C++ provides four different loops (well, three, actually) that we will examine today. These are called the *while* loop, the *do-while* loop, the *for* loop, and what we call the *forever* loop.

Getting Started.

Today's exercise is to make a calculator program that is even more functional and easy to use than the one we wrote last week. More precisely, the skeleton program in the `lab6` class directory differs from that in `lab5` in that the `lab6` version is a *five*-function calculator, that provides an *exponentiation operation*. Follow the usual procedure of copying the file(s) from the class directory into a `lab6` directory of your own, and then personalize the opening documentation of the file(s).

You may recall that exponentiation is available in C++ via the function `pow()` in the `math` library. Just for today (to learn about loops), we will not use `pow()`, but will instead pretend that we are C++ implementers and write our own exponentiation function, called `Power()`.

Since `Power()` performs an operation that already exists in a library, we will declare and define it within our source program, rather than in a library.

The Exponentiation Operation.

The exponentiation operation should be a familiar one, since the expression

$$X^n$$

performs exponentiation on the base X and the exponent n. We will implement this operation by writing a function `Power()`, such that a call:

```
Power(X, n)
```

will compute and return x^n.

Specification.

We can immediately identify the following objects are needed to solve our problem:

- *Base*, the (real) base used in the operation.
- *Exponent*, the (integer) exponent used in the operation.
- *Result*, the (real) result computed by the operation.

This gives us the following specification for the operation:

Receive: *Base*, a real value;
           Exponent, an integer value.
Return: *Result*, the real value $Base^{Exponent}$.

Using this specification, find the comment in your source program:

```
// ...declaration of Power() goes here ...
```

and replace it with a declaration for function `Power()` (see lab 4 if you need a reminder on function declarations). In the space below, write your declaration:

Then find the comment

```
// ... definition of Power() goes here ...
```

and replace it with a stub for `Power()` that is consistent with its declaration.

By convention, non-main functions are *defined* following the main function in C++. However, a function must be *declared* before it can be called, and so if it is called in the main function, then a declaration of the function should precede the main function.

Design.

To simplify the task of computing x^n, we will assume that n is nonnegative.

When faced with a new problem, it is sometimes helpful to solve it "by hand." For example, if we were to calculate `Power(2,0)`, `Power(2,1)`, `Power(2,3)` and `Power(2,5)` by hand, we might write:

<u>Power(2,0)</u>   <u>Power(2,1)</u>   <u>Power(2,3)</u>   <u>Power(2,5)</u>

Return 1;   1 * 2 = 2;   1 * 2 = 2;   1 * 2 = 2;
                     Return 2;   2 * 2 = 4;   2 * 2 = 4;
                                         4 * 2 = 8;   4 * 2 = 8;
                                         Return 8;   8 * 2 = 16;
                                                             16 * 2 = 32;
                                                             Return 32;

Now, remembering that our function must return the value *Result*, and examining the pattern in these "by-hand" computations, we might construct the following "open form" solution:

<u>Power(*Base, Exponent*)</u>

Initialize *Result* to 1;
Set *Result* to *Result * Base*; ⎫
Set *Result* to *Result * Base*; ⎬ *Exponent* times
      . . .   ⎪
Set *Result* to *Result * Base*; ⎭
Return *Result* ;

But notice, this solution simply calls for repeating the same operation *Exponent* times:

Set *Result* to *Result * Base*;

Repeating is the key word — to solve our problem, we want to use a *repetition statement* that counts from 1 to *Exponent*, executing the multiply-and-assign statement:

```
Result *= Base;
```

on each repetition. We can thus identify the following operations needed to solve our problem:

- assignment to a real variable;
- multiplication-and-assignment of real values;
- repetition of a statement for each value in a sequence of integers; and
- return of a real value.

We might thus organize these operations into the following algorithm:

Initialize *Result* to 1.
For each value *Count* **in the range 1 through** *Exponent*:
    Set *Result* to *Result * Base*;
End loop.
Return *Result*;

81

Coding.

The only one of these operations that we have not seen before is provided by the C++ **for loop**, whose general form is:

```
for (InitializationExpression ; LoopCondition ; StepExpression )
     Statement
```

When execution reaches this statement, a number of actions take place:

1. `InitializationExpression` is evaluated.
2. `LoopCondition` is evaluated:
3. If `LoopCondition` is false,
   then execution proceeds to the next statement in the program (bypassing `Statement`), otherwise execution proceeds to 4.
4. `Statement` is executed.
5. `StepExpression` is evaluated.
6. Execution returns to step 2.

By supplying appropriate `InitializationExpression`, `LoopCondition`, and `StepExpression` code, the for loop can be used to sequence an integer variable `Count` through an ascending integer range (`FirstValue`, `FirstValue+1`, ..., `LastValue`) as follows:

```
for (int Count = FirstValue; Count <= LastValue; Count++)
     Statement
```

Such a loop can be used to solve our problem because when execution reaches the statement:

1. The assignment expression int `Count` = `FirstValue` is evaluated.
2. The `LoopCondition`: `Count` <= `LastValue` is evaluated:
3. If `LoopCondition` is false,
   then execution proceeds to the next statement in the program (bypassing `Statement`), otherwise execution proceeds to 4.
4. `Statement` is executed.
5. The `StepExpression`: `Count++` is evaluated, incrementing `Count`.
6. Execution returns to step 2.

Using the following algorithm:

> Initialize *Result* to 1.
> For each value *Count* in the range 1 through *Exponent*::
>   Set *Result* to *Result * Base*;
> End loop.
> Return *Result*;

complete the definition of function `Power()` by filling in its stub with an assignment statement, a for loop, and a `return` statement.

When `Power()` is complete, uncomment the `Power()` call in the `switch` statement. Then translate your program, and test what you have written. Proceed when it is thoroughly tested.

Characterizing Loops.

Just as a condition is used to determine the flow of execution through a selection statement, a condition is used to control the repetition of a loop statement. The evaluation of this condition with respect to the statements repeated by the loop makes it possible to place a loop into one of three categories:

1. *Pretest* loops evaluate their condition *before* the loop's statements.
2. *Posttest* loops evaluate their condition *after* the loop's statements.
3. *Unrestricted* loops evaluate their condition *before*, *after*, or *within* the loop's statements.

The for loop that we saw earlier is a pretest loop, because it evaluates its condition before the loop's statement is executed (don't take my word for it — check back and see!) However, the for loop is designed primarily for problems that involve counting through ranges of numbers, or problems in which the number of repetitions can be determined in advance. As we shall see, there are many problems that do not fit this pattern.

The other three C++ loops differ from the for loop in that they are *general-purpose* loops, designed for problems where the number of repetitions to be performed is not known in advance. Why are there three of them? Because

1. The **while loop** provides a *general pretest* loop;
2. The **do-while loop** provides a *general posttest* loop; and
3. The **forever loop** provides a *general unrestricted* loop.

To see why this is significant, let's examine an alternate approach to fool-proofing a program. Currently, the algorithm employed by our calculator program is as follows:

0. Display an introductory message;
1. Display a menu of operations, and input a char, storing it in *Operation*;
2. Prompt for and input two real values, storing them in *Op1* and *Op2*;
3. If *Operation* is equal to '+',
    Then set *Result* to the sum of *Op1* and *Op2*;
    Else if *Operation* is equal to '-'
    Then set *Result* to the difference of *Op1* and *Op2*;
    Else if *Operation* is equal to '*',
    Then set *Result* to the product of *Op1* and *Op2*;
    Else if *Operation* is equal to '/',
    Then set *Result* to the quotient of *Op1* and *Op2*;
    Else if *Operation* is equal to '^',
    Then set *Result* to *Power(Op1, int(Op2))*;
    Else display an invalid menu choice message
    End if.
4. Display the value of *Result*.

The general-purpose loops give us an alternate means of handling user errors, by repeatedly displaying a prompt and inputting a value, until the user enters a valid value. By using a loop condition to test the validity of the input, this approach "traps" the user within the loop — execution is only permitted to proceed from the loop when a valid value has been entered.

To illustrate this technique, we might replace step 1 of our algorithm with the following pseudocode loop:

1. Cycle through the following steps, so long as *Operation* is not a valid menu choice:
   a. Display a menu of operations.
   b. Input a char, storing it in *Operation*.
   End loop.

In this step, the loop's condition is expressed by the phrase:

> *Operation* is not a valid menu choice

which we saw how to encode last time (this condition is a bit longer, since this menu has more operations). To encode this algorithm in C++, we must choose the appropriate loop.

The first decision is whether to use a for loop or one of the general-purpose loops. Since we cannot anticipate the number of times the user might enter an invalid menu choice, we should use a general-purpose loop, rather than a for loop.

The second decision is which general-purpose loop should be used. This decision is based on where the loop's condition should be evaluated with respect to steps (a) and (b). The condition involves the value of *Operation*, which is not defined until the input step (b). Therefore, the condition should be evaluated after (b) has executed, which implies that both (a) and (b) should execute prior to the evaluation of the loop condition. In other words, a *posttest* loop is the appropriate loop to solve this problem.

In C++, the posttest loop is called the **do-while loop**, and it has the following general form:

```
do
{
    StatementList
}
while ( Condition ) ;
```

where `StatementList` is a sequence of one or more C++ statements, and `Condition` is any C++ expression that evaluates to true or false.

When execution reaches this statement, the following actions occur:

1. `StatementList` is executed;
2. `Condition` is evaluated;
3. If `Condition` evaluates to true,
   Then control returns to step 1;
   Else control proceeds sequentially to the statement following the do-while loop;
   End if.

Since `Condition` is not evaluated until after the first execution of `StatementList`, the do-while loop guarantees that `StatementList` will be executed one or more times. For this reason, the do-while loop is said to exhibit **one-trip behavior** (i.e. `StatementList` is guaranteed to execute at least once).

In your source program, construct a do-while loop that encodes step 1 of our algorithm. Then translate and test it thoroughly before continuing.

As a second illustration, consider how we might "fool-proof" step 2 of our algorithm:

2. Prompt for and input two real values, storing them in *Op1* and *Op2*;

At first glance, this looks similar to step 1, which might lead us to choose a pretest loop, controlled by the `good()` member function of `cin`:

```
do
{
    // prompt for Op1 and Op2
    // input Op1 and Op2
}
while ( !cin.good() );
```

However, this approach is inappropriate because of two subtleties about numeric I/O. When the `>>` operator is expecting a real value, but gets a non-real value:

1. The status of `cin` is set so that its member function `good()` will return false (0), and
2. The non-real input value is left (unread) in the input stream.

Each of these actions causes a difficulty. The first difficulty is twofold:

a. No input operations can be performed with `cin` so long as `cin.good()` returns false.
b. In order to stop `cin.good()` from returning false, it must be explicitly *cleared* using the `clear()` member function of `cin`.

We must call `cin.clear()` before attempting another input operation, or else an **infinite loop** will result.

The second difficulty is that even after we have cleared the status of `cin`, the unread input is still sitting in the stream waiting to be read. That is, the next repetition of our loop, the input operation will try and read a real value, but instead get the same non-real value that caused our initial problem, unless we can somehow "skip" past that value. This can be accomplished using a different member function of `cin` named `ignore()`, whose general form is

```
cin.ignore(NumChars, UntilChar);
```

When execution reaches this statement, characters in the input stream will be skipped until *NumChars* have been skipped, or the character *UntilChar* is encountered, whichever comes first. Since lines are usually not more than 120 characters in length, and the end of a line is marked by the newline character (`'\n'`), we can use the following call to solve this difficulty:

```
cin.ignore(120, '\n');
```

This complicates our choice of which loop to use, because we now have four steps to perform:

2a. Display a prompt for two real values; // one or more times
2b. Input *Op1* and *Op2*;   // one or more times
2c. Clear status of `cin`;   // only if necessary (i.e., zero or more times)
2d. Skip invalid input;   // only if necessary (i.e., zero or more times)

This poses a dilemma. Some of the steps should be executed at least once, and others zero or more times. Which loop do we choose?

One solution is to use a pre-test loop with the statements arranged as follows:

2a. Display a prompt for two real values;
2b. Input *Op1* and *Op2*
2c. Cycle in a pretest loop, so long as a real value was not entered:
    1) Clear the status of `cin`;
    2) Skip the invalid input;
    3) Display a prompt for two real values;
    4) Input *Op1* and *Op2*;
    End loop.

By performing steps 2a and 2b outside of the loop, we ensure they are executed at least once. By performing steps 1), 2), 3) and 4) inside the pretest loop, they will be executed zero times, if the user enters a valid real value in step 2b.

The drawback to this approach is its *redundance*: steps 3) and 4) are exactly the same as steps 2a and 2b. This is not too much of an inefficiency, so long as one does not mind the extra typing.

Like many other languages the C++ pretest loop is called the **while loop**, and it has the following form:

```
while ( Condition )
    Statement
```

where: `Condition` is any C++ expression that evaluates to true or false, and
               `Statement` can be either a single or compound C++ statement.

When execution reaches this statement, the following actions occur:

1. `Condition` is evaluated (before `Statement` is executed);
2. If `Condition` evaluates to false, then
    `Statement` is bypassed, and control proceeds to the statement after the loop;
  Otherwise
    a. `Statement` is executed; and
    b. execution then returns to step 1;
  End if.

Since `Statement` may be executed zero or more times, the while loop is said to exhibit **zero-trip behavior** (i.e., the *Statement* controlled by a while loop may go unexecuted, if the loop's `Condition` is initially false).

Your source program currently has steps 2a and 2b encoded. Add a while loop to encode step 2c, as well as the statements to encode steps 1), 2), 3) and 4). Note that since the while loop must repeat multiple statements, its `Statement` must be a compound statement or else an infinite loop may result.

Then translate and thoroughly test what you have written. If you should happen to generate an infinite loop, it can usually be terminated by typing `Ctrl-C` (pressing the `Ctrl` and `C` keys simultaneously). On some systems, it may be necessary to type `Ctrl-C` several times.

Continue when you have thoroughly tested what you have written.

As a final illustration, let's wrap our program's statements (all but the introductory message) in a loop, so that with a single execution, we can perform as many calculations as we wish. That is, let's modify our overall algorithm as follows:

0. Display an introductory message;
1. **Cycle through the following statements,
   so long as the user does not want to quit:**
   A. Cycle through the following steps, so long as *Operation* is not a valid menu choice:
      1) Display a menu of operations.
      2) Input a char, storing it in *Operation*.
      End loop.
   B. Display a prompt for two real values;
   C. Input *Op1* and *Op2*
   D. Cycle in a pretest loop, so long as a real value was not entered:
      1) Clear the status of `cin`;
      2) Skip the invalid input;
      3) Display a prompt for two real values;
      4) Input *Op1* and *Op2*;
      End loop.
   E. If *Operation* is equal to '+',
      Then set *Result* to the sum of *Op1* and *Op2*;
      Else if *Operation* is equal to '-'
      Then set *Result* to the difference of *Op1* and *Op2*;
      Else if *Operation* is equal to '*',
      Then set *Result* to the product of *Op1* and *Op2*;
      Else if *Operation* is equal to '/',
      Then set *Result* to the quotient of *Op1* and *Op2*;
      Else if *Operation* is equal to '^',
      Then set *Result* to *Power(Op1, int(Op2))*;
      Else display an invalid menu choice message
      End if.
   F. Display the value of *Result*.
   End loop.

In order to determine which kind of loop to use, we must determine where to evaluate the loop's condition:

> the user does not want to quit

One way to have the user indicate that they want to quit is to view quitting as an operation, and provide a menu choice 'q' by which the user can indicate that they want to quit. The condition

```
Operation == 'q'
```

can then be used to test whether or not the user wishes to quit. If we take this approach, then we should evaluate our loop's condition immediately following step A in the preceding algorithm, since that is where *Operation* receives its value.

Put differently, if the user wants to quit, steps B through F should not be executed — execution should immediately leave the loop. We thus have a situation where the loop's condition should not be evaluated at the loop's beginning (eliminating the pretest loop), nor at its end (eliminating the posttest loop), but in its *middle* (suggesting the *unrestricted* loop).

In C++, the unrestricted loop is a simplification of the for loop that we call the **forever loop**, that has the following general form:

```
for (;;)
    Statement
```

That is, by leaving out the three expressions that normally control a for loop, it becomes an **infinite loop**, that repeats its `Statement` endlessly.

Of course, we do not want the behavior of an infinite loop, but instead want execution to leave the loop when some condition becomes true. This can be accomplished by placing an `if` statement in conjunction with a `break` statement (called an `if-break` combination) within the loop's `Statement`, as follows:

```
for (;;)
{
    StatementList₁

    if ( Condition ) break;

    StatementList₂
}
```

When a `break` statement is executed, execution is immediately transferred out of the forever loop to the first statement following the loop. By only selecting the `break` statement when `Condition` is true, a forever loop's repetition can be controlled in a manner similar to the other general-purpose loops.

As a result, this loop can be used to solve our problem, by making `StatementList₁` step A of our algorithm, and making `StatementList₂` steps B through F. Modify your source program to incorporate this approach, and then translate and test the newly added statements.

Note that this loop can be used to solve the preceding problem without redundant statements:

```
for (;;)
{
    // prompt for two real values      // executed one or more times
    // input Op1 and Op2               // executed one or more times

    if ( cin.good() ) break;

    // clear status of cin             // executed zero or more times
    // skip invalid input in stream    // executed zero or more times
}
```

For this reason, some programmers prefer the forever loop when some statements must be executed zero or more times and other statements must be executed one or more times.

Phrases You Should Now Understand.

Condition, Repetitive Execution, For Loop, While Loop, Do-While Loop, Forever Loop, General-Purpose Loop, Counting Loop, Zero-Trip Behavior, One-Trip Behavior, Pretest Loop, Posttest Loop, Unrestricted Loop, Break Statement, If-Break Combination.

Objectives.

1. Gain further experience using C++ loops.
2. Gain further experience constructing conditions.

Introduction.

Your instructor will assign one of the following projects, each of which involves the use of loops and the construction of conditions to control them.

Projects.

6.1. Modify your metric conversion program from last time to

a. Permit multiple metric conversions with a single execution; and
b. Use loops to make the two input steps "fool-proof".

6.2. Write a program that will read a sequence of numbers from the keyboard, and display the minimum, maximum, average, and range of the entered values. Make the input step "fool-proof".

6.3. Extend `calc.cc` into a six-function calculator, as follows:

1. Add a `factorial()` operation that, given an integer n,
   computes n! = 1 * 2 * ... * (n-1) * n.
2. Redesign `Power()` so that it handles negative exponents.

6.4. Design and implement a "fool-proof" menu-driver checkbook-balancing program whose menu provides the following operations:

```
b – set starting balance;
d – add deposit ;
w – deduct withdrawal;
c – deduct check;
i – add interest;
s – deduct service charge;
q – quit.
```

Project 6 Due Date _____

Turn in this grade sheet, attached to a hard copy of

a. your source program; and
b. an execution in which you show *all* functionality of your program

Name _____

Category	Points Possible	Points Received
Correctness............................	70	_____
Style & Readability......................	50	
Documentation.....................	30	_____
Meaningful Identifiers..................	10	_____
Use of White Space..................	10	_____
User-Friendliness........................	30	
Opening Message..................	10	_____
Menu Clarity.....................	10	_____
Labeled Output...................	10	_____
Total............................	**150**	_____

Lab 7

Parameter Passing and Scope

Note For the Instructor:

Today's exercise consists of two sets of experiments. The first set investigates the characteristics of value and reference parameters. The second set investigates the rules of scope in C++.

The intent of these experiment sets is to explore their respective topics. You should review these experiments, feeling free to replace, add or subtract any experiments that seem too easy or difficult for your students. (For example, you might want to add an experiment investigating what happens when the number of arguments in a function call doesn't match the number of parameters in its definition).

Be sure to inform your students of any changes of this sort.

You may also want to discuss the ideas of cutting (or copying) and pasting, if your students have not used these operations before.

Objectives.

1. Gain experience using reference parameters;
2. Gain experience writing functions;
3. Gain an understanding of the rules of scope.

Prelab Questions:

1. A parameter into which the value of its corresponding argument is *copied* is called a _____ parameter.

2. A parameter that becomes an *alias* for its corresponding argument is called a _____ parameter.

3. The scope of an object always starts at its declaration. The scope of an `auto` object ends at _____.

4. The scope of an object always starts at its declaration. The scope of an `extern` object ends at _____.

5. The scope of an object always starts at its declaration. The scope of a parameter object ends at _____.

Introduction.

Today's exercise involves two parts, each of which explores the writing of more sophisticated kinds of functions than the ones we have written thus far.

In the first part, we will begin by exploring the nature of function parameters, and what rules govern the relationship between parameters and their arguments.

In the second part, we will examine the relationship between definitions that appear in different functions.

Part I. Value and Reference Parameters.

The general form of a C++ function heading is:

```
ReturnType Name ( ParameterDeclarationList )
```

where `ParameterDeclarationList` is an optional sequence of one or more *Parameter-Declarations* separated by commas, each of which has the form:

```
Type ParameterName
```

where `Type` is a valid type, and `ParameterName` is a valid identifier.

Terminology:

1. A parameter whose `Type` is not followed by an ampersand (`&`) is called a *value parameter*.

> A value parameter is *a variable, local to the function, such that when the function is called,*
> ***it receives a copy of the value of the corresponding argument.***

2. A parameter whose `Type` is followed by an ampersand (`&`) is called a *reference parameter*.

> A reference parameter is an alias (another name) for its corresponding argument.

We have used parameters in several of our programs. In every case, which kind did we use ?

Getting Started.

Get and personalize the file(s) from the `lab7` class directory in your own `lab7` directory.

The Experiments.

Take a moment to look over the program in the file `params.cc`. It consists of 3 steps:

1. Initialize a set of variables to some initial value (-1 in this case);
2. Call function `Change()` that (in some way) tries to modify the values of those variables;
3. Output the values of those variables to view the effects of function `Change()`.

Function `Change()` is the "laboratory" in which we will experiment with parameters.

Experiment 1: Changing Value Parameters.

The Question: Our first experiment will try to answer the following questions:

> *Is it legal to alter (e.g., assign a value to) a value parameter ?*

Hypothesis: In the space below, construct a hypothesis that answers the question.
(Don't worry — hypotheses aren't graded - just make a guess.)

The Experiment: The `params` source program is set up to test your hypothesis. Function `Change()` is currently defined as follows:

```
void Change(int Param1, int Param2, int Param3)
{
    Param1 = 1;
    Param2 = 2;
    Param3 = 3;
}
```

and is called in the main program with the statement:

```
Change(Arg1, Arg2, Arg3);
```

so that if it is illegal to alter a value parameter, then compiling `params.cc` will produce errors.

Observation: Translate your source program. What is displayed ?

Conclusions: Review the definition of a value parameter, and record your conclusions.

Experiment 2: Value Parameters and their Arguments.

The Question:

> *Does altering a value parameter have any affect on its corresponding argument ?*

Hypothesis: Review the definition of value parameters, and then construct a hypothesis:

The Experiment: The current definition of `Params` takes the following steps:

1. Assign initial values to *Arg1*, *Arg2*, and *Arg3*;
2. Display those values on the screen;
3. Call `Change()` with *Arg1*, *Arg2*, and *Arg3* as arguments
   (and have `Change()` assign values to their corresponding parameters), and
4. Display the values of *Arg1*, *Arg2*, and *Arg3*.

By comparing the values displayed before the call with those displayed after the call, `Params` provides us with a means of testing our hypothesis.

Observation: Execute your program. What is displayed ?

Conclusions: Review the definition of value parameters, and record your conclusions.

Experiment 3: Value Parameters and Identical Argument Names.

The Question:

If a value parameter has the same name as its corresponding argument,
will altering it alter the corresponding argument ?

Hypothesis: Review the value parameter definition, and then construct a hypothesis.

The Experiment: Modify the definition of `Change()`, so that its parameter-names match the argument names:

```
void Change(int Arg1, int Arg2, int Arg3)
{

    Arg1 = 1;
    Arg2 = 2;
    Arg3 = 3;
}
```

As before, by comparing the values from before the call with those displayed after the call, `Params` and the new definition of `Change()` allow us to test our hypothesis.

Observation: Translate and execute your source program. What is displayed ?

Conclusions: Review the definition of a value parameter, and record your conclusions.

Experiment 4: Reference Parameters and Identical Parameter and Argument Names.

The Question:

> *If a reference parameter has the same name as its corresponding argument,*
> *will altering it alter the corresponding argument ?*

Hypothesis: Review the reference parameter definition, and construct a hypothesis.

The Experiment: Modify the definition of `Change()`, so that some of the parameters are reference parameters (Note: you will also need to modify the *declaration* of `Change()` in main):

```
void Change(int& Arg1, int& Arg2, int& Arg3)
{

    Arg1 = 1;
    Arg2 = 2;
    Arg3 = 3;
}
```

As before, by comparing the values from before the call with those displayed after the call, `Params` and the new definition of `Change()` allow us to test our hypothesis.

Observation: Translate and execute your source program. What is displayed ?

Conclusions: Review the definition of a reference parameter, and record your conclusions.

Experiment 5: Reference Parameters with Different Parameter and Argument Names.

<u>The Question</u>:

If a reference parameter has a name different from its corresponding argument, will altering it still alter the corresponding argument ?

<u>Hypothesis</u>: Review the reference parameter definition, and construct a hypothesis.

<u>The Experiment</u>: Modify the definition of `Change()`, so that some of the parameters are reference parameters whose names differ from their corresponding arguments:

```
void Change(int& Param1, int& Param2, int& Param3)
{

    Param1 = 1;
    Param2 = 2;
    Param3 = 3;
}
```

As before, comparing the values from before the call with those displayed after the call `Params` and the new definition of `Change()` allow us to test our hypothesis.

<u>Observation</u>: Translate and execute your source program. What is displayed ?

<u>Conclusions</u>: Review the definition of a reference parameter, and record your conclusions.

Experiment 6: Parameters and Argument Relationship.

<u>The Question</u>:

What rule determines the parameter with which an argument is associated?

<u>Hypothesis</u>: Construct a hypothesis.

<u>The Experiment</u>: Design an experiment to test your hypothesis, such that comparing the values from before the call with those displayed after the call tests your hypothesis:

<u>Observation</u>: Translate and execute your source program. What is displayed ?

<u>Conclusions</u>: Record your conclusions. If your hypothesis failed, revise it and redesign your experiment to test your new hypothesis, until you have answered the question.

Part II. Scope in C++.

A declaration can be thought of as giving the compiler a *meaning* for the name being declared.

However, think about this for a moment. In experiment 3, we saw that the name `Arg1` can be declared as an integer variable in the main program, and (again) as an integer value parameter in `Change()` — two different places. Moreover, altering `Arg1` in `Change()` has no affect on the value of `Arg1` in the main program. We might conclude from this that `Arg1` in main and `Arg1` in `Change()` are *two different variables*.

Put differently, *the same name can have different meanings in different places in a program.*

That is, there is nothing that prevents us from declaring the name x as an integer variable in main and then declaring the name x as a real variable in `Change()`. The same name will have different meanings, depending on whether execution is in main, or in `Change()`.

Once we realize that the same name can have different meanings at different places, it becomes important to understand the rules by which C++ determines the meaning of a name at a given spot in one's program.

> Definition: The set of all places in a program where a name has a particular meaning is called the **scope** of that name.

The C++ Rules of Scope.

The rules governing the scope of C++ names can be summarized as follows:

1. *A name may be declared anywhere that a statement can appear.*

2a. *The scope of any name declared within a pair of braces starts at its declaration and ends at the close-brace* (}). Such objects are described as `auto` (or sometimes local) names, because they <u>auto</u>matically come into existence whenever execution enters the surrounding braces.

2b. *The scope of any parameter starts at its declaration and ends at its function's close brace.*

3. *The scope of any name declared outside of all pairs of braces starts at its declaration and ends at the end of the file.* Such names are described as `extern`, since they are declared <u>extern</u>al to (i.e., outside of) all functions.

An exception to these rules is the C++ class, which we will examine in a later exercise.

Rule 1 sets C++ apart from other languages, since most languages restrict declarations to a particular region of your program (e.g., the beginning).

For example, a statement like:

```
for (int i = 1; i <= 10; i++) cout << i << '\n';
```

is illegal in most languages, since the name i is declared within the loop.

We will examine the implications of the other rules in the experiments that follow.

Experiment 7. Accessing an `auto` name before its open-brace.

The Question:

> *What happens if a function F() tries to access a name*
> *that is declared in a function G() that follows F() ?*

Hypothesis: Review the rules of scope, and construct a hypothesis:

Since there are two relevant kinds of names (parameters and variables), we'll examine each separately.

Experiment 7a: Parameters.

Modify the body of the main function, so that it attempts to display the values of one of the parameters of function `Change()` (e.g. `Param1`).

Since `Change()` follows main, this should be sufficient to determine whether or not a function can access a parameter declared in a function that follows it.

Observation: Translate your source program. What is displayed ?

Conclusions: Review the rules of scope and record your conclusions.

Experiment 7b: Local Variables.

Modify the body of `Change()`, so that it contains an `auto` variable (e.g., `LocalVar`). Then have main attempt to output the value of this variable.

Since `Change()` follows main, this should be sufficient to determine whether or not one function can access an `auto` variable declared in a function that follows it.

Observation: Translate your source program. What is displayed ?

Conclusions: Review the rules of scope and record your conclusions.

Experiment 8. Accessing an `auto` following its close-brace.

The Question:

> *What happens if a function G() tries to access an `auto` name*
> *that is declared in a function F() that precedes G() ?*

Hypothesis: Review the rules of scope, and construct a hypothesis.

Experiment: Remove the declarations inserted in the last experiment, and have `Change()` attempt to output one of the locals declared in main (e.g. `Arg1`).

Since `Change()` follows main, this should suffice to test our hypothesis.

Observation: Translate your source program. What is displayed ?

Conclusions: Review the rules of scope and record your conclusions.

Experiment 9: Accessing an `extern` prior to its declaration.

The Question:

What happens if a program (tries to) access an `extern` prior to its declaration ?

Hypothesis: Review the rules of scope, and construct a hypothesis.

Experiment: Remove the output statement from the last experiment. Then use **Cut** and **Paste** (under the **Edit** menu) to move the `#include` directive from where it is (before main) to after main, but before `Change()`.

This should suffice to test our hypothesis, since the use of `cout` in main will now precede the declaration of `cout` (in `<iostream.h>`).

Observation: Translate your source program. What is displayed?

Conclusions: Review the rules of scope, and record your conclusions.

Experiment 10: Accessing an `extern` following its declaration.

Actually, we'll just discuss this one.

It should be obvious, if you consider a bit, that accessing an `extern` anywhere after its declaration is perfectly legal - we've done it in every program we've written thus far, in using the directive:

```
#include <iostream.h>
```

This inserts (among other things) declarations of the names `cin` and `cout` into a program.

To see this, comment out the line with the `#include` directive and recompile.
What error is produced ?

This insertion occurs outside of any pair of braces, and so `cin` and `cout` are externs.

If you remember, we always include the `iostream` header file prior to main. According to the scoping rule, the declarations from `iostream` are then "visible" from the `#include` directive until the end of the file. This means that not only can main access `cin` and `cout`, but any other function in the file can access them as well.

Phrases You Should Now Understand:

Argument, Parameter, Value Parameter, Reference Parameter, Scope, Auto, Extern.

Objectives.

1. Practice using value and reference parameters;
2. Practice constructing "normal" and void functions; and
3. More practice constructing libraries and programs.

Introduction.

Each of the following projects involves the construction of a function that uses reference parameters. Your instructor will inform you of which project you are to complete.

Projects.

7.1. White water rapids are classified by their *gradient* (the number of feet per mile they descend), and their *class* (a number in the range 1-6 indicating the difficulty of the rapids, with 1 being *calm* and 6 being *unnavigable*.) Popular white water rafting trips in Pennsylvania and West Virginia include the lower Youghiogheny (gradient 15, class 3), the New (gradient 25, class 4), the Cheat (gradient 35, class 4), and the upper Youghiogheny (gradient 125, class 5). Write a menu-driven program that displays a menu of the trips, and displays the gradient and class of whichever trip the user selects. Your program should include a function that, given the trip selected by the user, returns the gradient and class of that trip to the caller.

7.2. Write a function `Sort3()` that, given three integer (variable) arguments `Int1`, `Int2` and `Int3`, changes the values of those arguments so that their values are in ascending order (i.e., `Int1` ≤ `Int2` ≤ `Int3`). Write a driver program that demonstrates the correctness of `Sort3()`.

7.3. Your local painting supplies store would like a paint-mixing "expert system." Write a function that, given a non-primary color (e.g., orange, green, purple) will return the two primary colors that must be mixed to produce that color (e.g., red and yellow must be mixed to produce orange, yellow and blue to produce green, and blue and red to produce purple). Each color should be declared as a named constant. You should also write a function that, given a color, displays its corresponding character string. Then write a menu-driven program that allows its user to enter, process and display the solution of as many paint-mixing problems as s/he wishes.

7.4. Write a `Statistics()` function that inputs a series of real values from the keyboard, and returns the *mean*, *variance* and *standard deviation* of those values, as efficiently as possible. If the list contains n values:

$$V_1, V_2, ..., V_n$$

then the *mean* and *variance* of the list are given by the formulas

$$mean = \overline{V} = \frac{1}{n} \times \sum_{i=1}^{n} V_i \qquad variance = \frac{1}{n} \times \sum_{i=1}^{n} (V_i - \overline{V})^2$$

and the *standard deviation* of the list is the square root of the *variance*.

Store your function in a `Stats` library. Then write a driver program that includes the library's header file and tests the correctness of `Statistics()`.

Project 7 Due Date _____

Turn in this grade sheet, attached to hard copies of

a. your source program,
b. an execution of your program, in which you demonstrate its correctness.

Name _____

Category	Points Possible	Points Received
Correctness and efficiency.	60	_____
Structure.	30	
Appropriate use of functions.	10	_____
Appropriate use of parameters.	10	_____
No extern variables.	10	_____
Style and Readability.	20	
Horizontal White Space.	5	_____
Vertical White Space.	5	_____
Meaningful Identifiers.	10	_____
Documentation.	30	
Opening Documentation.	10	_____
Specifications.	20	_____
Total.	**140**	_____

Lab 8

File I/O

Objectives.

1. Learn more about `iostream` objects.
2. Gain familiarity with the fundamentals of file I/O.
3. Learn about simple encryption techniques.

Prelab Questions:

1. In the `iostream` library, a connection between an executing program and a file stored on disk is called an _____.

2. The operation of actually establishing a connection between a program and a file is called _____ that connection.

3. The normal input operator (>>) skips leading white space characters. What member function of `cin` can be used to read white space characters?

4. When one is done reading from an `fstream`, what operation should be performed on it?

5. How does the Caesar cipher encode a character?

Introduction.

Throughout this manual, we have made extensive use of **files** — containers on hard or floppy disk that can be used to store information for long periods of time. For example, each source program that we have written has been stored in a file, and each binary executable program has also been stored in a file. While they may seem to be the same, files differ from programs in that a program is a sequence of instructions, and a file is a container in which a program (among other things) can be stored.

A different use for files is for storing data. That is, where each of our exercises have thus far read data from the keyboard and written data to the screen, an alternative approach is to read data from a file (in which the data has been stored) and write data to a file. This approach is particular useful for problems where the amount of data to be processed is so large that entering the data each time the program is executed (interactively) becomes inconvenient. That inconvenience can be eliminated by storing the data in a file, and then having the program read from the file, instead of the keyboard. Today's exercise is to learn how to do so.

When many of us were young, we enjoyed writing secret messages, in which messages were *encoded* in such a way as to prevent others from reading them, unless they were in possession of a secret key that enabled them to *decode* the message. Coded messages of this sort have a long history. For example, the **Caesar cipher** is a simple means of encoding messages that dates from Roman times. To illustrate, the Caesar cipher produces the encoded sentence:

```
Rqh li eb odqg, wzr li eb vhd.
```

when applied to the historic phrase:

```
One if by land, two if by sea.
```

What is the relationship between the letters in the original sentence and their counterparts in the encoded sentence?

Today's exercise is to write programs that use the Caesar cipher to encode and decode messages that are stored in files.

Getting Started.

Copy the file(s) from the `lab8` class directory into your own `lab8` directory. Look at the contents of `lab8`, and then personalize the documentation in the file `Encode.cc`, taking a few moments to study its contents.

Designing an Encoding Program.

Our first problem is to write a program that can be used to encode a message that is stored in a file. In order to demonstrate both input from and output to a file, we will store the encoded message in a second file. For the sake of simplicity, we will assume that the name of the input file is `encode.dat`, and that the name of the output file is `decode.dat` (in the next exercise, we will see how this restriction can be eliminated.)

Our problem might thus be specified as follows:

> Input(`encode.dat`), a sequence of unencoded characters.
> Output(`decode.dat`), a sequence of encoded characters.

The algorithm employed by our program can be summarized as follows:

1. Display an introductory message.
2. Open a connection for input to `encode.dat`, and a connection for output to `decode.dat`.
3. If either part of step 2 was unsuccessful, display an appropriate error message and quit.
4. Cycle through the following steps:
   a. read a character from the input file.
   b. if end-of-file was reached, then terminate repetition.
   c. encode the character.
   d. write the encoded character to the output file.
   End cycle.
5. Close the input and output connections.
6. Display a "successful completion" message.

It should be evident that steps 1 and 6 can be performed with familiar output statements, and step 4 can be accomplished using a forever loop, using an `if-break` combination in step 4b to control the repetition. Step 4c can be accomplished using the `CaesarEncode()` function that appears after the main function. That leaves the file-related operations in steps 2, 3, 4a, 4d, and 5 for us to learn how to perform.

Opening a Connection to a File.

An executing program is unable to interact directly with a file for a very simple reason: an executing program resides *in main memory* and a file resides *on disk*. However, an executing program can interact indirectly with a file, by *opening a connection* between the program and that file. In C++, such connections are called `fstream` objects.

Like any other object, an `fstream` must be declared before it can be used. The declaration

```
fstream
    FStreamName;
```

constructs *FStreamName* as a *potential connection* to a file. Such a potential connection is turned into an actual connection to a particular file named *FileName* using the member function `open()`:

```
FStreamName.open(FileName, OpenMode) ;
```

Alternately, an `fstream` can be declared and opened in one easy step:

```
fstream
    FStreamName(FileName, OpenMode) ;
```

Regardless of which approach is used:

`fstream` is a type declared in the header file `<fstream.h>`,
FStreamName is an identifier that we wish to use as the name of the `fstream`,
FileName is the (character string) name of the file to which we wish to establish a
    connection, and
OpenMode states how we intend to use the `fstream`:

- `ios::in` will open the `fstream` for input.
- `ios::out` will open the `fstream` for output (any data in the file is destroyed).
- `ios::app` will open the `fstream` for output (any data in the file is preserved,
    and data written to the `fstream` will be appended to the file).
- `ios::in | ios::out` will open the `fstream` for both input and output.

When opening an `fstream` to a file, *OpenMode* allows us to state how we intend to use that connection: for input, for output, or for both. This allows the C++ compiler to generate an error if we should inadvertently write to an `fstream` opened for input, or read from an `fstream` opened for output.

In the space below and in the appropriate place in your source program, write the necessary statement(s) to (1) open an `fstream` named `InStream` as an input connection to the file `encode.dat`, and (2) open an `fstream` named `OutStream` as an output connection to the file `decode.dat`. Be sure that you make `encode.dat` and `decode.dat` character strings.

Then test what you have written by using the compiler to translate your source program. Unless you're ahead of the game, the compiler should generate an error message. Record it in the space below:

The reason for this error message is that `fstream` is itself an identifier, declared in the header file `<fstream.h>`, and so that file must be included, in order for `fstream` to be declared. Add the necessary `#include` directive to do so, and then recompile your source program.

When your source program compiles correctly, do *not* execute your source program yet (or an infinite loop will occur.) Instead, continue to the next part of the exercise.

Test for Success.

Opening files is an operation that is highly susceptible to user errors. For example, suppose the user has accidentally deleted the file `encode.dat` and our program tries to open a connection to it? Or suppose that the disk is full, so that there is no room for `decode.dat`? In such circumstances, the open operation is said to *fail*. To detect such failures, all `fstream` objects contain a member function named `fail()` whose form is as follows:

```
FStreamName.fail()
```

When execution reaches this function, it is evaluated and returns true (1), if the last operation on `FStreamName` failed, and returns false (0), if that operation was successful.

Note that the member function `good()` (that we have used before) could also be used. The call

```
FStreamName.good()
```

generally returns true (1) if the last operation on `FStreamName` was successful, and returns false (0), if that operation was unsuccessful. The functions `good()` and `fail()` typically return the opposite values, so that the call

```
!FStreamName.good()
```

would have to be used in our current problem. Since this requires an additional operation (the negation operation using `!`), the use of `fail()` is to be preferred in solving our problem.

We should thus use the `fail()` member function in performing step 3 of our algorithm, by using calls to it as the conditions controlling a following `if-else-if` statement:

```
if ( /* our attempt to open InStream failed */ )
{
  cerr << "\n*** Unable to open input file: 'encode.dat' !\n";
  exit(-1);
}
else if ( /* our attempt to open OutStream failed */)
{
  cerr << "\n*** Unable to open output file: 'decode.dat' !\n";
  exit(-1);
}
```

In order for the name `exit()` to be declared, the header file `<stdlib.h>` must be included.

Enter this `if-else-if` statement in your source program, replacing the comments with appropriate calls to `fail()`. Then compile your source program to check the correctness of what you have written. Use the space below to record any difficulties you encounter.

Continue when what you have written is free of syntax errors.

Input from an `fstream`.

Just as we have used the >> operator is used to read data from the `istream` named `cin`, the >> operator can be used to read data from an `fstream` opened for input. Since the `fstream` connects a file to a program, applying >> to it transfers data from the file to the program. For this reason, this operation is described as *reading from the file*, even though we are actually operating on the `fstream`. An expression of the form:

        FStreamName >> *VariableName*

thus serves to read values from an `fstream` named *FStreamName* that has been opened for input (and thus from the file to which *FStreamName* is a connection) into the variable *VariableName*. Of course, the type of the value being read must match the type of *VariableName*, or the operation will fail.

While the input operator is the appropriate operator to solve many problems involving file input, it is not the appropriate operator for our problem. The reason is that like its interactive counter-part, the >> operator *skips leading white space characters*. That is, if our input were

        One if by land.
        Two if by sea.

and we were to use the >> operator (in a loop) to read each of these characters:

        InStream >> Ch;

then all white space characters (blanks, tabs and newlines) would be skipped, so that only non-white space characters would be processed and output. Our encoded message would then appear as follows:

        Rqhliebodqg.wzrliebvhd.

To avoid this problem, `fstream` objects (and `istream` objects) contain a member function named `get()`, whose statement form is as follows:

        FStreamName.get(*CharacterVariable*) ;

When execution reaches such a statement, the next character is read from *FStreamName* and stored in *CharacterVariable*, even if it is a white space character.

The `get()` member function of `InStream` can thus be used to perform step 4a of our algorithm. In your source program, place a call to `get()` in the appropriate place to perform this step. Then compile your source program, to test that what you have written is syntactically correct. Use the space below to record any problems you encounter.

When your source program is syntactically correct, continue to the next part of the exercise.

Controlling a File Input Loop.

Files are created by a computer's operating system. When the operating system creates a file, it marks the end of the file with a special **end-of-file mark**. Input operations are then implemented in such a way as to prevent them from reading beyond the end-of-file mark, since doing so could allow a programmer unauthorized access to the files of another programmer.

This end-of-file mark can be used to control a loop that is reading data from the file. Just as the `istream` member function `eof()` can be used to control an interactive input loop, the `fstream` member function `eof()` can be used to control a file input loop, with the form:

```
FStreamName.eof()
```

When execution reaches this expression, the `eof()` function returns true (1) if the last read from `FStreamName` tried to read the end-of-file mark, and returns false(0) otherwise.

In a forever loop like the one in the source program, the `eof()` function can be used to prevent infinite loop behavior. By placing an `if-break` combination:

```
if ( /*end-of-file has been reached */ ) break;
```

following the input step, repetition will be terminated when all of the data in the file has been processed.

In your source program, place an `if-break` combination in the appropriate place to perform step 4b of our algorithm, using the `eof()` member function of `InStream` as the condition in the `if` statement. Then compile your source program, to check the syntax of what you have written. When it is syntactically correct, continue to the next part of the exercise.

File Output.

Just as we have used the `<<` operator to write data to the `ostream` named `cout`, the `<<` operator can be used to write data to an `fstream` opened for output. Since the `fstream` connects a program to a file, applying `<<` to it transfers data from the program to the file. This operation is thus described as *writing to the file*, even though it is an `fstream` operation. The general form is similar to what we have seen before:

```
FStreamName << Value ;
```

where `FStreamName` is an `fstream` opened for output, and `Value` is a character or constant we wish to store in the file to which `FStreamName` is a connection.

Alternatively, we could use the `fstream` member function `put()`, whose form is

```
FStreamName.put( CharValue ) ;
```

which achieves the same effect, but can be used only for characters.

Use either of these statements to write the encoded character to `decode.dat` via `OutStream`, to perform step 4d of our algorithm. Then compile your source program to test the syntax of what you have written, continuing when it is correct.

Closing Files.

Once we are done using an `fstream` to read from or write to a file, we should *close* it, to break the connection between our program and the file. This is accomplished using the fstream member function `close()`, whose statement form is

```
FStreamName.close() ;
```

When execution reaches this statement, the connection named *FStreamName* between the program and the file is broken.

In the appropriate place in the source program, place calls to `close()` to

- break the connection between the program and `encode.dat`; and
- break the connection between the program and `decode.dat`.

Then translate your source program, and ensure that it is free of syntax errors. When it is, test it using the provided file named `encode.dat`. If what you have written is correct, then your program should produce the file `decode.dat`, containing the output:

```
Rqh li eb odqg,
Wzr li eb vhd.
```

If this file is not produced, then your program contains a logical error. Retrace your steps, comparing the statements in your source program to those described in the preceding parts of the exercise, until you find your error. Correct it, retranslate your source program and then re-test your program, until it performs correctly.

Applying What We Have Learned.

The last part of today's exercise is for you to apply what you have learned to the problem of decoding a file encoded using the Caesar cipher. Complete the skeleton program `Decode.cc`, that can be used to decode a message encoded using the Caesar cipher. Do all that is necessary to get this program operational, so that messages encoded with `Encode` can be decoded with `Decode`. Note that if `Decode` is written to read from `decode.dat` and write to `encode.dat`, then the two programs will be complementary.

Use the next page to record any observations you make, new error messages you encounter and how they were corrected, and so on.

Phrases You Should Now Understand.

File, `fstream`, Opening An `fstream` To A File For Input, Opening An `fstream` To A File For Output, File Input, File Output, Closing A File.

Notes:

Objectives.

1. Practice performing file I/O via `fstreams`.
2. Practice designing and implementing programs.

Introduction.

Each of the following projects involves the use of file I/O. Your instructor will tell you which of them you are to do, and will provide any input files to be used to test your program.

Projects.

8.1. Write a program that reads from a file of real numbers, and displays the *minimum*, *maximum*, *average*, and *range* of the numbers in the file.

8.2. Write a program that reads the contents of a file and creates an exact copy of the file, except that each line is numbered. For example, if the first line of the input file is

```
Four score and seven years ago,
```

then the first line of the output file should appear something like the following:

```
1: Four score and seven years ago,
```

8.3. Write a single menu-driven program by which a user can either encode a message using the Caesar cipher, or decode a message that has been encoded using the Caesar cipher. In either case, the message is to be read from a file and the output from the program should be stored in a file. Store the functions `CaesarEncode()` and `CaesarDecode()` in a separately compiled library named `codes`, so that they can be used again by any program that needs them.

8.4. Write a text-analysis program that reads an essay or composition stored in a text file, and determines the number of words, the number of sentences, the average number of words per sentence, the average number of letters per word, and a *Complexity* rating, using:

$$Complexity = 0.5 \times AverageSentenceLength + 0.5 \times AverageWordLength.$$

Based on these calculations, your program should assess the writing level of the essay as:

- *Grammar School*, if *Complexity* < 6.
- *Junior High*, if 6 ≤ *Complexity* < 7.
- *High School*, if 7 ≤ *Complexity* < 8.
- *College*, if 8 ≤ *Complexity* < 9.
- *Graduate*, if *Complexity* ≥ 9.

Alternative Writing Project: A number of recent (1994) newspaper and magazine articles have discussed the *clipper chip*. Write a research paper on the clipper chip, explaining what it is, what issue(s) it is designed to address, who is in favor of it, who is against it, and your own viewpoints on the issue(s).

Project 8 Due Date _____

Turn in this grade sheet, attached to a hard copy of

a. your source program,
b. the input files used to test your program,
c. the output files (if any) produced by your program, and
d. a sample execution of your program.

Name _____

Category	Points Possible	Points Received
Correctness and efficiency...................	60	_____
Design and Structure.......................	20	_____
Style and Readability......................	20	
Horizontal White Space...............	5	_____
Vertical White Space.................	5	_____
Meaningful Identifiers...............	10	_____
Documentation...........................	20	
Opening Documentation...............	10	_____
Specification(s)....................	10	_____
Total................................	**120**	_____

Lab 9

Character Strings

Note to the Instructor:

Preparation for this lab includes the following steps:

1. Ensure that the class directory contains a directory `MyLib`, containing the files `Strings.h` and `Strings.cc`.

2. Within the `lab9` class directory, define the `Makefile` macro `CLASSLIB` with the absolute name of the `MyLib` class directory.

These must be done in order for students to be able to translate their (separately compiled) source programs, since those programs must be linked to the `Strings` library or else translation will fail.

Special Note: This exercise uses class `Strings` to replace all occurrences of one string, called the *Target*, with another string, called the *Replacement*. Because replacement searches always begin at the beginning of a Strings object, *Target* should not be a substring of *Replacement* (i.e., *Replacement* should not contain *Target*.)

Objectives.

1. Learn about variables capable of storing character strings.
2. Learn about operations on character strings.
3. Learn more about computing with files.

Prelab Questions:

1. The number of characters in a character string is called the _____ of that string.

2. The operation of creating a string by selecting a portion of another string is called the _____ operation.

3. The operation of determining whether one (sub)string occurs within another string is called the _____ operation.

4. The operation of forming a string by combining two separate strings is called the _____ operation.

5. The operation of deleting a substring from a string and inserting another string in place of the deleted substring is called the _____ operation.

Introduction.

In the last exercise, we learned about files — containers for information stored on secondary memory devices — and how to manipulate them indirectly using fstream objects. Today's exercise involves learning about character strings, and how they can be used to process files more conveniently, in some problems.

One of the uses of character strings is to represent an object's name. For example, in the last exercise, the name of our input file was encode.dat. To represent this name within our program, we used the character string constant

```
"encode.dat"
```

That is, to open an fstream connection to that file, we wrote:

```
fstream
       InStream("encode.dat", ios::in),
       ...
```

The problem with this approach is that the name of our input file is "hard-wired" into our program — if we wish to read from a file whose name is something other than encode.dat, then that file must be renamed encode.dat, or our program cannot read from it.

A solution to this problem is to declare a variable *InFileName* capable of holding a character string. Given such an object, we can prompt for and read the name of the input file from the keyboard and store it in *InFileName*, and then open an fstream to the file whose name is in *InFileName*.

```
// declare InFileName

cout << "\nPlease enter the name of the input file: "
cin >> InFileName;

fstream
       InStream (InFileName, ios::in);
```

By doing so, we avoid "hard-wiring" the name of a file into our program, resulting in a program that can be used to process any file.

To declare and operate on *InFileName*, a type is needed whose objects can store character strings, along with operations on such objects. Unfortunately, C++ does not (at this time) provide such a type. For this reason, we have used the C++ *class* mechanism to define our own (new) type named Strings. This type can be used to declare objects that are capable of storing and processing character strings. Today's exercise is to become familiar declaring and operating on objects of this type.

Getting Started.

Begin by changing directory to the `MyLib` class directory. If you examine its contents, you will see the files `Strings.h` and `Strings.cc`. These are the header and implementation files of a `Strings` library, in which the type `Strings` is declared.

Each of the operations provided for `strings` objects is described in the documentation within these files. While we will utilize several of these operations in today's exercise, we will not use all of them. See the documentation in `Strings.h` or the discussion in C++: An Introduction To Computing for further information about `strings`.

To begin today's exercise, create and change directory to `labs/lab9`, and copy the file(s) from the `lab9` class directory. Then begin editing `replace.cc`, and familiarize yourself with the contents of that file.

The Problem.

Today's exercise is to write a program that performs an operation provided by most text editors. The problem the program is to solve is to replace all occurrences of one string (called the target string) with another string (called the replacement string) within a given file. For the sake of convenience, we should enter the name of this file from the keyboard, rather than "hard-wiring" it into our program.

It is usually a good idea to avoid overwriting an input file, so we will store the changes to the input file in a second file distinct from the input file. We can thus identify the following objects:

- The input file, whose name we will describe as *InFileName*;
- The string being replaced, whose name we will describe as *TargetString*;
- The replacement string, whose name we will describe as *ReplacementString*; and
- The output file, whose name we will describe as *OutFileName*.

In terms of these objects, we can now specify our problem, as follows:

Output (screen):	Messages and prompts for input.
Input (keyboard):	The name of the input file, stored in *InFileName*;
	The string to be replaced, stored in *TargetString*;
	The replacement string, stored in *ReplacementString*.
Input(*InFileName*):	Each line of the file.
Output(*OutFileName*):	Each line of the input file, with all occurrences of *TargetString* replaced with *ReplacementString*.

Note that in specifying this problem, we specify *where input comes from*, and *where output goes to*, since it can go either to an interactive I/O device, or a secondary memory device.

Designing A Solution.

The algorithm that we will use to solve our problem is as follows:

1. Display an introductory message.
2. Prompt for the name of the input file, and input a character string, storing it in *InFileName*.
3. Build *OutFileName*, consisting of *InFileName*, with its extension (if any) replaced with the extension .REP.
4. Open an fstream for input named *InStream* to *InFileName*, and an fstream for output named *OutStream* to *OutFileName*.
5. Verify that each fstream opened successfully.
6. Prompt for the string to be replaced, and input a character string, storing it in *TargetString*.
7. Prompt for the replacement string, and input a character string, storing it in *ReplacementString*.
8. Cycle through the following steps:
   a. Input a line of text through *InStream*, storing it in *Line*;
   b. If the end of file mark was read, then terminate repetition.
   c. For each occurrence of *TargetString* within *Line*:
      Replace *TargetString* in *Line* with *ReplacementString*.
      End loop.
   d. Output *Line* through *OutStream*.
   End cycle.
9. Close *InStream* and *OutStream*.
10. Display a "successful completion of processing" message.

Declaring A strings Object.

Before we can complete step 2 of our algorithm, we must be able to declare a variable capable of storing a character string. As described previously, the class strings is a type that can be used to declare such variables. To declare such variables, a declaration of the form:

```
Strings StringName1, StringName2, ..., StringNamen;
```

constructs the objects $StringName_1$, $StringName_2$, ..., $StringName_n$; as variables capable of holding character string values.

Using this form, declare two strings objects InFileName and OutFileName in your source program, in the appropriate place. Be sure to add the appropriate #include directive to insert the header file of library strings, using double-quotes (" and ") instead of angle-brackets (< and >) around the name of the file. Then check the syntax of what you have written by compiling your source program. When it is free of syntax errors, continue.

If desired, a strings variable *StringName* can optionally be initialized at its declaration with a character string constant *CharacterStringConstant*, as follows:

```
Strings StringName ( CharacterStringConstant ) ;
```

An uninitialized strings object (like InFileName or OutFileName) is initialized as an **empty string**, containing no characters (i.e., whose *length* is zero).

Strings Input.

Step 2 of our algorithm involves inputting a character string. There are two ways this can be accomplished. The first is the traditional method, using the >> operator, with an expression of the form:

```
InputStream >> StringName
```

This expression begins by skipping over any white space characters in *InputStream*, until a non-white space character is encountered. It then reads non-white space characters until a white space character (or the end-of-file mark) is encountered, which remains unread. The non-white space characters are stored in *StringName*, which grows or shrinks as necessary to hold the input characters.

The important thing to remember is that the >> operator acts like a *get word* operation, because once it starts reading non-white space characters, any white space character (blank, tab or newline) causes the reading to halt.

An alternative means of inputting a character string is provided by the strings member function GetLine(), whose statement form is as follows:

```
StringName.GetLine(InputStream);
```

As its name implies, this function acts as a *get line* operation. More precisely, it reads characters from *InputStream* into *StringName* without skipping leading white space, until a newline character (or the end-of-file mark) is encountered, which is read, but not stored within *StringName*. *StringName* grows or shrinks to the size needed to hold the input characters, which are then stored in it.

Which of these operations should we use? In general, the >> operator should be used if a single word is to be input, but GetLine() should be used if multiple words are to be read.

In our particular problem, we must input the name of a file. UNIX permits file names to consist of multiple words, and so in order for our program to handle such names, we should use the GetLine() operation.

In the appropriate place in your source program, write a call to GetLine() that when executed, will fill InFileName with a character string from the input stream cin. By placing this call after the prompt for the name of the input file, the name entered by the user in response to that prompt will be stored in InFileName. Then use the compiler to check the correctness of what you have written, and continue when it is syntactically correct.

Because of the differences in their behavior, care must be taken if calls to the >> operator and GetLine() are mixed in the same program. In particular, suppose that the >> operator is used to read a word entered at the keyboard, and then GetLine() is used to read a line from the keyboard. Because >> does not read the newline that terminates its input, that newline will remain unread in cin. Then, because GetLine() (1) does not skip leading white space and (2) terminates as soon as it encounters a newline, that newline will be the first character read by GetLine(), which will cause it to terminate immediately. This can be circumvented by calling

```
cin.get(Ch);
```

after the call to >>, to explicitly read the newline from cin.

Constructing The Output File Name.

In step 3, we come to an interesting problem. Rather than simply input the name of the output file, our algorithm calls for us to

> 3. Build *OutFileName*, consisting of *InFileName*, with its extension (if any) replaced with the extension `.REP`.

Since a file name with an extension always has a period in it, we can solve this problem by refining it into the following substeps:

> 3a. Find *Pos*, the position of the period in *InFileName* (if *InFileName* has a period).
> 3b. If there is no period:
>   Assign *OutFileName* the concatenation of *InFileName* and `".REP"`.
>   Else
>   Assign *OutFileName* the concatenation of
>   the substring *InFileName*(0, *Pos*-1) and `".REP"`.
>   End if.

These steps involve the use of some `Strings` operations that are new to us.

The Pattern-Matching Operation.

Step 3a can be performed using the `Position()` member function (which performs the *pattern-matching* operation), whose usage in a statement form is

```
int Pos = StringName.Position(StringValue);
```

When execution reaches such a statement, the `Position()` function searches `StringName` for `StringValue`. If `StringValue` is not in `StringName`, then `Position()` returns a negative value. Otherwise, `Position()` returns the number or index of the character within `StringName` where `StringValue` starts. In a `Strings` object of n characters, the index of the first character is always 0, the index of the second character is always 1, ..., and the index of the nth character is always n-1.

In your source program, write a statement that uses `Position()` to search `InFileName` for a period, and stores its return value in an integer variable `Pos`. Then use the compiler to check what you have written, continuing when it is correct.

We clearly need an `if` statement to perform step 3b. To control it, we can use the value of `Pos`, since it contains the return value from `Position()`, which is negative if `InFileName` contains no period, and is zero or positive otherwise. Write such an `if` statement in the appropriate place in your source program, leaving its statements empty.

The Assignment Operation (=).

To fill in the statements of our `if` statement, we can use the assignment operator (=) that allows us to assign a `Strings` expression to a `Strings` variable in the usual manner:

```
StringsVariable = StringsExpression
```

The Concatenation Operation (&).

To construct the appropriate *StringsExpression* for our assignment, we must be able to join two Strings values into one, an operation called *concatenating* the two strings. This can be done using the concatenation operator (&) with an expression of the form:

    StringsValue₁ & StringsValue₂

which returns the single Strings value *StringsValue₁* followed by *StringsValue₂*.

In the appropriate place in your source program, encode the first assignment from our algorithm:

Assign *OutFileName* the concatenation of *InFileName* and ".REP".

The Substring Operation.

To encode the second assignment, we will need to be able to select a part of a Strings object, which is usually called a *substring*. The operation to do so is accordingly called the substring operation, whose form is:

    StringsName(FirstIndex, LastIndex)

When execution reaches such an expression, this function returns the portion of *StringsName* beginning with the character whose index is *FirstIndex* and ending at the character whose index is *LastIndex*. Since 0 is always the index of the first character in a Strings object, $0 \le$ *FirstIndex* $\le$ *LastIndex* $< n$, if *StringsName* contains n characters.

In our problem of building OutFileName for an InFileName that contains a period (i.e., an extension), we want to select the substring of InFileName starting with its first character and ending with the character before the period. This is quite easy, since the index of the first character is 0, and the index of the period is stored in Pos. In your source program, write a statement in the appropriate place that uses the assignment, substring, and concatenation operators to perform the second assignment from our algorithm:

Assign *OutFileName* the concatenation of
the substring *InFileName*(0, *Pos*-1) and ".REP".

Then, use the compiler to check the syntax of the statements you have added, and continue when they are correct.

One way to understand the substring and concatenation operations is to view them as complementary operations. That is, by enabling you to select a portion of a string, substring allows you to partition one string into two or more of its components. By contrast, concatenation enables you to take two or more substrings and combine them together into a single string. The two operations can thus be used in a complementary fashion.

Opening an `fstream` to `InFileName`.

Step 4 of our algorithm is to open `fstream`s to the files whose names are stored in *InFileName* and *OutFileName*. Last time, we saw how to open an `fstream` to a file whose name was represented as a character string constant. Opening an `fstream` to a file whose name is stored in a `Strings` object is just as easy, with a declaration of the form:

```
fstream StreamName (StringsName, Mode);
```

When execution reaches such a statement, an `fstream` named *StreamName* is established as a connection between the program and the file whose name is stored in *StringsName*. As we saw before, *Mode* is used to specify the nature of the connection: `ios::in` if we intend to read from the file, `ios::out` if we intend to write to the file, and so on.

In the appropriate place in your source program, declare `InStream` as a connection to the file whose name is stored in `InFileName`, and declare `OutStream` as a connection to the file whose name is stored in `OutFileName`. Then use the compiler to check the syntax of what you have written, continuing when it is correct.

Verifying the Open.

Step 5 of our algorithm is to verify the success of our attempts to open the `fstream`s. As we saw last time, it is usually a good idea to do so, in case the operation cannot be performed for some reason. If the operation should fail, then an informative error message should be displayed and the program should be terminated using `exit()`, from `<stdlib.h>`. The error messages and `exit()` statement are already present in your source program, so appropriately position an `if` statement that uses the `fail()` member of `InStream` and `OutStream` to verify that these `fstream`s opened successfully. Continue when what you have written is syntactically correct.

Getting the Two Strings.

Steps 6 and 7 of our algorithm are essentially to input the two character strings needed to solve our problem — the values for *TargetString* and *ReplacementString*. These steps are quite similar to step 2, and so doing them requires no new information.

At the appropriate place in your source file, declare the two `Strings` objects `TargetString` and `ReplacementString`. Then position calls to their `GetLine()` members to fill them with keyboard-entered character strings, after their respective prompts. Check the syntax of what you have written, and continue when it is correct.

Processing via `InStream`.

To perform step 8 requires an input loop, which we have implemented using a forever loop, because the condition controlling the repetition is best tested in the middle of the loop.

Step 8a is to input a line of text from the input file via *InStream*. This is easily accomplished using the same `Strings` member function `GetLine()` function that we used to fill *InFileName*, *TargetString*, and *ReplacementString*.

To hold the line of text, declare a new `Strings` object `Line` (before the loop) in your source file. Then write a call to the `GetLine()` member of `Line`, to fill `Line` with a line of text from `InStream` (as opposed to `cin`).

Step 8b requires nothing new, either. Using `InStream`'s `eof()` function, write an `if-break` combination in your source program that terminates repetition if the end-of-file mark is read.

`Strings` Replacement.

Step 8c of our algorithm is as follows:

> c. For each occurrence of *TargetString* within *Line*:
> Replace each occurrence of *TargetString* in *Line* with *ReplacementString*.
> End loop.

This is not a trivial step, so let's refine it a bit. The difficulty is that there might be multiple occurrences of *TargetString* within *Line*. We might break it down as follows:

> c. Cycle through the following steps:
> 1) Determine whether or not *TargetString* occurs within *Line*.
> 2) If it does not, terminate repetition.
> 3) Replace *TargetString* in *Line* with *ReplacementString*.
> End cycle.

This clearly involves a second loop, nested within the first loop. Moreover, we must do c1) at least once, but should do c3) zero times at times, implying that we should terminate the repetition between c1) and c3). We thus choose another forever loop, rather than the while or do-while. Write such a forever loop in your source program.

It should be evident that we can determine whether or not *TargetString* occurs in *Line* using the same `Position()` function we used to perform step 2. Write an assignment statement that uses the `Position()` function to search `Line` for `TargetString`, and stores the result in `Pos`.

Encode step c2) by using `Pos` to control an `if-break` combination, such that repetition will be terminated if `TargetString` was not present in `Line`.

To encode step c3), we need two new `Strings` operations. The name of the first operation is `Replace()`, which can be called with the statement form:

```
StringsName.Replace(FirstIndex, LastIndex, StringsValue);
```

It can be used to replace the characters in `StringsName` that occur at positions `FirstIndex` through `LastIndex` with `StringsValue`. We thus want to write

```
Line.Replace(FirstIndex, LastIndex, ReplacementString);
```

with appropriate values for `FirstIndex` and `LastIndex`. Since `Pos` contains the index of the first character, we can use it for `FirstIndex`:

```
Line.Replace(Pos, LastIndex, ReplacementString);
```

But how can we determine the index of the last character of `TargetString` within `Line`?

`strings` Length.

This is where the second `strings` operation is useful. Every `strings` object has a member function named `Length()`, such that the call:

        `StringsName.Length()`

returns the number of characters in `StringsName`. That is, the call

        `TargetString.Length()`

returns the number of characters in `TargetString`, so the expression

        `Pos + TargetString.Length() - 1`

can be used to compute the index of the last character in `TargetString` within `Line`. We thus write:

        `Line.Replace(Pos, Pos+TargetString.Length()-1, ReplacementString);`

to replace the characters of `TargetString` with those of `ReplacementString`. By executing this statement within our loop, each occurrence of `TargetString` will be replaced by `ReplacementString`.

Add this statement to your source program, and then continue.

`strings` Output.

The final step in our processing loop is

  d. Output *Line* through *OutStream*.

Our final `strings` operation is thus to output a `strings` value, which is accomplished using the `<<` operator in the usual manner. The form of such an expression is

        `StreamName << StringsName`

When execution reaches this expression, the characters in `StringsName` are output via `StreamName`, regardless of whether it is an `ostream` to the screen or an `fstream` to a file.

Add an output statement to your source program that will write the contents of `Line` to our output file via `OutStream`. Since we are outputting a line of characters, be sure to output a newline after `Line`. This is necessary because while `GetLine()` reads the newline at the end of a line, it does not store that character in `Line`.

Closing Streams.

Using the `iostream` member function `close()` (see Lab 8, if you have forgotten), add the necessary statements to your source program to perform step 9 of our algorithm:

  9.   Close *InStream* and *OutStream*.

Wrapping Things Up.

The final step in our algorithm is

> 10. Display a "successful completion of processing" message.

The variable Count maintains a count of the number of occurrences of TargetString that are replaced by ReplacementString. Add a final output statement that tells the user

1. How many replacements were performed, and
2. The name of the output file.

Then translate your program using the Makefile (one of the files you copied from the class directory). When it is free of compilation errors, test it thoroughly for logical errors, either using the provided input file lab9.dat, or another that you supply.

About the Makefile.

The Makefile provided with this exercise has several new features that merit discussion. One feature is that it uses a **macro** (like a named constant declaration) something like the following:

```
CLASSLIB = /home/CS-1/MyLib
```

The part that follows the = is the absolute name of your MyLib class directory. To *use* the macro, you must place $(before its name and) following its name. This allows us to write

```
Strings.o: $(CLASSLIB)/Strings.cc $(CLASSLIB)/Strings.h
```

which is more convenient than writing:

```
Strings.o: /home/CS-1/MyLib/Strings.cc /home/CS-1/MyLib/Strings.h
```

A second feature is its use of the -I switch that tells g++ where to look for include files. The line

```
        g++ -c -I$(CLASSLIB) replace.cc
```

has g++ search your MyLib class directory, so that it can find Strings.h. The final feature is

```
clean:
        rm -f replace *~ *# *.o
```

This means that at the system prompt (i.e., enter at the command-line), you can enter

```
        % make clean
```

to remove replace, all emacs backup and save files, and all object files, respectively.

Phrases You Should Now Understand.

String, Substring, Concatenation, String Input, String Output, String Length, String Replacement, String Position, String Pattern Matching.

Objectives.

1. Practice solving problems that involve character string objects
2. Gain familiarity with remaining character string operations.

Introduction.

Each of the following projects involves the use of character strings, and can be solved using the `strings` library. Your instructor will inform you of which project you are to do.

Projects.

9.1. A character string is said to be a **palindrome** if it reads the same when the order of its characters is reversed. For example, the following are all palindromes:

```
madam
smada bob adams
able was I ere I saw elba
```

Write a program that inputs a character string and identifies whether or not it is a palindrome. Use a boolean function that, given the input string, returns true if that string is a palindrome and returns false otherwise.

9.2. In Lab 8, we used the functions `CaesarEncode()` and `CaesarDecode()` to encrypt a character. An even simpler encryption method is to reverse the order of the characters in a string, so that if the characters in the message

```
UOHT TRA EROFEREHW OEMOR OEMOR
```

are reversed as a line, then the decoded message reads:

```
ROMEO ROMEO WHEREFORE ART THOU
```

A variation is to reverse the characters in each word, while preserving the order of the words, in which case the coded message is:

```
EOMOR EOMOR EROFEREHW TRA UOHT
```

Write a function `Reverse()` that reverses the order of the characters in a character string. Then write a menu-driver program that, using this function and one of these approaches, encrypts or decrypts a message stored in a file, whose name the user enters from the keyboard.

9.3. Professor Diskus keeps student exam scores in a file, each line of which has the form:

```
FirstName LastName Exam1 Exam2 Exam3
```

where `FirstName` and `LastName` are character strings representing a student's name, and `Exam1`, `Exam2` and `Exam3` are the percentages scored by that student on each of the three exams. Write a program that, given the name of such a file, uses its data to create another file, in which each line has the form:

```
LastName, FirstInitial    ExamAverage
```

In the new file, `LastName` again represents the student's last name, but `FirstInitial` is the first initial of the first name and `ExamAverage` is the average of the student's three exam percentages. Make the name of the output file a variation of the name of the input file, as we did in this lab exercise (i.e., if the input file is `exams.dat`, then the output file might be `exams.avg`).

9.4. The table below illustrates the relationship between words in English and Pig-Latin:

English	Pig-Latin	English	Pig-Latin
circus	ircuscay	parrot	arootpay
flying	yingflay	snapshots	apshotssnay
silly	illysay	granny	annygray
shrink	inkshray	inquisition	inquisitionyay
albatross	albatrossyay	upside-down	upside-downyay

From these examples, it should be fairly easy to infer the rules by which a Pig-Latin word is derived from an English word. Write an English-to-Pig-Latin translating function that, given a word in English, returns the corresponding word in Pig-Latin. Then use this function to write a program that, given the name of a file containing a message and the name of an output file, translates that message from English into Pig-Latin, storing the translation in the output file.

Project 9 Due Date _____

Turn in this grade sheet, attached to a hard copy of

a. your source program
b. a sample execution,
c. any input files used in your sample execution, and
d. any output files produced by your sample execution.

Name _____

Category	Points Possible	Points Received
Correctness and efficiency	60	_____
Design and Structure	30	_____
Style and Readability	20	
Horizontal White Space	5	_____
Vertical White Space	5	_____
Meaningful Identifiers	10	_____
Documentation	20	
Opening Documentation	10	_____
Specification(s)	10	_____
Total	**130**	_____

Lab 10

Classes and Types

Objectives.

1. Introduce the class — the primary C++ mechanism for creating new types.
2. Become proficient defining the data and function members of classes.
3. Learn how to overload C++ operators.

Prelab Questions:

1. The members of a class cannot be accessed outside of the class, because they are (by default) _____ .

2. The objects within a class that are used to store the attributes of a class object are called the _____ of the class.

3. The member functions of a class provide a means by which the _____ on a class object can be performed.

4. A member function that automatically initializes a class object when it is defined is called a class _____ function.

5. How can the `Simplify()` member function of a `Fraction` object named `Result` be called?

Introduction.

Most of the problems we have examined to this point have had relatively simple solutions, because the data objects in the problem could be represented using the predefined C++ types. For example, we can represent a *Menu* with a character string, a *Choice* from that menu with a character, the *Radius* of a circle with a real, and so on.

The problem is that real-world problems often involve data objects that cannot be directly represented using the predefined C++ types. For example, suppose that we know a certain gourmet chef named Pièrre whose recipes are written to make 12 servings. The difficulty is

1. Pièrre frequently must prepare a dish for fewer than 12 customers
   (e.g., 1 customer = $\frac{1}{12}$ of a recipe, 2 customers = $\frac{1}{6}$ of a recipe, and so on.)

2. Pièrre's recipes are written using fractions (e.g., $\frac{1}{2}$ tsp., $\frac{3}{4}$ cup, etc.) so that he must multiply fractions to reduce the size of a recipe, and

3. Pièrre is so poor at multiplying fractions, that he has hired us to write a program that will enable him to conveniently multiply two fractions.

Getting Started.

Create and change directory to `labs/lab10`, and then copy the files from the `lab10` class directory to this directory. If you examine the program in `convert.cc`, it's logic is as follows:

```
Fraction
      OldMeasure,
      ScaleFactor;

cout << "\nEnter the fractional measure you want to convert: ";
cin >> OldMeasure;

cout << "\nEnter the fractional amount to reduce/increase it by: ";
cin >> ScaleFactor;

Fraction
      NewMeasure = OldMeasure * ScaleFactor;

cout << "\nThe converted measurement is: " << NewMeasure << "\n\n";
```

Note that a solution to Pièrre's problem is quite simple, given the ability to define, input, multiply and output `Fraction` data objects. The difficulty is that there is no predefined C++ type `Fraction` by which such data objects can be defined or operated upon.

In such situations, C++ provides a mechanism by which a programmer can create a new type and its operations. This mechanism is called the *class*, which is the subject of today's exercise.

Creating Classes.

In C++, a new type can be created by

1. Defining the data objects that make up the **attributes** of an object of the new type (i.e., the things of which an object of that type consists); and

2. Surrounding those definitions with a **class structure**, which has the form:

```
class TypeName
{
};
```

where *TypeName* is an appropriate name describing the new type.

For example, if we wished to define a new type whose objects could be used to store Cartesian coordinates, such an object has two attributes: an x value, and a y value, both reals, which we might define as follows:

```
double
    x_,
    y_;
```

To distinguish attribute identifiers from other identifiers, we will place an underscore at the end of a data member's name. We then surround them with an appropriately-named class structure:

```
class Coordinate
{
    double
        x_,
        y_;
};
```

The result is a new type, named `Coordinate`, which can be used to declare data objects, such as a point:

```
Coordinate
    Point;
```

The object `Point` then has two real components, one named `x_` and the other named `y_`.

In general, the data portion of a class definition can be thought of as having the general form:

```
class TypeName
{
    Type1 AttributeList1;
    Type2 AttributeList2;
    ...
    TypeN AttributeListN;
};
```

where each $Type_i$ is any defined type; and each $AttributeList_i$ is a list of the $Type_i$ attributes of an object of type *TypeName*.

Now, if we apply this approach to the problem we are trying to solve, we see that we need to identify the attributes of a `Fraction` object. If we examine a few fractions

$$\frac{1}{2} \qquad \frac{4}{3} \qquad \frac{4}{16} \qquad \frac{16}{4}$$

we can see that each fraction has the form:

$$\frac{Number_1}{Number_2}$$

where *Number₁* is called the **numerator** and *Number₂* is called the **denominator**. A fraction thus has two attributes, its numerator and its denominator, both of which are integers.

Begin editing the file `Fraction.h`, and define two integer data objects named `Numerator_` and `Denominator_` to represent these two attributes (Yes, you should append an underscore character to the end of each name, for reasons that will be apparent shortly). Then surround these definitions with a class structure that defines the name `Fraction` as a new type whose objects contain these two attributes.

Given this definition of `Fraction`, the declarations in our source program:

```
Fraction
    OldMeasure,
    ScaleFactor;
```

can be thought of as defining two data objects with the following forms:

OldMeasure   ScaleFactor

	Numerator_			Numerator_
---	---		---	---
	Denominator_			Denominator_

Note that each data object of type `Fraction` has each of the attributes we defined. Since a class may contain an arbitrary number of attributes, a software model can be constructed for virtually any real-world object, simply by defining data objects for each of its attributes, and then surrounding those data objects with an appropriately-named class structure.

The data objects within a class object are usually called the **data members** of that object. That is, each of the `Fraction` objects `OldMeasure` and `ScaleFactor` contain two data members, the first of which is named `Numerator_` and the second of which is named `Denominator_`.

In the source program `convert.cc`, the declarations of `OldMeasure` and `ScaleFactor` are currently commented out. Modify your source program so that the declarations are no longer commented out (but the subsequent lines are) and then compile your source program, to test the syntax of what you have written. When you have successfully tested it, continue to the next part of today's exercise.

Function Members.

Besides having data members, a class can also contain function declarations and definitions, which are called the *function members* (or member functions) of the class. Member functions provide a means by which the **operations** on a class object can be encoded.

Class Structure and Information Hiding.

One of the characteristics of a class is that its members (whether data or function) are by default *private*, meaning they cannot be directly accessed from outside of the class, say, by a program using the class. While it is a good idea for the data members of a class to be kept private[1], we want users of the class to be able to perform operations on class objects. As a result, the operations should be declared as *public* members, in contrast to the data members.

This is accomplished by placing the keyword `public:` after the data members of the class, and then declaring the functions for the operations, as follows:

```
class TypeName
{
    // Class Attribute Declarations - private!

  public:

    // Class Operation Declarations - public!
};
```

All of the declarations that precede the keyword `public:` in a class cannot be accessed outside of the class. All declarations between `public:` and the end of the class (or the keyword `private:`) can be accessed outside of the class. The keyword `public:` (and `private:`) can appear an arbitrary number of times in a class definition, if multiple public sections are needed.

The Class Constructor.

The action of declaring and initializing an object is called *constructing* that object. In order to allow the designer of a class to control the construction of class objects, C++ allows us to define a function called a **constructor** that specifies exactly what actions are to be taken when a class object is constructed. When a class object is declared, the C++ compiler calls this function to initialize the object's data members.

For example, suppose we would like for a declaration of a `Coordinate` object:

```
Coordinate
   Point;
```

to initialize the data members of `Point` to zeros. Then we can define a `Coordinate` constructor function to do so, as follows:

---

[1] It is a good idea because a program that directly accesses the data members of a class is dependent on those particular data members. If those data members are changed (which is not uncommon in class maintenance), then such programs must also be changed, increasing the cost of software maintenance.

```
Coordinate::Coordinate(void)
{
    x_ = 0.0;
    y_ = 0.0;
}
```

We can then declare this function in the public section of class `Coordinate`, as follows:

```
class Coordinate
{
    double x_, y_;
  public:
    Coordinate(void);
};
```

Then when a `Coordinate` object is defined, the C++ compiler will call this function, which initializes its `x` and `y` members to zero values.

There are several things to learn from this example:

1. A constructor has no return type (not even `void`.)

2. When a member function like a constructor is defined outside of the class, its full name must be given, which includes the name of the class of which it is a member, followed by the scoping operator (`::`), followed by the name of the function.

3. The name of a constructor is always the same as the name of its class.

4. When a member function like a constructor is declared (or defined) within the class, its full name need not be given.

5. A member function has access to the private members of a class.

The general form of a constructor function definition is thus:

```
ClassName::ClassName(ParameterList)
{
    StatementList
}
```

where the first `ClassName` refers to the name of the class, and the second `ClassName` names the constructor function. Constructors can take parameters, which are defined as they would be for any other function, and any valid C++ statement can appear in the body of such a function.

Using this example as a pattern, define a `Fraction` constructor, such that a declaration:

```
Fraction
    Example;
```

will initialize the `Numerator_` member of `Example` to zero and its `Denominator_` member to 1. Store this definition in the `Fraction` implementation file. Then add a declaration of this constructor to the public section of class `Fraction` in the `Fraction` header file.

Like other functions, constructor functions can be overloaded with multiple definitions, so long as each definition is distinct in either the number or the type of its arguments.

For example, suppose that we would like to be able to initialize the x_ and y_ members of a `Coordinate` object to two non-zero values when it is defined. We can do this by overloading the `Coordinate` constructor with another definition that takes two real arguments and initializes its members to them:

```
Coordinate::Coordinate(double xValue, double yValue)
{
   x_ = xValue;
   y_ = yValue;
}
```

If we add a declaration of this constructor to the public section of class `Coordinate`:

```
class Coordinate
{
   double x_, y_;
  public:
   Coordinate(void);
   Coordinate(double xValue, double yValue);
};
```

then the C++ compiler will process a `Coordinate` declaration

```
Coordinate
   Point1,
   Point2(1.2, 3.4);
```

by using our first constructor to initialize `Point1` (since it has no arguments), and use our second constructor to initialize `Point2` (since it has two arguments), resulting in objects that we might visualize as follows:

```
   Point1                        Point2
  ┌─────────┐                   ┌─────────┐
  │   0.0   │ x_                │   1.2   │ x_
  ├─────────┤                   ├─────────┤
  │   0.0   │ y_                │   3.4   │ y_
  └─────────┘                   └─────────┘
```

Add whatever code is necessary to the implementation and header files of library `Fraction` in order for the declarations

```
Fraction
   Fract1,
   Fract2(3,4);
```

to initialize `Fract1` to $\frac{0}{1}$ and initialize `Fract2` to $\frac{3}{4}$ (If you are looking for more of a challenge, use the *default-arguments mechanism* to do both of these with a single constructor function).

Then use the C++ compiler to test the syntax of what you have written, and continue when it is correct.

Extractor Functions.

Whatever operations we wish to perform on a class object can be declared as public functions within the class. For example, it might be useful to be able to extract the x (or the y) value of a `Coordinate` object. To do so, we might write:

```
class Coordinate
{
    double x_, y_;
 public:
    Coordinate(void);
    Coordinate(double xValue, double yValue);
    double x(void) const { return x_; }
};
```

There are two things to note in this example:

1. If a function does not modify the data members of a class it should be declared (and defined) as a *constant function*, by placing the keyword `const` after its parameter list.

2. If a function is extremely simple (i.e., one or two lines), then it can be defined within the class itself, rather than in the implementation file of the class library. Doing so has the benefit of making the function an `inline` function, meaning that a call to such a function does not incur the overhead of a normal function call. In fact, the constructor definitions we defined previously are simple enough that you may if you wish place them within the class definition.

Given such a function, if two `Coordinate` objects `Point1` and `Point2` are as follows:

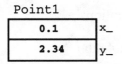

then the expression:

```
Point1.x()
```

evaluates to `0.1`, while the expression

```
Point2.x()
```

evaluates to `5.67`. Note that a member function like `x()` must be invoked using **dot notation**, that specifies the `Coordinate` object whose `x()` function we wish to call.

We should mention that this is the reason for our convention of appending an underscore to the names of the data members of a class — we can then use the names (without the underscore) as the name of a member function that extracts the value of that data member.

Add extractor functions `Numerator()` and `Denominator()` to class `Fraction`, and then test their correctness (and that of your constructors) by displaying the values of some `Fraction` objects constructed using your two constructors. Continue when what you have written has been thoroughly tested.

Output.

The next operation we would like to be able to perform is output, so that we can conveniently display the value of a `Fraction` object. Doing so requires us to learn a bit more about operators, namely, how they can be overloaded.

Recall that overloading is providing multiple definitions of a function's name, that differ in the number of types of their arguments. For example, we overloaded the `Coordinate` constructor:

```
Coordinate(void);
Coordinate(double xValue, double yValue);
```

within class `Coordinate`.

Besides allowing a programmer to overload function names, C++ allows a programmer to overload operators, so that they can be applied to class objects. For example, it would be convenient to be able to write:

```
cout << Point << endl;
```

to display a `Coordinate` object named `Point`. To do so, we must overload the output operator (`<<`) with a definition that takes an `ostream` (e.g., `cout`) and a `Coordinate` (e.g., `Point`) as its operands. That is, we might define the following function in the implementation file:

```
ostream& operator<<(ostream& Out, const Coordinate& Coord)
{
    Out << Coord.x_ << ' ' << Coord.y_;
    return Out;
}
```

There are a number of things we can learn from this definition:

1. In general, for any overloadable operator Δ, the notation

   ```
   operatorΔ
   ```

   can be used as the name of Δ in overloading it with a new definition.

2. In an output expression of the form:

   ```
   cout << Value ;
   ```

   we see that an output operator takes two operands. The left operand is `cout`, an `ostream`, which is altered by the operation (i.e., *Value* gets inserted into the `ostream`), and an `ostream` reference parameter must thus be defined for this operand. The right operand is *Value* (of whatever type is being displayed).

   From this, it should be evident that whenever we overload `operator<<` as the output operator, it must have two parameters, the first of which is a reference to an `ostream`, and the second of which is the class-type for which `operator<<` is being overloaded. For the sake of efficiency, this second parameter is a constant reference parameter, since a value parameter would waste time copying each of the data members of the corresponding argument.

3. In an output statement of the form:

```
cout << Value₁ << Value₂ << ... << Valuen;
```

we see that output expressions can be chained together. That is, the leftmost << is applied first, and the value it returns becomes the left operand to the second <<. Similarly, the value returned by the second << becomes the left operand of the third <<, and so on, down the chain.

Now, since the left operand of << must be an ostream (which is changed by the output operation), the value returned by the output operator must be a reference to an ostream, namely *the one it received as its left operand*. The return-type of operator<< is thus a reference to an ostream, and in its return statement, the function returns Out, the parameter used to hold its left (ostream) operand.

Unfortunately, because the left operand of operator<< must be an ostream, the function cannot be overloaded as a member function of class Coordinate, because member functions are called using the notation

ObjectName.MemberFunctionName(ArgumentList)

That is, the left operand of a member function of class Coordinate must be a Coordinate, not an ostream, so (since the left operand of the output operator must be an ostream) we are unable to define operator<< as a member function of class Coordinate (though it could be defined as a member of class ostream, if we had access to it...).

But non-member functions are unable to access the (private) data members of a class object, and the output operator must be able to access those data members to display them. How can we resolve this difficulty?

For such situations, a C++ class can permit a non-member function to access its private members, by preceding its declaration (within the class) with the keyword friend, as follows:

```
class Coordinate
{
   double x_, y_;
 public:
   Coordinate(void);
   Coordinate(double xValue, double yValue);
   double x(void) const { return x_; }
   friend  ostream& operator<<(ostream& Out, const Coordinate& Coord);
};
```

Note that a friend function differs from a member function — a member function receives the class object to be operated on implicitly, but a friend function receives it via a parameter.

Using this as a pattern, overload the output operator so that if the value of Fract is $\frac{1}{2}$, then

```
cout << Fract << endl;
```

causes the characters 1/2 to be displayed on the screen. Then test your function thoroughly.

Input.

Now that we've learned how to do output, input is easy. To illustrate, if we wanted to input a `Coordinate`, entered as

```
3,4
```

then we could define:

```
istream& operator>>(istream& In, Coordinate& Coord)
{
   char
        Separator;

   In >> Coord.x_;
   In.get(Separator);    // clean out the comma
   In >> Coord.y_;

   return In;
}
```

From this, we can see that the primary differences are

1. To perform input, we overload `operator>>` instead of `operator<<`.

2. The left operand of the input operator (i.e., `cin`) is an `istream` instead of an `ostream`.

3. The right operand is a `Coordinate` reference, rather than a constant `Coordinate` reference.

4. The function returns its left operand (i.e., the `istream`) to permit input expressions to be "chained" together into an input statement.

As with the output operator, we must declare this function as a friend within the class:

```
class Coordinate
{
   double x_, y_;
 public:
   Coordinate(void);
   Coordinate(double xValue, double yValue);
   double x(void) const { return x_; }
   friend ostream& operator<<(ostream& Out, const Coordinate& Coord);
   friend istream& operator>>(istream& In, Coordinate& Coord);
};
```

Using this as a pattern, overload the input operator for class `Fraction`, so that a user can enter

```
3/4
```

to input the fraction $\frac{3}{4}$. Then test the correctness of this operation, using your source program. Continue when you have thoroughly tested its correctness.

Fractional Multiplication.

Any of the arithmetic operators (+, -, *, /, and %) can also be overloaded. For example, if we wanted to permit two `Coordinate` objects to be added together, we might define:

```
Coordinate operator+(const Coordinate& Coord1, const Coordinate& Coord2)
{
   Coordinate
       Result;

   Result.x_ = Coord1.x_ + Coord2.x_;
   Result.y_ = Coord1.y_ + Coord2.y_;

   return Result;
}
```

Once such a function has been declared as a friend inside of class `Coordinate`, we can write normal looking expressions, such as

```
   Point1 + Point2
```

to compute the sum of two `Coordinate` objects `Point1` and `Point2`.

While it is useful to overload all of the arithmetic operators for a `Fraction`, the final operation that we need in order to solve our problem is multiplication (the others, we leave for the exercises). From the preceding discussion, it should be evident that we need to overload `operator*` so that an expression of the form:

```
   OldMeasure * ScaleFactor
```

can be used to multiply two `Fraction` objects named `OldMeasure` and `ScaleFactor`.

The specification for such an operation can be written as follows:

> Receive: *Left* and *Right*, two `Fraction` operands.
> Return: The `Fraction` product of *Left* and *Right*.

The definition of this operation can be determined by working some simple examples:

$$\frac{1}{2} \times \frac{2}{3} = \frac{2}{6} = \frac{1}{3} \qquad\qquad \frac{3}{4} \times \frac{2}{3} = \frac{6}{12} = \frac{1}{2}$$

From these examples, it should be apparent that the `Numerator_` and `Denominator_` members of the `Fraction` value to be returned by `operator*` can be computed by multiplying the `Numerator_` and `Denominator_` members (respectively) of the two operands *Left* and *Right*, and then simplifying the resulting `Fraction`.

For moment, let's ignore the problem of simplifying an improper `Fraction` value. Update your `Fraction` class library with a definition of `operator*` that can be used to multiply two `Fraction` objects. Then test the correctness of what you have written using your source program. Continue when your multiplication operation has been thoroughly tested.

Fraction Simplification.

The main deficiency of our implementation of `operator*` is its inability to simplify fractions. That is, our multiplication operation would be improved if class `Fraction` had a `Simplify()` operation, such that fractions like:

$$\frac{2}{6}, \frac{6}{12} \text{ and } \frac{12}{4}$$

could be simplified to:

$$\frac{1}{3}, \frac{1}{2} \text{ and } \frac{3}{1},$$

respectively. Such an operation is useful to keep fractional results as simple and easy to read as possible. To provide this capability, we will implement a `Fraction` member function named `Simplify()`, such that a function like `operator*` can call

```
Fraction operator*(const Fraction& Left, const Fraction& Right)
{
    Fraction Result;

    // compute Result...

    Result.Simplify();

    return Result;
}
```

in order to reduce a `Fraction` object's value.

There are a number of ways to simplify a fraction. One straightforward way is the following algorithm:

> Find *GCD*, the greatest common divisor of *Numerator* and *Denominator*.
> If *GCD* > 1, then
> > Replace *Numerator* by *Numerator/GCD*.
> > Replace *Denominator* by *Denominator/GCD*.
> End if.

The implementation file of library `Fraction` contains a function `GreatestCommonDivisor()` that uses Euclid's algorithm for finding the greatest common divisor of two integers.

Using this function, define function `Simplify()` by encoding the preceding algorithm. Don't forget to define `Simplify()` as a member function, by prefacing its name with the name of its class and the scope operator.

Then use your source program to test what you have written. We have now provided all of the operations needed to solve chef Pièrre's problem, so the original version of our program should be operable and can be used to test the operations of our class.

Phrases You Should Now Understand.

Class, Constructor, Name Overloading, Operator Overloading, Data Member, Function Member, Friend Function, Scope Operator.

Objectives.

1. Gain experience designing, defining and using classes.
2. Practice defining member functions.
3. Practice defining friend functions.

Introduction.

Each of these projects deals with objects that are not readily modeled using the predefined C++ data types. In each project, you are to use a class to build a software representation of the object described, as well as the operations appropriate for the object.

Projects.

10.1. Extend class `Fraction` by overloading the remaining arithmetic operators (for addition, subtraction and division). Then construct a menu-driven 4-function calculator that an elementary school student can use to check his or her fractional homework assignments.

Alternatively, create a "drill" program that generates random fractions (using `RandomInt` from the `MyLib` class directory), that young students can use to practice their fractional arithmetic.

10.2. A phone number consists of three separate pieces of information: an area code, an exchange, and a local number. Write a class `PhoneNum` that models a phone number, containing operations to construct, input, output, and extract each of the data members of a `PhoneNum`. Then write a program that simulates an intelligent computer modem dialer by (1) reading a `PhoneNum`, (2) determining (for your locality) whether or not that number is a long distance number, and (3) displaying the number to be dialed on the screen (i.e., if the number is long distance, it should be preceded by `1-`. Otherwise, it should be displayed normally.)

10.3. A person's name consists of three separate pieces of information: their last and first names (each of which is a character string) and their middle initial, a character. Write a class `Name` that models a person's name, containing operations to construct, initialize, assign, input, output, compare, and extract the data members of a `Name` object. Then use classes `Name` and `PhoneNum` to write a directory assistance program that allows its user to enter a person's *name*. The program should then open a file containing a list of people's names and their phone numbers and search for the given *name*. If *name* is present in the file, then have the program display the corresponding phone number. Otherwise, display an appropriate error message.

10.4. A quadratic equation has the form

$$ax^2 + bx + c = 0$$

where `a`, `b` and `c` are all real values. Write a class `Quadratic` that can be used to model a quadratic equation, containing operations to construct, input, output, extract the data members of, evaluate (for a given x value), and find the x value at which the value of the `Quadratic` is minimized (or maximized). Then write a menu-driven program that allows a user to enter a quadratic and then apply any of the `Quadratic` operations to in order to process that quadratic.

Project 10 Due Date _____

Turn in this grade sheet, attached to a hard copy of

a. your program,
b. the header file for your class library, and
c. the implementation file for your class library.

Name _____

Category	Points Possible	Points Received
Correctness and efficiency.................	75	_____
Design and Structure.....................	25	_____
Style and Readability....................	20	
Horizontal White Space..............	5	_____
Vertical White Space................	5	_____
Meaningful Identifiers...............	10	_____
Documentation..........................	30	
Opening Documentation...............	9	_____
Specification(s).....................	21	_____
Total..............................	**150**	_____

Lab 11

Enumeration Classes

Note to the Instructor:

Preparation for this lab includes the following step:

- Within the lab11 class directory, define the Makefile macro CLASSLIB with the absolute name of the MyLib class directory.

You may, if you wish, have your students do this (for practice) after they copy the Makefile from the lab11 class directory. Doing so is necessary for the use of the Boolean class the students build in this exercise, because it uses class Strings to simplify the function to input a Boolean value.

Objectives.

1. More practice designing, building and using classes.
2. Learn about using enumerations with classes.
3. Gain further experience creating types.

Prelab Questions:

1. The _____ provides a mechanism whereby a type can be created whose values are identifiers.

2. A function that the C++ compiler can use to automatically convert an object of one type into an object of a class type is called a _____ of the class.

3. The identifiers that make up the values of an enumeration are called the _____ of the enumeration.

4. Providing new definitions of each of the operators so that they can be applied to a new type is called _____ those operators.

5. In an enumeration

```
enum TypeName {Identifier1, Identifier2, ... IdentifierN};
```

the compiler associates the integer value _____ with $Identifier_N$.

Introduction.

A common technique in writing functions is to have a function return the boolean value *true* if it executed successfully, and return the boolean value *false* if its execution was for some reason unsuccessful. By doing so, the caller of the function can determine the success or failure of the operation by saving and examining this return value.

The difficulty is that C++ represents the boolean value *false* with the integer zero and the boolean value *true* with any non-zero integer. This can lead to confusion and less readable programs, since variables intended to store boolean values must be defined as integers.

We can eliminate this difficulty, if we construct a type `Boolean`, whose values are either `True` or `False`. Such a type should allow us to define and initialize objects:

```
Boolean Ok = True;
```

enter the boolean values *true* and *false* from the keyboard:

```
cin >> Ok;
```

output, assign, and in general, manipulate boolean values conveniently.

Getting Started.

Create and change directory to `labs/lab11` and copy the files from the `lab11` class directory. Then begin editing the file `Boolean.h`.

We have seen before that the C++ class provides a mechanism for defining new types. That is, the stub definition

```
class Boolean
{
};
```

defines the name `Boolean` as a new type. Take a few moments to enter this stub in the appropriate place in `Boolean.h`. Our task today is to complete this definition with the necessary data and function members so that boolean values can be conveniently manipulated.

To illustrate how to solve our problem (without completely giving away the answers), we will in parallel solve a problem whose solution is similar to our `Boolean` problem. This problem is to construct a new type `Gender`, whose values are `Male` and `Female`, starting with the class definition:

```
class Gender
{
};
```

Enumerations.

Our first hurdle is to determine how to make the words `True` and `False` acceptable to the C++ compiler as boolean values. The key to doing so is to recognize that the C++ compiler will treat them as identifiers — words whose meaning must be explicitly defined.

To cross this hurdle, C++ provides the **enumeration** — a mechanism for creating a type whose values are identifiers. To illustrate, suppose that we wish to use the identifiers `Male` and `Female` as values for a new type `Gender`. Then we might write

```
enum Gender_ {Male, Female};
```

When the C++ compiler processes this line, the identifier `Gender_` becomes the name of a new type, whose values are the identifiers `Male` and `Female` (We use the name `Gender_` because we are going to use this name to define a data member within class `Gender`.) The identifiers `Male` and `Female` are called the *enumerators* of the enumeration.

Given such a definition, we can use it to define the primary data member of a class `Gender`, as follows:

```
class Gender
{
   Gender_
      theValue;
};
```

after which objects of type `Gender` can be defined.

You may be thinking, "Wait a minute. You said that the enumeration `Gender_` is the name of a new type, whose values are identifiers `Male` and `Female`. Why do we need to define `Gender` as a class, if an enumeration creates a new type?"

We *could* define `Gender` as an enumeration. The problem is that most operators cannot be overloaded for enumerations, the way they can for classes. By defining `Gender` as a class, we can overload whatever operators we need.

It is worth noting that the C++ compiler treats our `Gender_` enumeration as if we had written:

```
const int Male = 0;
const int Female = 1;
```

More generally, an enumeration declaration

```
enum TypeName {Identifier1, Identifier2, ... IdentifierN};
```

names *TypeName* as a new type, whose valid values are *Identifier$_1$* through *Identifier$_N$*. 0 is associated with *Identifier$_1$*, 1 with *Identifier$_2$*, ..., and N-1 with *Identifier$_N$*.

Take a few minutes and define an enumeration named `Boolean_`, with enumerators `True` and `False`, such that the C++ compiler will process `False` as 0 , and `True` as 1. Then use `Boolean_` to declare a private data member `theValue` within class `Boolean`. Check the syntax of what you have written by compiling `driver.cc`, continuing when it is correct.

The Class Constructor.

The first operation defined for a class is usually its constructor. For our `Gender` class, we might define a constructor so that the definitions

```
Gender
    Gender1(Female),
    Gender2(Male),
    Gender3;
```

define the objects `Gender1`, `Gender2` and `Gender3` as `Female`, `Male` and `Female`, respectively. To accomplish this, we can define a Gender constructor whose specification is as follows:

Precondition: A `Gender` object has been defined.
Receive: `Gend`, a `Gender_` value (default value, `Female`).
Postcondition: The `theValue` member of the object has been initialized to `Gend`.

Performing this function is sufficiently simple that we can define it internally within (the public portion of) class `Gender`:

```
class Gender
{
    Gender_
        theValue;

  public:

    Gender(Gender_ Gend = Female)
    {
        theValue = Gend;
    }
};
```

Given this definition, the declarations

```
Gender
    Gender1(Female),
    Gender2(Male),
    Gender3;
```

will use explicit arguments to initialize `Gender1` and `Gender2` to `Female` and `Male`, and will use the default argument mechanism to initialize `Gender3` to `Female`.

Define a constructor function for class `Boolean`, so that definitions like the following:

```
Boolean
    Bool1,
    Bool2(True),
    Bool3(False);
```

can be used to define and initialize `Bool1` to `False` (using the default argument mechanism), `Bool2` to `True`, and `Bool3` to `False`. Then test what you have written using your driver program, continuing when it has been thoroughly tested.

Output.

In order to verify that the other operations are working correctly, it is important to be able to display the value of a class object, so the output operation should be implemented early in the development of a class. For `iostream` output on our `Gender` class, we might specify this operation as follows:

Receive: `Out`, an `ostream`;
                     `Gend`, a `Gender` value.
Output: The `Gender_` value within `Gend`.
Pass Back: `Out`, with the `Gender_` value inserted onto it.
Return: `Out` (for chaining).

From this, we can declare `operator<<` as a friend function in the public portion of class `Gender` (don't forget to `#include` the file `<iostream.h>`, so that `ostream` is declared).

```
friend ostream& operator<<(ostream& Out, const Gender& Gend);
```

Now, how do we output the value of `Gend.theValue`? The first key is to recognize that all I/O is performed as sequences of characters, meaning that we don't want to actually output the values `Male` or `Female`, but rather the character strings `"Male"` and `"Female"` (i.e., the character sequences corresponding to `Male` and `Female`).

The second key is to recognize that we really have two (valid) cases to consider: if `theValue` is `Male`, then we have to output one string, but if `theValue` is `Female`, then we have to output a different string.

We might use this logic to define `operator<<` as follows:

```
ostream& operator<<(ostream& Out, const Gender& Gend)
{
    switch(Gend.theValue)
    {
        case Male:
                Out << "Male";
                break;
        case Female:
                Out << "Female";
                break;
        default:
                cerr << "\n*** operator<<: Gender value is "
                    << "neither Male nor Female !\n";
    }
    return Out;
}
```

We can then declare this function within class `Gender`, as a friend function. Note that while the error message in this function should never be generated, it is always a good idea to anticipate potential problems, such as the value of `theValue` being (somehow) erroneous.

Following this approach, do all that is necessary in order for `Boolean` values to be output using `operator<<`. Then use your driver program to thoroughly test what you have written.

Input.

It is similarly useful to able to input `Boolean` values from the keyboard. The primary key is to again remember that all I/O proceeds as character sequences, so that if the user types `True`, the character string `"True"` is actually present in the input stream. To overload `operator>>` for class `Gender`, we can thus specify:

Receive: `In`, an istream; and `Gend`, a `Gender` object.
Input: A character string, presumed to be either `"Male"` or `"Female"`;
Return: `In`, the character string extracted from it;
              `Gend`, its `theValue` member set to the `Gender_` value
                  corresponding to the extracted character string.

We can thus declare `operator>>` as a friend in the public portion of class `Gender`, as follows:

```
friend istream& operator>>(istream& In, Gender& Gend);
```

It should be evident that if the input string is `"Male"`, then we want to set `Gend.theValue` to `Male`, while if the input string is `"Female"`, then we want to set it to `Female` (and if it is neither, then we should generate an appropriate error message). To allow this input string to be input and compared conveniently, we can make use of class `Strings` as shown below:

```
#include "Strings.h"    // provides Strings
#include <ctype.h>      // provides isupper(), tolower()

istream& operator>>(istream& In, Gender& Gend)
{
   // input a character string
   Strings Buffer;
   In >> Buffer;

   // convert it to lowercase (to permit male, MALE, Male, etc.)
   for (int i = 0; i < Buffer.Length(); i++)
        if (isupper(Buffer[i])
              Buffer[i] = tolower(Buffer[i]);

   // set theValue according to the input value
   if (Buffer == "male")
        Gend.theValue = Male;
   else if (Buffer == "female")
        Gend.theValue = Female;
   else
        cerr << "\n*** operator>> expected Male or Female, but read "
              << Buffer << endl;

   return In; // permit chaining
}
```

Using this approach, overload `operator>>` for class `Boolean`, so that boolean values can be input and processed as usual. Note that your `Makefile` should be set up to link the `Strings` object to your driver program's object file, in addition to linking in the `Boolean` object file.

Use your driver program to check what you have written, continuing when it has been thoroughly tested.

Relational Operations.

Of the six relational operations (==, !=, <, >, <=, >=), it makes sense to overload the first two of these for `Boolean` values. That is, some people like to write code like

```
if ((Ok == True) && (Done != False)) ...
```

We can permit them to do so, if we overload the equality and inequality operators for class `Boolean`. We can specify the equality operation as follows:

> Receive: `Bool1` and `Bool2`, two `Boolean` values;
> Return: The `Boolean` value `True`, if the two `theValue` members are the same;
> the `Boolean` value `False`, otherwise.

We can thus declare this operation as a public friend of class `Gender`, as follows:

```
friend Boolean operator==(const Boolean& Bool1, const Boolean& Bool2);
```

To define this operation, we must compare `Bool1.theValue` and `Bool2.theValue`, returning `True` if they are the same and returning `False` if they are different. We might encode this logic as follows:

```
Boolean operator==(const Boolean& Bool1, const Boolean& Bool2)
{
   if (Bool1.theValue == Bool2.theValue)
        return True;
   else
        return False;
}
```

We have provided the declaration and definition of this function in the appropriate files of our `Boolean` library. Take a few moments and define `operator!=` to perform the corresponding inequality comparison, given two `Boolean` values.

Before continuing, take a moment to carefully study the behavior of `operator==`. It's return type is `Boolean`, but the values we are returning are `Boolean_` values. How can a function of one type return a value of a different type?

The trick here is that we have defined a constructor that, given a `Boolean_` value, constructs the corresponding `Boolean` value. That is, suppose that `operator==` executes its

```
return True;
```

statement. This is a `Boolean_` value, and since the return type of `operator==` is `Boolean`, we might expect a type error. The reason that we do not is that we have told the C++ compiler how to build `Boolean` values from `Boolean_` values, with our `Boolean` constructor. Put differently, if the C++ compiler is in a context where it expects a value of type *T1*, but it sees a value of type *T2*, and a *T1* constructor exists to build a *T1* object from a *T2* value, the compiler will use that constructor to convert the *T2* value into a *T1* object, which it then returns. The C++ compiler thus uses constructors like type converters when the context suggests it.

A similar type conversion is performed by the compiler in processing a condition like

```
if (Ok == True) ...
```

That is, we have defined `operator==` to compare two `Boolean` values, but it is receiving a `Boolean` and a `Boolean_`. Given our constructor, the compiler converts the `True` into the corresponding `Boolean` object, which is then passed as the second operand to `operator==`.

As a final illustration suppose we had defined `operator==` as follows:

```
Boolean operator==(const Boolean& Bool1, const Boolean& Bool2)
{
    return (Bool1.theValue == Bool2.theValue);
}
```

Take a moment and try this form, recording the error message in the margin...

The reason this doesn't work is not immediately obvious. The logic seems fine — if the two `theValue` members are equal, the expression evaluates to *true*, which we return; otherwise, the expression evaluates to *false*, which we return.

The problem is that the expression doesn't actually evaluate to *true* or *false*, but evaluates to `1` or `0`. Because C++ represents false as zero and true as non-zero, the result of the comparison

```
    Bool1.theValue == Bool2.theValue
```

is the integer `1` if the two operands are equal, and the integer `0` otherwise. Put differently, we have a `Boolean` function that is returning an `int`; and while we have provided a constructor capable of building a `Boolean` out of a `Boolean_`, we have not provided a constructor that the compiler can use to build a `Boolean` from an `int`! Doing so is a good idea, so that the compiler can handle situations like this correctly.

A Second Constructor.

We can specify the problem this constructor must solve as follows:

> Precondition: A `Boolean` object has been defined.
> Receive: `i`, an `int` value.
> Postcondition: If i is equal to 0, then the `theValue` member is set to `False`;
>   otherwise, the `theValue` member is set to `True`.

Using this specification, overload the `Boolean` constructor with a second declaration that the compiler can use to convert an `int` into a `Boolean` when necessary (If you define it in the implementation file, don't forget to define it as a member function.)

Once you have defined this constructor, check its correctness using the second version of `operator==`, which should now compile correctly. Then convert your definition of `operator!=` to utilize this same approach.

Note that unlike the first constructor, parameter `i` should have no default argument; otherwise, the compiler will not know which constructor to use in a declaration like the following:

```
    Boolean Bool;
```

resulting in a compilation error.

The Logical Operators.

The final operators that are commonly applied to boolean values are the logical operations AND (`&&`), OR (`||`) and NOT (`!`). To make our class a well-rounded, reuseable piece of software, we should thus implement these operations for the type `Boolean`.

We can specify the behavior of the logical AND operation as follows:

Receive:	`Bool1` and `Bool2`, two `Boolean` values.
Return:	`True`, if `Bool1` and `Bool2` are both `True`, `False`, otherwise.

Similarly, we can specify the behavior of the logical OR operation as follows:

Receive:	`Bool1` and `Bool2`, two `Boolean` values.
Return:	`False`, if `Bool1` and `Bool2` are both `False`, `True`, otherwise.

Finally, we can specify the behavior of the logical NOT operation as follows:

Receive:	`Bool`, a `Boolean` value.
Return:	`True`, if `Bool` is `False`, `False`, otherwise.

Each of these functions is simple enough to define within class `Boolean`. Take the next few minutes to do so, thoroughly testing each function as you finish its implementation.

When you have completed this, we now have a fully functional `Boolean` class, that can be used to define `Boolean` objects and functions.

Phrases You Should Now Understand.

Enumeration, Enumerator, Type Converting Constructor.

Objectives.

1. Practice defining classes.
2. Gain experience using enumerations.

Introduction.

Each of the following projects requires you to build two or more classes:

- `Month`, that uses an enumeration `Month_` whose values are appropriate identifiers for the names of the months, with operations to conveniently manipulate `Month` values; and

- `Date`, with data members for a date's month, day and year, as well as operations to conveniently manipulate `Date` values.

Projects.

11.1. Extend class `Month` with a function that, given a year, returns the number of days in that month. Don't forget to consider leap years — a year is a leap year if it is evenly divisible by 4, unless it is also divisible by 100, in which case it must also be evenly divisible by 400. Write a driver program that illustrates the correctness of your function.

11.2. Write a program that, given two `Date` values, computes the number of days between those dates. Don't forget to consider leap years (see 11.1) in your computation.

11.3. In Project 10.3, we constructed a `Person` class. Extend this class by using the `Date` class to add a data member to a `Person` in which their birthday can be stored, adjusting the operations on a `Person` to include the new member, as appropriate. Then write a program that, given a `Date`, searches a data file of `Person` values and displays the name and age of anyone whose birthday falls on that date.

11.4. Reverend Zeller developed a formula for computing the day of the week on which a given date fell or will fall. Let C be the century in which the year falls, Y be the year in that century, M be an integer representation of the month, with March = 1, April = 2, and so on (and January and February counted as months 11 and 12 of the preceding year) and D be the day of the month. If we compute

$$a = (13*M - 1)/5$$
$$b = Y/4$$
$$c = C/4$$
$$d = a + b + c + D + Y - 2C$$
$$r = d \% 7$$

then $r = 0$ implies the date falls on Sunday, $r = 1$ implies it falls on Monday, and so on.

Build a `Day` class, using an enumeration `Day_` whose values are appropriate identifiers for the names of the days of the week, with operations to conveniently manipulate `Day` values. Add an operation to the `Date` class that computes the `Day` on which a given `Date` falls. Write a program that uses this function to allow a user to find the `Day` on which an arbitrary `Date` falls.

Project 11 Due Date _____

Turn in this grade sheet, attached to a hard copy of

a. your program,
b. the header file for each class library,
c. the implementation file for each class library, and
d. an execution of your program illustrating its correctness.

Name _____

Category	Points Possible	Points Received
Correctness and efficiency	100	_____
Design and Structure	30	_____
Style and Readability	20	
Horizontal White Space	5	_____
Vertical White Space	5	_____
Meaningful Identifiers	10	_____
Documentation	50	
Opening Documentation	15	_____
Specification(s)	35	_____
Total	**200**	_____

Lab 12

One-Dimensional Arrays

Note to the Instructor:

Labs 12 and 13 comprise a two-part sequence that illustrate the implementation of array-based classes. Lab 12 begins the process in a "traditional" manner, by building a general purpose array-based class named `RealArray`. Lab 13 introduces the "object-oriented" approach of the C++ inheritance mechanism, by deriving a new `DataSet` from the `RealArray` class built in Lab 12.

We believe that this approach is preferable for a number of reasons:

1. Experience has taught us that students find arrays sufficiently difficult that they must not be given a superficial treatment. It is thus prudent to examine arrays in some depth.

2. The topic of inheritance plays a central role in object-oriented programming. It is thus also prudent to examine inheritance in some depth.

3. Trying to introduce both arrays and inheritance within the same exercise (a) is too many new, complicated ideas for a student to assimilate; and (b) leads to superficial coverage of these important topics.

4. In order for programmers to truly appreciate the amount of work the inheritance mechanism saves them, they must have done that work themselves, at least once.

If for some reason you do not wish to do both of these exercises, Lab 13 derives class `DataSet` from the `RealArray` class derived in Lab 12; Lab 13 can be easily omitted. Lab 12 can be omitted if you provide the students with the `RealArray` class implemented in this exercise.

Objectives.

1. Practice defining and using arrays.
2. Implement some common array operations.
3. Practice defining array-based classes.

Prelab Questions:

1. The most efficient algorithm for searching an unordered list of values for a particular value is called what?

2. A storage structure for multiple values of the same type is called an _____.

3. The _____ operator allows you to access the element of an array at a given index.

4. The number used to access a given array element is called its _____?

5. A component of an array in which a value can be stored is called an _____?

Introduction.

It is often the case that one of the data objects in a problem is a *list* of data values. Solving the problem involves processing each of the values in the list in some manner. While files provide one means of storing such lists, files suffer from two drawbacks:

1. Accessing a value from a file takes a very long time, relative to CPU speed, so that accessing the values stored in such a list is quite *slow*; and
2. Values in a file must typically be *accessed sequentially*: we are unable to directly access the ith value in a file, without first accessing each of the elements preceding it.

The **array** provides a means of storing a list of values that does not suffer these drawbacks. More precisely, an array is a data object in a program, in which multiple values of the same type can be stored. Since the array is a data object in a program, it resides in main memory, allowing much *faster* access to the values in the list. In addition, values stored in an array can be *accessed directly*, without the need to access those elements that precede it.

Today's exercise is to practice using arrays by building an array-based class named `RealArray` in which lists of numbers can be conveniently stored and processed.

Getting Started.

Create and change directory to `labs/lab12` and then copy and begin editing the files `RealArray.h` and `driver12.cc` from the class `lab12` directory. This directory contains the files `driver12.cc` and `driver13.cc`, because both of Labs 12 and 13 will be done in this directory.

Defining Arrays.

To illustrate the definition of an array, suppose that we need to declare an array capable of storing eight integers, and wish to name it `anArray`. To do so, we could write:

```
enum {Capacity = 8};  // an alternative to: const int Capacity = 8;
int anArray[Capacity];
```

We might visualize the resulting object `anArray` as follows:

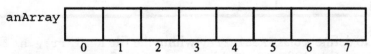

Each compartment within `anArray` represents a different *element* of the array, and is capable of storing one integer. The numbers drawn beneath each element are called *indices*: the element whose index is `i` can be accessed using the notation `anArray[i]` (if `i` is between 0 and 7, inclusive). One thing to remember is that *the index of the first element of a C++ array is always zero*, so that the indices of our array of 8 elements range from 0 to 7.

The general form of an array definition can be given as follows:

```
Type ArrayName [ Size ] ;
```

Here, *Type* is the type of value we wish to store in the array, *ArrayName* is the name of the object being defined, and *Size* is the number of values that can be stored in the object.

To facilitate expanding the capacity of an array, it is a good style to avoid giving *Size* as a literal number (e.g., 8). A better approach is to define a named constant (e.g., Capacity) and use it to refer to the *Size* of the array, both in defining the array and within its operations. By doing so, the capacity of the array can be modified with one change (both in its definition and throughout its operations) rather than many changes.

Because an array may not be full (i.e., fewer than all of its elements may be in use), operations on an array need to be able to access not only the array, but also the number of values that are stored in the array. To accomplish this, a second object NumValues_ is useful, such as

```
unsigned NumValues_;
```

in which can be stored the number of values to be stored in anArray. If these definitions are surrounded with a class structure:

```
class MyArray
{
 public:
   enum {Capacity = 8};
 protected:
   int anArray[Capacity];    // an array of integers
   unsigned NumValues_;      // will indicate # of elems to be used
};
```

then these definitions become the data members in a class, which can be used to define objects:

```
MyArray A1;
```

Note that we define Capacity publicly so that users of the class can ascertain the capacity of a MyArray object with the notation MyArray::Capacity. Note also that members anArray and NumValues_ are defined as protected: (which is like private: but slightly weaker) for reasons that will be made clear in Lab 13. We might visualize the resulting object as follows:

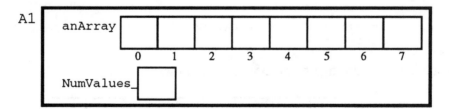

Use this approach to define a class RealArray within the file RealArray.h. Define a named constant Capacity equal to 128, and use this constant to define an array named theArray capable of storing 128 real values. Then define an integer named NumValues_ in which the number of values in theArray can be stored. Surround these definitions with a class structure named RealArray. Then test what you have written by compiling your driver program (since it includes RealArray.h), continuing when class RealArray is syntactically correct.

Array Operations.

An important part of the design of any class is the selection of its operations. For today, we want to implement only the most general operations appropriate for an array of real values. Some of these might include:

- Construct and initialize a real array.
- Display the values in a real array on the screen (or write it to a file).
- Fill a real array with values entered at the keyboard (or read from a file).
- Determine the number of values in the data set.
- Access the value stored at a given index.

These are just a few of the operations that can be performed with an array of reals. Others will be left for the future. To illustrate their implementation, we will define each of these operations using our MyArray class.

The Class Constructor.

An array's declaration should indicate how many of the array's elements we intend to use (i.e., how many values we intend to store in the array). For example, we might want to write:

```
MyArray A1(5);
```

to invoke the MyArray constructor to build A1, passing it the argument 5 to indicate the number of values we wish to store. We can specify this problem as follows:

```
Precondition:   A MyArray object has been declared.
Receive:        Size, the number of elements to be used.
Postcondition:  The object's data members have been initialized
                appropriately as an array of Size values.
```

Since the purpose of the NumValues_ member is to indicate the number of values in the array, the class constructor can solve this problem, by (1) checking that Size is within our array's capacity (i.e., $0 \leq$ Size $<$ Capacity); (2) setting the NumValues_ member to Size; and (3) initializing each of the elements to zero. This is complicated enough to define separately:

```
#include "MyArray.h"            // class MyArray
#include <stdlib.h>             // function exit()

MyArray::MyArray(unsigned Size)
{
   if (Size > Capacity)
   {
        cerr << "\n*** MyArray: " << Size
             << " exceeds maximum capacity ("
             << unsigned(Capacity) << ")\n";
        exit (-1);
   }

   NumValues_ = Size;

   for (int i = 0; i < NumValues_; i++)
        anArray[i] = 0;
}
```

Note our use of a for loop to conveniently sequence through the elements of `anArray`. In general, if an operation must access *all* of the elements used in an array named `anArray`, then that operation can be implemented as follows:

```
for (int IndexVar = FirstIndex; IndexVar < NumValues; IndexVar++)
        // access anArray[IndexVar]
```

where `NumValues` is the number of values stored in `anArray`. When executed, the value of `IndexVar` will iterate through the range `FirstIndex` through `NumValues-1`, so that each element of `anArray` is accessed in turn.

We then declare our constructor in the public portion of class `MyArray`:

```
class MyArray
{
 public:
   enum {Capacity = 8};
 protected:
   int anArray[Capacity];
   unsigned NumValues_;
 public:
   MyArray(unsigned Size);
};
```

Note that because a constructor function is called at run-time, the value of the argument corresponding to parameter `Size` need not be known at compile-time (unlike "normal" arrays). That is, a programmer can write:

```
cout << "How big an array do you want (8 maximum)? ";
cin >> N;

MyArray A1(N);
```

If the user of the program enters 5, then `A1` will be constructed as shown below:

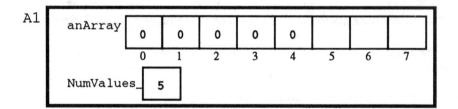

Note that only the first five elements are initialized. The remaining elements are left undefined, since the user only intends to use five of the array's elements.

Using `MyArray::MyArray()` as a pattern, write a constructor for class `RealArray`, so that a declaration of the form

```
RealArray RArray(100);
```

can be used to construct a `RealArray` object named `RArray` as an array of 100 elements (each initially zero).

Number Of Values.

To verify that our constructor is working correctly, we can write a function to extract the `NumValues_` member of a `MyArray` object. That is, if we have declared

```
MyArray A1(5);
```

then the expression

```
A1.NumValues()
```

should return the value 5. If we display this return value, we can verify that (at least part of) our constructor is working correctly.

We can specify this problem as follows:

> Receive: A `MyArray` object.
> Return: The number of elements in use in the array data member of the object.

If we declare this operation as a member function, then we can avoid having to define a parameter to hold the `MyArray` object being operated on. Moreover, since `NumValues_` is always supposed to correctly indicate the number of elements in `anArray` that are available for use, our function can simply return the value of `NumValues_`; a function simple enough to define within class `MyArray`:

```
class MyArray
{
 public:
   enum {Capacity = 8};
 protected:
   int anArray[Capacity];
   unsigned NumValues_;
 public:
   MyArray(unsigned Size);
   unsigned NumValues() const { return NumValues_; }
};
```

Note that we define function `NumValues()` as a *constant function*:

```
unsigned NumValues() const { return NumValues_; }
```

Member functions that do not in any way modify the data members of the class should be defined as constant functions.

Using this function as a model, implement a `NumValues()` function for class `RealArray`, such that the expression:

```
RArray.NumValues()
```

can be used to find the number of values that are stored in `RArray`. Then have your driver program display the value returned by this function to check that it and your constructor are working properly.

Output.

As usual, it is a good idea to implement the output operation early in the design of an object, so that operator<< can be used to aid in debugging the subsequent operations by viewing an object's contents. We can specify the problem of operator<< for class MyArray as follows:

Receive:	*Out*, an ostream object;
	MArray, a MyArray object.
Output:	The contents of *MArray*.
Return(parameters):	*Out*, containing the values from *MArray*.
Return(function):	*Out*, to permit chaining of output operators.

As we have seen before, we declare operator<< within class MyArray as a friend function:

```
class MyArray
{
 public:
   enum {Capacity = 8};
 protected:
   int anArray[Capacity];
   unsigned NumValues_;
 public:
   MyArray(unsigned Size);
   unsigned NumValues() const { return NumValues_; }
   friend ostream& operator<<(ostream& Out, const MyArray& MArray);
};
```

To define this function, we must display each of the values in the anArray member of MArray. The important word here is each — when we must access each of the elements of an array, the for loop form discussed previously can be used to access them conveniently:

```
for (int IndexVar = FirstIndex; IndexVar < NumValues; IndexVar++)
        // access anArray[IndexVar]
```

In our particular problem, the "access" step is to display the value, and then display a space character (to keep values from running together). Since the resulting function is non-trivial, we encode it in our class implementation file as follows:

```
ostream& operator<<(ostream& Out, const MyArray& MArray)
{
   for (int i = 0; i < MArray.NumValues(); i++)
        Out << MArray.anArray[i] << ' ';
   return Out;
}
```

Given this function, a programmer can output the values stored in the MyArray object A1 in the same manner as they would display the value of any other object.

Using this function as a pattern, do all that is necessary to overload operator<< for class RealArray. Then test what you have written using your source program, continuing when it has been thoroughly tested.

Input.

In order to verify that `operator<<` is working correctly, we need to be able to store values in a class object. One way that this can be done is by overloading `operator>>` to fill class objects with input values. Doing so is straightforward, if we assume that the array's `NumValues_` member indicates the number of values to be entered, which is accomplished as follows:

```
cout << "How many values do you have to enter ("
     << MyArray::Capacity << " maximum)? ";
cin >> N;

MyArray A1(N);

cout << "\nEnter your values now: ";
cin >> A1;
```

That is, if the user tells us how many entries they have and we pass that number to our class constructor, then the constructor will set `NumValues_` to that number, solving our problem.

We can specify the input problem for a `MyArray` object as follows:

Receive:	*In*, an `istream` object;
	MArray, a `MyArray` object.
Input:	A sequence of values.
Return(parameters):	*In*, with the input values extracted from it;
	MArray, containing the input values.
Return(function):	*Out*, to permit chaining of output operators.

As usual, we declare this operation as a friend function in class `MyArray`:

```
class MyArray
{
   // ... members omitted to save space ...
 public:
   MyArray(unsigned Size);
   unsigned NumValues() const { return NumValues_; }
   friend ostream& operator<<(ostream& Out, const MyArray& MArray);
   friend istream& operator>>(istream& In, MyArray& MArray);
};
```

Given our assumptions, encoding this operation separately is straightforward:

```
istream& operator>>(istream& In, MyArray& MArray)
{
   for (int i = 0; i < MArray.NumValues(); i++)
        In >> MArray.anArray[i];
   return In;
}
```

Using this as a pattern, overload `operator>>` for class `RealArray`, and continue when you have thoroughly tested all of the `RealArray` operations implemented thus far.

Searching for a Value.

The next operation we will examine is searching an array for a given value, to determine whether or not it is present in the array. One way this operation can be specified is as follows:

> Receive: A `MyArray` object;
> *Val*, a data value.
> Return(Function): The index of the element containing *Val* (if *Val* is in the array)
> -1, otherwise.

Note that rather than simply returning a boolean value (0 or 1) to indicate the presence of *Val*, this approach goes a step further and returns the index of *Val* (a number between 0 and `NumValues-1`) if *Val* is in the array, and returns -1 (an invalid index value) otherwise.

We can avoid declaring a parameter to hold the `MyArray` object if we declare this function (which we call `LSearch()` for reasons explained below) as a member of class `MyArray`:

```
class MyArray
{
    // ... members omitted to save space ...

    friend istream& operator>>(istream& In, MyArray& MArray);
    int LSearch(int Val) const;
};
```

To search the array, we must clearly examine each array element in the worst case (i.e., *Val* is not present in the array). Put differently, we can only return -1 after every array element has been examined. This is best done with a for loop, as we have seen before. As we examine a given element within the for loop, if *Val* is equal to that element, then we want to immediately return its index. These constraints suggest the following algorithm:

> For each index *i* in the range 0 through `NumValues-1`:
>   If the value in element *i* of `anArray` equals *Val*,
>   Return *i*;
>   End if.
> End for.
> Return -1.

This algorithm is called the **Linear** (or **Sequential**) **Search Algorithm**. This is the reason we named the function `LSearch()`, which we encode in the `MyArray` implementation file:

```
int MyArray::LSearch(int Val) const
{
    for (int i = 0; i < NumValues_; i++)
        if (anArray[i] == Val)
            return i;

    return -1;
}
```

Using this function as a model, implement an `LSearch()` function for class `RealArray`. Verify the correctness of your function, continuing when it has been thoroughly tested.

Subscript.

Our final operation is the subscript operation, which allows the subscript operator [] to be applied to an array-based class object. That is, a programmer should be able to use the "normal" array notation:

```
A1[i]
```

to access the value stored in the element whose index is i of the anArray member of a MyArray object A1. We can specify this operation for class MyArray as follows:

> Receive: A MyArray object
>   An (unsigned) integer *Index*
> Return: A reference to the element of anArray whose index is *Index*.

Note that operator[] must return a *reference* to the element, because this operator can be invoked on the left-hand side of an assignment statement:

```
A[i] = j;
```

If operator[] simply returns an integer, than a *copy* of the element will be returned. As a result, assignments will change the value of this copy, rather than changing the value stored in the array, producing an incorrect result.

Something else to keep in mind is that operator[] is one of the operators that *must be declared as a member function*. A compilation error will result otherwise.

The final complication is that operator[] can be applied to either a constant MyArray object, or to a non-constant MyArray object. When applied to a constant MyArray object, operator[] must behave as a constant function, but when applied to a non-constant MyArray object, operator[] must permit modification of that object.

Circumventing this difficulty requires that we overload operator[] *twice* — once for constant MyArray objects and once for non-constant MyArray objects:

```
class MyArray
{
 public:
    enum {Capacity = 8};
 protected:
    int anArray[Capacity];
    unsigned NumValues_;
 public:
    MyArray(unsigned Size);
    unsigned NumValues() const { return NumValues_; }
    friend ostream& operator<<(ostream& Out, const MyArray& MArray);
    friend istream& operator>>(istream& In, MyArray& MArray);
    int LSearch(int Val) const;
    const int& operator[](unsigned Index) const;      // for constants
    int& operator[](unsigned Index);                   // for non-constants
};
```

Both functions will utilize exactly the same logic, but the compiler will apply the first of them to constant MyArray objects, and apply the second to non-constant MyArray objects.

Aside from checking the validity of the value of *Index*, these functions are straightforward, as illustrated by the following algorithm:

> If *Index* is a valid array index,
>> Return the element of anArray whose index is *Index*.
> End if.
> Display an appropriate error message and halt.

Using this algorithm, we define both functions in the MyArray implementation file:

```
const int& MyArray::operator[] (unsigned Index) const
{
    if (Index >= NumValues_)
    {
        cerr << "\n*** invalid index " << Index
             << " received by operator[]!\n";
        exit (-1);
    }
    return anArray[Index];

}

int& MyArray::operator[] (unsigned Index)
{
    if (Index >= NumValues_)
    {
        cerr << "\n*** invalid index " << Index
             << " received by operator[]!\n";
        exit (-1);
    }
    return anArray[Index];
}
```

Note that the logic of each function is identical (i.e., the second function can be written using cut-and-paste and some editing, rather than writing it from scratch). But where the first function returns a reference to anArray[Index] that cannot be modified, the second function returns a reference to anArray[Index] that can be modified. The compiler will apply the first function to calls A1[i] where A1 is a constant MyArray object, and apply the second function to calls A1[i] where A1 is not a constant MyArray object.

Using these functions as models, do all that is necessary to overload operator[] for class RealArray. Then use your driver program to test what you have written on both constant and non-constant arrays of real values, continuing when they have been thoroughly tested.

This completes our implementation of the class MyArray (and your class RealArray).

Phrases You Should Now Understand.

Array, Element, Index, Subscript Operator.

Objectives.

1. Practice the implementation of array-based class operations.
2. Solve a problem using a `RealArray` object.

Introduction.

The first part of this week's project is to extend the capabilities of class `RealArray` with the following additional operations:

- An input function to fill a `RealArray` with values stored in a given file.
- An output function to write the values of a `RealArray` to a given file.

Your instructor will tell you if your input function can assume that the first value in the file is the number of values in the file. If so, then your output function should create a file with this same format (i.e., whose first entry is the number of values in the file).

Your instructor will also tell you which of the following projects you are to do:

Projects.

12.1. Extend class `RealArray` with a member function `Sort()` that returns a sorted copy of its `RealArray` (without changing that `RealArray`). Your instructor will tell you which of the following sorting algorithms to use: Insertion Sort, Selection Sort, Quick Sort, Merge Sort.

12.2. Professor Diskus records student exam scores in a text file. Write a program that (using class `RealArray`) the professor can use to analyze student performance on an exam. The program should input the name of the text file, and then display the worst score, the best score, and the average score. For extra credit, have your program display a *histogram* — a bar graph indicating the frequency with which given values occur in a data set. For example, if three people scored 74, five people scored 75, six people scored 76, no one scored 77 and two people scored 78, then that portion of the histogram should appear as:

```
74: ***
75: *****
76: ******
77:
78: **
```

Entries below the worst or above the best should not be displayed.

12.3. Each year, the well-known meteorologist Dr. H. Tu Oh creates a file containing the year's 12 monthly precipitation totals (e.g., `rain1990.dat`). Write a program that, given the names of two of these files, will create a file containing an easy-to-read analysis comparing the two sets of readings, including which of the two years was the wettest (and by how much), the average monthly precipitation for each year, and the wettest and driest months in each year.

12.4. Dr. Oh has created the files described in 12.3 over many years. Write a program that, given the names of an "arbitrary" number (less than 128) of files for consecutive years, builds a list whose values are the precipitation totals for each year. Your program should output this list to a file, and display the average annual precipitation over these years on the screen.

Project 12 Due Date _____

Turn in this grade sheet, attached to a hard copy of

a. your program,
b. the header file for your class library,
c. the implementation file for your class library, and
d. an execution of your program illustrating its correctness.

Name _____

Category	Points Possible	Points Received
Correctness and efficiency	90	_____
Design and Structure	40	_____
Style and Readability	20	
Horizontal White Space	5	_____
Vertical White Space	5	_____
Meaningful Identifiers	10	_____
Documentation	50	
Opening Documentation	15	_____
Specification(s)	35	_____
Total	**200**	_____

Lab 13

Inheritance

Note to the Instructor:

If you have not yet read the instructor's note for Lab 12, please do so before proceeding.

Lab 13 introduces the topic of inheritance, to illustrate how a derived class inherits the members of its base class. This is a central topic in object-oriented programming, particularly when programming in an environment providing predefined classes.

The key idea that must be emphasized to students is that inheritance is a way to avoid re-inventing the wheel. To illustrate, suppose that we have available to us a working, general-purpose Array class, and a problem requires operations on an array that this class does not provide.

The "old-fashioned" approach might be to add new member functions to this class that implement the needed operations. However, in doing so, we tamper with a tested, operational class — and the file that previously compiled correctly may no longer do so after we add our new operations. This creates a problem for other programs sharing that class.

By contrast, the object-oriented approach is to define a new class (say, DerivedArray) and *derive* this new class from class Array, which is called the *parent* class of DerivedArray. By doing so, the derived class inherits all of the members of its parent class (including its operations) allowing us to avoid "re-inventing the wheel" since we need not re-implement its operations. Moreover, any mistakes we make in the construction of DerivedArray will be local to it — our original Array class remains untainted and other programs sharing it are unaffected by our work.

This exercise uses this approach to derive a new class DataSet from the RealArray class that was built in Lab 12.

Objectives.

1. More practice defining and using arrays.
2. Implement more common array operations.
3. Introduce inheritance as a way to avoid "reinventing the wheel."

Prelab Questions:

1. The mechanism whereby one class can have the same members as another class without redefining those members is called the _____ mechanism.

2. A class that inherits the members of another class is said to be _____ from that other class

3. In order for a derived class to be able to access the data members of its parent class (and still ensure that programs and other classes are unable to access them), those members should be designated _____ instead of private.

4. What is the only member function that a derived class does not inherit from its parent?

5. The constructor of a derived class can invoke the constructor of its parent class using the _____ mechanism.

Introduction.

When a child is born having some similarity to one of its parents (e.g., eyes, hair, etc.), we describe the child as having *inherited* that feature from that parent. A statement like "I think you have your mother's eyes," is based on this idea. The child does nothing to inherit the feature — it is automatically a part of him or her.

In object-oriented programming languages, inheritance plays a similar role. More precisely, a new class can be built in such a way that it inherits the members (data and function) of another already existing class. The already existing class is called the *parent* class and the new class is called the *derived* class, so the derived class inherits the members of its parent class. Of course, if the parent class was derived itself from a *grandparent* class, then the new class also inherits those members (similar to you inheriting your grandfather's nose through your mother).

In Lab 12, we built a class `RealArray` that provided the basic array operations for an array of real values, including construction, input, output, searching, and subscript. Depending on the kind of data being stored in a `RealArray`, it is possible (in fact, quite likely) that additional operations would be useful. For example, if the array is used to store a list of exam scores, then we might wish to compute the minimum, maximum, and average of the scores (see Project 12.1). This kind of an array, that is designed to store and process *measurements* is called a **data set**. For example, a list of students' exam scores comprise a data set, as do a list of daily air quality readings, or a list of the daily per share prices of a company's stock. Through the processing of such data sets, patterns can sometimes be detected, allowing the prediction of trends in the future, such as a student's performance, the air quality, or the price of a company's stock.

Today's exercise is to build an array-based class named `DataSet` in which such lists can be conveniently stored and processed.

Getting Started.

Begin by changing directory to `labs/lab12`. We will conduct Lab 13 within the directory `lab12`, since we wish to experiment with inheritance by re-using the work we did in Lab 12.

Take a moment to re-familiarize yourself with the files stored in `lab12`, with particular emphasis on the various operations that were implemented for class `RealArray`.

Then use emacs to begin editing the files `driver13.cc` and `DataSet.h`.

Running Example.

To illustrate today's topics, we will again use the MyArray class that served to illustrate last week's topics. Recall that a MyArray object had the following structure:

```
class MyArray
{
 public:
    enum {Capacity = 8};
 protected:
    int anArray[Capacity];   // an array of integers
    unsigned NumValues_;     // will indicate # of values in anArray
 public:
    // ... function members omitted ...
};
```

so that a MyArray object named A1 could be visualized as follows:

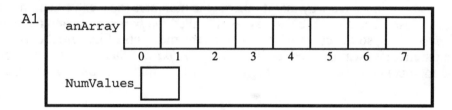

Take a moment to compare this structure with that of your RealArray class. The two classes should be quite similar, and we will use class MyArray to illustrate the construction of a DataSet class.

Class Design — Operations.

Let's begin with the operations on a data set. Some operations are similar to those we built last week:

- Construct a data set;
- Input and output a data set;
- Search a data set for a particular value; and
- Access the value in a data set at a given location (i.e., subscripting).

Others are particular to a data set:

- Find the maximum value in the data set;
- Find the minimum value in the data set;
- Find the average value in the data set;
- Add a value to the data set;
- Delete a value from the data set;

Now, if we consider these latter operations, it should be evident that the number of values in a data set can change, if values are added or deleted from the data set. This has implications for our data members — we must keep track of the number of values, not simply the maximum number of elements that will be used.

Class Design — Data Members.

We thus need the following *data members* to represent a `DataSet` object:

- A member to store the values in the data set (an array).
- A member to indicate the number of values actually stored in the array .

If we think about the members that are needed to represent a `DataSet` object, it should be evident that some of those operations are the same as those needed to represent a `MyArray` object. One approach would be to start "from scratch" to define a `DataSet`:

```
class DataSet
{
 public:
   enum {Capacity = 8};
 private
   int anArray[Capacity];
   int NumValues_;
 public:
   // ... constructor, I/O functions, etc.
};
```

But doing so is "reinventing the wheel" because we already defined these back in `MyArray`. A preferable approach would be to somehow reuse the work we invested in building `MyArray`.

The C++ **inheritance mechanism** makes this easy, by allowing one class to have all of the members of another class *without redefining those members*. To illustrate, we just write:

```
class DataSet : public MyArray
{
};
```

and class `DataSet` automatically has a `Capacity` constant whose value is 8, an 8-element integer array member named `anArray`, and an integer member named `NumValues_`, without further ado. Class `DataSet` also inherits the member functions from class `MyArray`, so as it stands, `DataSet` is exactly the same as class `MyArray`.

Since class `DataSet` has all of the members of `MyArray`, `DataSet` is described as being **derived from** `MyArray`. Conversely, since class `MyArray` was used to create `DataSet`, `MyArray` is called the **parent** of class `DataSet`.

In `DataSet.h`, use this approach to derive class `DataSet` from your `RealArray` class. However, don't test your code yet — we must provide a constructor before we can actually define a `DataSet` object.

DataSet Operations.

As just described, class `DataSet` inherits all of the member functions of class `MyArray`, with the exception of the class constructor — a parent's constructor function(s) is not inherited by a derived class (though as we shall see, that constructor is easily reused). Since the constructor is needed to define objects, we will start with this function.

The DataSet Constructor.

The constructor must initialize all of the data members of class DataSet — both those defined explicitly, and those inherited from class MyArray. Ideally, a programmer should be able to write:

```
DataSet DSet1(5);
```

and the data members of DSet1 should be initialized as follows:

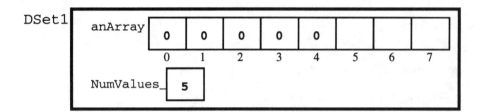

However, it may be the case that we want to initialize an empty DataSet object:

```
DataSet DSet2;
```

should construct DSet2 as a DataSet containing no values:

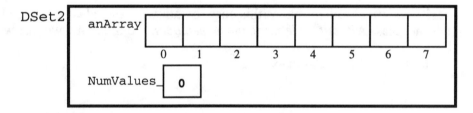

To allow this, the parameter of our constructor should have a default argument of zero, as shown in the following stub:

```
class DataSet : public MyArray
{
 public:
   DataSet(unsigned Size = 0)
   {}
};
```

Our constructor must then ensure that the NumValues_ and anArray members get initialized appropriately. While we could do this explicitly in the DataSet constructor, doing so would involve

- setting NumValues_ to Size, and
- initializing elements 0 through Size-1 of anArray to zero.

But these steps are exactly the same as those performed by the MyArray constructor. A preferable approach would be to somehow reuse the work we invested in writing the MyArray constructor by having it initialize those members for us, since that is its purpose.

The question is, how can the `DataSet` constructor invoke the `MyArray` constructor?

C++ makes this easy by supplying a *member initialization mechanism*, that can only be used by constructor functions. To illustrate, we can write

```
class DataSet : public MyArray
{
 public:
    DataSet(unsigned Size) : MyArray(Size)
    {}
};
```

The effect of this definition is that when the `DataSet` constructor is called, the first thing it does is invoke the `MyArray` constructor, passing it `Size` as an argument. Since that function initializes the `anArray` and `NumValues_` members, this invocation serves to initialize those data members that were inherited from `MyArray`.

Class `DataSet` has no data members except those it inherits from class `MyArray`. If it did, then these data members could then be initialized in its *StatementList*, as usual. In the absence of such members, the *StatementList* of the `DataSet` constructor is simply left empty.

In general, a derived class constructor can invoke its parent class constructor with the notation:

```
DerivedClassName ( ParameterList ) : ParentClassName ( ArgumentList )
{
    StatementList
}
```

In `DataSet.h`, use this as a model to build a `DataSet` constructor that invokes the `RealArray` constructor. If you then examine your driver program, you can see that it (1) constructs a `DataSet` capable of holding 10 elements, and (2) displays that `DataSet` object on the screen. Using this program, test the correctness of your `DataSet` constructor, continuing when it has been thoroughly tested.

When you execute your driver program, something very interesting should occur: the contents of the initialized `DataSet` should appear on the screen! That is, we are able to use `<<` to display a `DataSet` object without having overloaded `operator<<` for class `DataSet`!

The key to understanding why this occurs is to remember that as far as the compiler is concerned, a `DataSet` object *is a* `RealArray` object that happens to have some extra members. Thus, when the compiler sees a statement like:

```
cout << DSet << endl;
```

it invokes the definition of `operator<<` that `DSet` inherits from `RealArray`. In exactly the same way, all of the other operations that we defined for a `RealArray` object (e.g., `LSearch()`, `operator[]`, etc.) can now be applied to a `DataSet` object without alteration.

Understanding this **is a** relationship (i.e., a derived class object *is a* parent class object with additional members) is critical to understanding much of object-oriented programming (OOP). By carefully designing general-purpose classes that will serve as parent classes, much of the tedium can be removed from problem-solving by re-using their functionality.

Appending a Value to a DataSet.

One approach to building a data set is to start with an empty set and add values to it, one by one. This *add* operation is useful enough to encode as a member function. Since the operation can fail (i.e., if anArray is full), we can specify this operation for class MyArray as follows:

Receive:	A DataSet object;
	Val, a data value.
Return(Parameters):	The DataSet, containing *Val* as its newest values.
Return(Function):	*True*, if the operation succeeds, *False* otherwise.

If we declare this operation as a member of class DataSet, then we can avoid declaring a parameter to hold the DataSet object to which *Val* is being added:

```
class DataSet : public MyArray
{
 public:
    DataSet(unsigned Size) : MyArray(Size) {}
    int Append(int Val);
};
```

To implement this operation, we need only note that NumValues_ not only indicates the number of values in the array, it also indicates the index of the next empty array element (e.g., if NumValues_ is 2, then there are values in the elements whose indices are 0 and 1). Our algorithm thus utilizes NumValues_ to determine the index of the element in which to store *Val*:

If (NumValues_ >= Capacity)
    Display a "Full" error message.
    Return *False*.
End if.
Store *Val* in the element of anArray whose index is NumValues_ .
Increment NumValues_.
Return *True*.

Since this algorithm is non-trivial, we encode it in the implementation file of DataSet:

```
int DataSet::Append(int Val)
{
    if (NumValues_ >= Capacity)
    {
        cerr << "\n*** Append: Data set is full!\n";
        return 0;
    }
    anArray[NumValues_] = Val;
    NumValues_++;
    return 1;
}
```

Note that Append() is able to access the data members anArray and NumValues_ directly. If these members were declared as private within class MyArray, Append() would be unable to do so. This is the reason we declared them as *protected* instead of *private* — where private members cannot be accessed outside of their class (i.e., not even within derived classes), protected members can be accessed within a derived class, but remain inaccessible to programs or non-derived classes that use the class.

To illustrate the behavior of this operation, suppose that DSet2 is defined as follows:

```
DataSet DSet2;
```

Then as we saw earlier, DSet2 is an empty data set, that we can picture as follows:

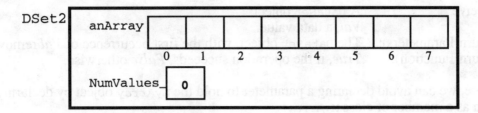

Now consider the execution of the following loop:

```
for (int i = 0; i < 3; i++)
{
    DSet2.Append(10+i);
}
```

The first repetition, the value 10+0 = 10 is appended, giving us:

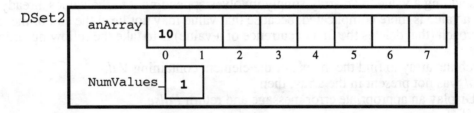

the second, the value 10+1 = 11 is appended, giving us:

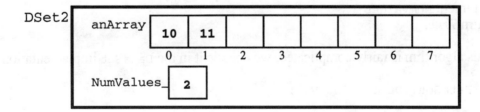

and the final repetition, the value 10+2 = 12 is appended, giving us

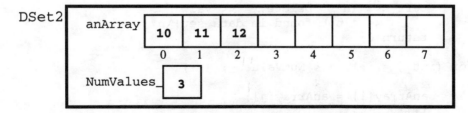

Use this function as a model and write an Append() function for your DataSet class. Use your driver program to verify its correctness , continuing when it is thoroughly tested.

Deleting a Value.

Just as it is useful to be able to add values to a data set, it is useful to be able to delete them. Since this operation can fail if the value is not present in the set, we can specify our operation for class `DataSet` as follows:

Receive:	A `DataSet` object;
	Val, a data value.
Return(Parameters):	The `DataSet` object, with the first occurrence of *Val* removed.
Return(Function):	*True*, if the operation succeeds, *False* otherwise.

As before, we can avoid declaring a parameter to hold the `MyArray` object by declaring this function as a member of class `MyArray`:

```
class DataSet : public MyArray
{
 public:
    DataSet(unsigned Size) : MyArray(Size) {}
    int Append(int Val);
    int Delete(int Val);
};
```

Whereas adding a value to an array simply involves appending it to the values already present, deleting a value is more complicated, because that value may not lie at the end of the array. One approach (that deletes the first occurrence of a value) is to take the following actions:

Search the array to find the index *i* of the element containing *Val*.
If *Val* was not present in the array, then
    Display an appropriate error message and return *False*.
End if.
Copy the values in elements *i+1* through `NumValues_-1`
    into elements *i* through `NumValues_-2`, respectively.
Decrement `NumValues_`.
Return *True*.

Since this algorithm is fairly complicated, we encode it in the `DataSet` implementation file:

```
int DataSet::Delete(int Val)
{
    int i = LSearch(Val);
    if (i < 0)
    {
        cerr << "\n*** Delete: " << Val
            << " not found in data set!\n";
        return 0;
    }
    for (int j = i+1; j < NumValues_; j++)
    {
        anArray[i] = anArray[j];
        i++;
    }
    NumValues_--;
    return 1;
}
```

Note that searching is accomplished using the LSearch() function from class MyArray — a quick return on the labor we invested in writing it.

To illustrate the behavior of Delete(), suppose that DSet2 is as follows:

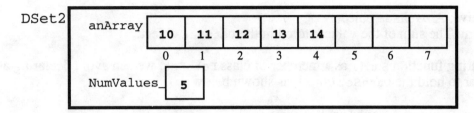

and the call

```
    DSet2.Delete(12);
```

is executed. Then LSearch() finds that 12 is in element 2 of anArray, and so execution passes to the for loop. The first repetition, the 12 in element 2 is replaced with the 13 from element 3:

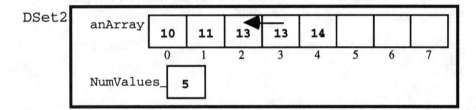

The second iteration the 13 in element 3 is replaced with the 14 from element 4:

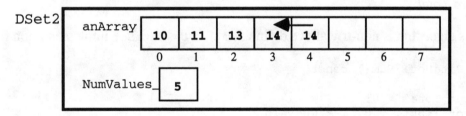

This completes the shifting of values, and so NumValues_ is decremented to indicate that there is one fewer value in the data set. As a result, the values in the array whose indices are 4 and higher will be subsequently out of bounds, and thus can be ignored:

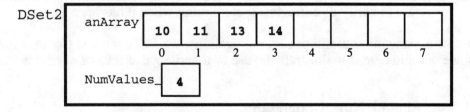

Using this function as a model, encode a Delete() function for your DataSet class. Verify its correctness with your driver program, continuing when it has been thoroughly tested.

Sum.

There are a number of useful operations that can be applied to a data set. One of them is to compute the sum of the values in the data set. We can specify this operation as follows:

Receive: A DataSet object.
Return: The sum of the values stored in the DataSet object.

By declaring function Sum() as a member of class DataSet, we can avoid declaring a parameter to hold the DataSet object, as shown below:

```
class DataSet : public MyArray
{
 public:
   DataSet(unsigned Size) : MyArray(Size) {}
   int Append(int Val);
   int Delete(int Val);
   int Sum() const;
};
```

Note that unlike Append() and Delete(), Sum() does not alter the data members of its DataSet, and so it is best declared as a constant function.

Since each value in anArray must be examined to compute their sum, a for loop plays a central role in our algorithm:

Initialize *Total* to zero.
For each index *i* in the range 0 through NumValues_-1:
    Add the value in element *i* of anArray to *Total*.
End for.
Return *Total*.

Since this algorithm is non-trivial, we define Sum() in the DataSet implementation file:

```
int DataSet::Sum() const
{
    int Total = 0;
    for (int i = 0; i < NumValues_; i++)
         Total += anArray[i];
    return Total;
}
```

Using this function as a model, define a Sum() function for your DataSet class. Then use your driver program to verify its correctness, continuing when it has been thoroughly tested.

While there are many other useful DataSet operations, we will conclude (for now) with Sum(), since our aim here is to illustrate the use of inheritance as a labor-saving mechanism.

Phrases You Should Now Understand.

Inheritance, Parent Class, Derived Class, Private, Protected, Member Initialization Mechanism.

Objectives.

1. Practice the implementation of derived class operations.
2. Solve a problem using a DataSet object.

Introduction.

This week's project has two parts: (1) a 2-person group part in which different group members work on enhancing the DataSet class with additional operations; and (2) an individual part in which each individual uses the resulting DataSet class to solve a particular problem.

Group Part. Each group member must choose one of the following groups of operations:

A.   • Fill a DataSet with values input from a given file.
       • Find the maximum value in the DataSet
       • Compute the average of the values in a DataSet
       • Insert a value into a DataSet at a given position (without losing any values)

B.   • Write the values of a DataSet to a given file
       • Find the minimum value in the DataSet
       • Compute the standard deviation of the values in a DataSet (see Project 7.4).

You are free to discuss and collaborate in the design of these operations, but each group member should write their own functions. A group member's grade will not be influenced by the functions written by their partner.

Individual Part.

Once you have assembled you and your partner's functions into a unified DataSet class definition, make certain that each of you has a copy of the class. Your instructor will then assign you one of the problems from Project 12 to solve using your DataSet class.

If you are unable to fulfill all of the requirements of your project because your partner was unable to complete their group of functions, you may either (1) implement them yourself (they're good practice), or (2) discuss the situation with your instructor, who may provide them for you, or else not require your project to satisfy those requirements that depended upon your partner's work.

Project 13 Due Date _____

Turn in this grade sheet, attached to a hard copy of

a. your program,
b. the header file for your unified class library,
c. the implementation file for your unified class library, and
d. an execution of your program illustrating its correctness.

(Functions written by one group member will only affect the grade of that group member)

Name _____

Functions for which I was responsible: _____

Category	Points Possible	Points Received
Correctness and efficiency...................	100	_____
Design and Structure.......................	30	_____
Style and Readability.......................	20	
Horizontal White Space...............	5	_____
Vertical White Space.................	5	_____
Meaningful Identifiers................	10	_____
Documentation...........................	50	
Opening Documentation...............	15	_____
Specification(s).....................	35	_____
Total.................................	**200**	_____

Lab 14

Multi-dimensional Arrays

Note to the Instructor:

This lab exercise involves the creation of a simple software model of a tic-tac-toe board. To illustrate the development of this class and its operations, we (in parallel) create a software model of a grade report card, of the type commonly used in (elementary and secondary) schools in the United States. If you are using this exercise in another country, you may wish to adjust the examples so that they are appropriate for academic reports in your country.

Objectives.

1. Learn to define and operate on a multi-dimensional array.
2. Practice class implementation.

Prelab Questions:

1. Describe the dimension of a one-dimensional array.

2. Describe the dimensions of a two-dimensional array.

3. A two-dimensional array can be thought of as a one-dimensional array whose elements are _____.

4. To access the element in row r and column c of a two-dimensional array A, the notation _____ can be used.

5. Whereas a single for loop can be used to conveniently process a one-dimensional array, _____ are needed to conveniently process a two-dimensional array, either explicity or implicity.

Introduction.

Previously, we have seen that declarations of the form:

```
int Capacity = 8;
double Alpha [ Capacity ];
```

can be used to define a single object named `Alpha` that is capable of storing eight different real values, indexed from zero through seven, that we can visualize as follows:

	0	1	2	3	4	5	6	7
Alpha								

An object like `Alpha` is called a **one-dimensional array**, because such objects have a single dimension, namely the number of elements in the array.

While one-dimensional arrays are useful for storing simple sequences of values (e.g., lists), it is sometimes the case that a data object in a problem has more than one dimension. For example, a grade report card can be thought of as two-dimensional structure, consisting of a given number of rows (e.g., 4) and a given number of columns (e.g., 6):

Marking Period

	1	2	3	4	5	6
Language	A	B	A			
History	B	A	A			
Math	A	B	A			
Phys.Ed.	B	A	A			

Such an object can be modeled in software using a **two-dimensional array** of characters. Similarly, a tic-tac-toe board is a two-dimensional structure of characters, consisting of three rows and three columns:

	1	2	3
1	X		O
2		X	O
3	X	O	X

Today's exercise involves the implementation of such objects. We will demonstrate the implementation through the construction of a `ReportCard` class, and have you apply the same techniques in the implementation of a `TicTacToe` board class.

Getting Started.

Create and change directory to labs/lab14 and copy the files from the lab14 class directory. Then open the file Row.h and take a few moments to examine its contents.

A two-dimensional array can be thought of as a one-dimensional array, whose elements are themselves one-dimensional arrays. That is, our report card can be thought of as a one-dimensional array of four rows, the elements of which are one-dimensional arrays of six characters:

	1	2	3	4	5	6
Language	A	B	A			
History	B	A	A			
Math	A	B	A			
Phys.Ed.	B	A	A			

It turns out that this is the best way to think of representing a two-dimensional structure via classes. We therefore need a class Row containing a one-dimensional array of characters. Given the capability to define Row objects, then we can represent a ReportCard as a one-dimensional array of Row objects.

Modifying Class Row.

In order to practice code maintenance, we have provided a Row class appropriate for a report card, which you can modify to make it appropriate for a tic-tac-toe Row class:

```
class Row
{
    enum {Capacity_ = 6};
    char Alpha [ Capacity_ ];
    unsigned NumValues_
  public:
    Row();
    const char operator[] (unsigned Index) const;
    char operator[] (unsigned Index);
    friend ostream& operator<<(ostream& Out, const Row& R);
    friend istream& operator>>(istream& In, Row& R);
    unsigned NumValues() const { return NumValues_;}
    unsigned Capacity() const { return Capacity_;}
};
```

What modifications are needed? The most obvious is that for a tic-tac-toe board, there are only three elements in a row, as opposed to six for a report card.

A more subtle difference is that whereas we can ignore the empty spaces in a report card row, this is not the case in a tic-tac-toe row:

	1	2	3
1	X		O
2		X	O
3	X	O	X

That is, when displaying a tic-tac-toe row, *every* element in the Row must be displayed, so the for loop in operator<< should be modified to display all of the elements of Alpha, rather than just some of them.

This brings up the third difference. If we try and display a Row, and one of its elements is "empty," but has not been initialized to some character value (e.g., the space character), then whatever "garbage" value happens to be in that element (left over from the prior use of the storage) will be displayed, instead of an empty space. One simple way to resolve this difficulty is to use a for loop to initialize every element of a Row to the space character when it is constructed (i.e., in the constructor function). By doing so, each element of a Row will be appropriately initialized when that Row is created.

In the light of these observations, it should be evident that the NumValues_ member is effectively useless. In particular, it does not really provide any useful information for a tic-tac-toe board row, and so it can be eliminated (along with function NumValues()).

Take a few minutes to make these changes before continuing, and use the driver program to verify the correctness of your changes, continuing when Row has been thoroughly tested.

Using Class Row.

Now that we have a functional Row class, we should be ready to use it to build other, two-dimensional classes. For example, to declare a ReportCard class, we first define a one-dimensional array of four Row objects:

```
enum {Capacity_ = 4};
Row Beta [ Capacity_ ];
```

which we then surround with an appropriately named class structure:

```
class ReportCard
{
   enum {Capacity_ = 4};
   Row Beta [ Capacity_ ];
 public:
   ReportCard() {}
   unsigned Capacity() const { return Capacity_; }
};
```

Note that the class constructor is a "dummy" class constructor that does nothing. No actions are needed because Beta is an array of Row objects, so the Row constructor will be automatically called for each element in Beta when a ReportCard object is declared, and there are no other data members to be initialized. The Capacity() function is almost as trivial.

Open the file TTToe.h and construct an equivalent TicTacToe class structure.

Operations For Our New Class.

A minimal set of operations (beyond those given above) for our new class might include:

- A subscript operation, whereby an element of a ReportCard can be accessed; and
- Input and output operations, to read and display a ReportCard.

The Subscript Operation.

The first operation we will implement is the subscript operation, so that the notation

```
RepCard[r][c]
```

can be utilized to access an arbitrary row r and column c of a ReportCard object named RepCard. The key to understanding how to do this is to

1. Recognize that two calls to operator[] are being used in this expression;
2. Remember that operator[] is a left-associative operator, so that the left-most operator[] will be applied first and the rightmost operator[] applied second;
3. Recognize that the first application of operator[]

```
RepCard[r]
```

must return the Row within RepCard whose index is r. The second application of operator[] will then return the character whose index is c within that Row.

That is, we can specify the problem ReportCard::operator[] must solve, as follows:

Receive: A ReportCard object;
            Index, an integer;
Return: The element of the ReportCard object whose index is *Index*.

As before, operator[] must be defined as a member function, so there is no need to declare a parameter to hold the ReportCard object. Since the function should check that the value of *Index* is a valid subscript, we declare (but do not define) operator[] within class ReportCard. Since the function might be applied to either constant or non-constant ReportCard objects, we supply declarations for each kind of ReportCard:

```
class ReportCard
{
   enum {Capacity_ = 4};
   Row Beta [ Capacity_ ];
 public:
   Row() {}
   unsigned Capacity() const { return Capacity_; }
   const Row operator[] (unsigned Index) const;
   Row operator[] (unsigned Index);
};
```

We can then encode the two definitions of operator[] in the ReportCard implementation file, as follows:

```
const Row ReportCard::operator[] (unsigned Index) const
{
   if (Index < Capacity_)
        return Beta[Index];

   cerr << "\n*** invalid index " << Index
        << " received by ReportCard::operator[]\n";
   exit(-1);
}
```

```
Row ReportCard::operator[] (unsigned Index)
{
   if (Index < Capacity_)
         return Beta[Index];

   cerr << "\n*** invalid index " << Index
        << " received by ReportCard::operator[]\n";
   exit(-1);
}
```

Given these definitions, the expression

```
    RepCard[r]
```

can be used to access the Row element of RepCard whose index is r, and

```
    RepCard[r][c]
```

can be used to access the character element at column c within that Row.

Using this approach, overload operator[] for class TicTacToe so that the notation

```
    Board[r][c]
```

can be used to access the element at row r, column c of a TicTacToe object named Board.
Then use your driver program to verify the correctness of what you have written, continuing
when it has been thoroughly tested.

The Output Operation.

We can specify the problem of the output operator as follows:

Receive:	*Out*, an ostream;
	RCard, a ReportCard.
Output:	Each Row in *RCard*.
Return(Parameters):	*Out*, containing the output values.
Return(Function):	*Out* (for chaining).

As usual, we declare this operation as a friend of class ReportCard:

```
class ReportCard
{
   enum {Capacity_ = 4};
   Row Beta [ Capacity_ ];
 public:
   Row() {}
   unsigned Capacity() const { return Capacity_; }
   const Row operator[] (unsigned Index) const;
   Row operator[] (unsigned Index);
   friend ostream& operator<<(ostream& Out, const ReportCard& RCard);
};
```

Since our function must output each Row in RCard, we can do so using a for loop that iterates
through the index values of RCard.Beta, as shown in the following function:

197

```
ostream& operator<<(ostream& Out, const ReportCard& RCard)
{
    for (int i = 0; i < RCard.Capacity(); i++)
       Out << RCard.Beta[i] << endl;

    return Out;
}
```

Note that the `endl` is necessary to prevent each `Row` from being displayed on one line. However, the subtle part of this function is the part before the `endl`:

```
        Out << RCard.Beta[i]
```

It's subtle because it's not immediately obvious that it is the `Row` function:

```
        operator<<(ostream& Out, const Row& Rw)
```

that is being invoked. That is, since `RCard.Beta[i]` is a `Row` object, this function call is invoking the output operator from class `Row`, whose for loop does the actual work of displaying each of the elements in the `Alpha` member of that `Row`. Our function thus uses two nested for loops to process this two-dimensional structure, although the inner loop is hidden by the call to `operator<<` of class `Row`.

An Alternative Approach.

If the output operator were not defined for class `Row`, an alternative approach would be to define the `ReportCard` output operation using two explicitly nested for loops:

```
ostream& operator<<(ostream& Out, const ReportCard& RCard)
{
    for (int r = 0; r < RCard.Capacity(); r++)
       for (int c = 0; c < RCard.Beta[i].NumValues(); c++)
          Out << RCard[r][c] << ' ';
       Out << endl;

    return Out;
}
```

Here, the outer loop is used to sequence through the rows of the `ReportCard` object `RCard`, and the inner loop is used to pass from column to column within each row. The notation

```
        RCard[r][c]
```

uses the double-subscript operation, the first of which (`ReportCard::operator[]`) returns the `Row` whose index is `r` within `RCard`; to which the second subscript operation is applied, returning the value of the element whose index is `c` in that `Row`.

Using either of these approaches, define `operator<<` for your `TicTacToe` class so that

```
        cout << Board << endl;
```

can be used to to display a `TicTacToe` object named `Board`. Then using your driver program, verify that `operator<<` works correctly when applied to `TicTacToe` board objects.

The Input Operation.

Given the output operation, a ReportCard can be written to a file (just as a tic-tac-toe game in progress might be saved to a file). In order to update such a ReportCard, it would be useful to be able to fill a ReportCard object with input values (just as it would be useful to be able to resume a saved tic-tac-toe game).

The problem this function must solve can be specified as follows:

Receive:	*In*, an istream;
	RCard, a ReportCard.
Input:	Each Row in *RCard*.
Return(Parameters):	*In*, with the input values extracted from it;
	RCard, containing those values.
Return(Function):	*In* (for chaining).

We therefore declare this function as a friend in class ReportCard:

```
class ReportCard
{
    enum {Capacity_ = 4};
    Row Beta [ Capacity_ ];
 public:
    Row() {}
    unsigned Capacity() const { return Capacity_; }
    const Row operator[] (unsigned Index) const;
    Row operator[] (unsigned Index);
    friend ostream& operator<<(ostream& Out, const ReportCard& RCard);
    friend istream& operator>>(istream& In, ReportCard& RCard);
};
```

and then define the function in the ReportCard implementation file:

```
istream& operator>>(istream& In, ReportCard& RCard)
{
    for (int r = 0; r < RCard.Capacity(); r++)
        In >> RCard.Beta[r];

    return In;
}
```

Similar to our version of the output operation, this function is simplified by making use of the input operation from class Row, which deserves further examination. In particular, the Row input operation must use the get() member of class iostream, because entries in a Row can be spaces (and operator>> ignores white spaces).

Note also that since a Row might contain fewer than Row::Capacity_ values, repetition is terminated if the character separating valid data entries is the newline character.

Using this function as a pattern, overload the input operator for class TicTacToe so that TicTacToe objects can be filled with values from the keyboard or a file. Then use your driver program to verify that your operation works correctly

The `Mark()` Function.

We conclude with a final tic-tac-toe operation for you to implement, which we call `Mark()`. Write a function, so that the call

```
Board.Mark(0, 0, 'X');
```

can be used to place an x in the top-left corner of a `TicTacToe` object `Board`,

```
Board.Mark(2, 2, 'O');
```

can be used to place an o in the bottom-right corner of `Board`, and in general

```
Board.Mark(i, j, Ch);
```

will place a char `Ch` (whose value should be verified as either x or o) in the `Board` entry whose row-index is `i` and whose column-index is `j`. `Mark()` should prevent cheating, by displaying an error message if there is already a mark in `Board[i][j]` and leaving `Board` unchanged.

A Word About the `Makefile`.

The `Makefile` for this project must coordinate the translation of *three* different source files: and thus requires *four* pairs of lines. The first pair:

```
driver: driver.o Row.o TTToe.o
     g++ driver.o Row.o TTToe.o -o driver
```

makes `driver` by linking together the three object files; the second pair:

```
driver.o: driver.cc TTToe.h Row.h
     g++ -c driver.cc
```

makes the `driver` object file by separately compiling the `driver` source file; the third pair

```
TToe.o: TTToe.cc TTToe.h Row.h
     g++ -c TTToe.cc
```

makes the `TTToe` object file from the `TTToe` implementation file; and the fourth pair

```
Row.o: Row.cc Row.h
     g++ -c Row.cc
```

makes the `Row` object file from the `Row` implementation file. Note that both `driver.o` and `TTToe.o` are dependent upon `Row.h` (since each of their source files include `TTToe.h`, which includes `Row.h`) and so the first line of each pair names `Row.h` to reflect this dependence.

Phrases You Should Now Understand.

Two-Dimensional Array, Row, Column, Row Subscript, Column Subscript.

Objectives.

1. Practice using two-dimensional objects.
2. Practice maintaining or creating classes.

Projects.

14.1. Use dashes (-) and vertical bars (|) to enhance the `TicTacToe` output operation, so that a `TicTacToe` object is displayed with "grid lines" between its elements:

```
X |   | O
-----------
  | X | O
-----------
X | O | X
```

Then write a program that allows two people to play tic-tac-toe against one another.

14.2. A *matrix* is a two-dimensional array of real values, on which arithmetic operations like addition, subtraction and multiplication are defined. For example, the sum of two matrices *M1* and *M2* produces a third matrix *M3*, as follows:

$$
M1 \quad\quad M2 \quad\quad\quad M3
$$

$$
\begin{bmatrix} 1 & 2 & 3 \\ 4 & 5 & 6 \\ 7 & 8 & 9 \end{bmatrix} + \begin{bmatrix} 1 & 4 & 7 \\ 2 & 5 & 8 \\ 3 & 6 & 9 \end{bmatrix} = \begin{bmatrix} 2 & 6 & 10 \\ 6 & 10 & 14 \\ 10 & 14 & 18 \end{bmatrix}
$$

Create a class `Matrix`, and overload the +, - , *, <<, >> and [] operators to perform the addition, subtraction, multiplication, output, input and subscript operations for matrices. Then write a menu-driven matrix calculator program, that allows the user to perform numeric calculations on matrices in an easy-to-use manner.

14.3. A year might be modeled as a two-dimensional structure, with its rows indexed by months (January-December), its columns indexed by the day number (1-31) within that month, and each element [m][d] containing the day (Monday-Sunday) on which that date falls. Create whatever classes are necessary in order for the notation:

```
Year Y(1994);
```

to correctly construct a `Year` object `Y` for a given year; and the notation

```
Y[M][D]
```

to indicate the day on which month `M` and day number `D` falls within year `Y`. Build a driver program that lets the user enter a date (a month, a day number and a year), and displays the day on which that date falls.

14.4. Do all that is necessary to enhance the program in 14.1, so that the user of the program can choose whether to play against another person or against the program itself.

Project 14 Due Date _____

Turn in this grade sheet, attached to a hard copy of

a. a sample execution of your program;
b. your source program; and
c. the header and implementation files for each class used by your program.

Name _____

Category	Points Possible	Points Received
Correctness and efficiency..................	80	_____
Design and Structure......................	50	_____
Style and Readability.....................	20	
Horizontal White Space...............	5	_____
Vertical White Space.................	5	_____
Meaningful Identifiers...............	10	_____
Documentation...........................	50	
Opening Documentation...............	15	_____
Specification(s)....................	35	_____
Total...............................	**200**	_____

Lab 15

Pointers & Run-Time Allocation

Note to the Instructor:

Today's exercise introduces pointers and run-time allocation, and is divided into two parts:

1. The first part introduces the student to the basics of using pointers
   (i.e., addresses, pointer variables, dereferencing, and so on).

2. The second part introduces the student to using pointers as a means of accessing arrays whose storage is allocated at run-time.

The exercise may be divided across two weeks, if there is insufficient time during your lab period to cover both of these parts.

Objectives.

1. Introduce pointers as a means of storing addresses
2. Introduce dynamic allocation and deallocation of memory.

Prelab Questions:

1. In C++, memory is allocated and deallocated using the _____ and _____ operators.

2. A variable capable of storing an object's address is called a _____ variable.

3. A class member function that is automatically executed at the end of an object's lifetime is called a _____ function.

4. When applied to an object as a unary, prefix operator in an expression, the & operator produces the _____ of that object.

5. When applied to a pointer variable as a unary, prefix operator in an expression, the * operator is said to _____ that pointer.

Introduction.

A variable data object can be thought of as having four components:

- The variable's *name* is the way we normally refer to it in a program.
- The variable's *address* is the memory location associated with its name.
- The variable's *type* indicates the kind of value to be stored in its memory location, which in turn determines its size, or the number of bytes needed for the variable.
- The variable's *value* is the contents of its memory location.

Now, suppose that characters are stored in 1 byte of memory and that long integers are stored in four bytes of memory. Then when the compiler processes a set of declarations:

```
char Ch;
long IntVal;
```

it sets aside (or **allocates**) memory for the variables Ch and IntVal. If the memory location set aside for Ch is 0x08, and the compiler allocates Ch and IntVal in adjacent memory locations, then we might picture memory as follows:

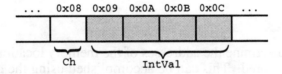

Note that the memory address associated with IntVal is 0x09, even though IntVal actually consists of locations 0x09 through 0x0C, as indicated by the shaded part of the picture. Such a picture is called a **memory map**, because it represents a mapping between a program's variable names and its memory addresses, which are given in *hexadecimal* (base 16) notation.

A variable's name can be thought of as a symbolic replacement for its address, because an access to a variable is really an access to its memory location. To illustrate, assigning a value to a variable:

```
Ch = 'A';
```

simply changes the value of the variable's memory location. If the ASCII code is in use, then we can picture the result of such an assignment as follows::

...	0x08	0x09	0x0A	0x0B	0x0C	...
	65					

As you do this exercise, keep in mind the distinction between these four parts of a variable.

Today's Exercise.

Today's exercise consists of two distinct parts, each of which examines a different facet of a new topic. This topic is a new kind of variable — a variable whose *value* is the address of some memory location. In the first part, we give a simple introduction to such variables, and introduce the operators that facilitate their use. In the second part, we investigate how these variables can be used to access arrays whose memory is allocated at run-time. Next time, we will investigate the construction of lists, consisting of nodes linked together using this idea.

The exercise is highly experimental in nature: you will be designing experiments in order to answer certain questions.

Getting Started.

Begin by creating and changing directory to `labs/lab15`. Then copy and examine the files from the `lab15` class directory. The two files `driver1.cc` and `driver2.cc` will be used in parts I and II, respectively; so to get started with part I, begin editing `driver1.cc`.

Part I — Indirect Access.

The `driver1` source program currently does very little, besides declare some integer variables `Int1`, `Int2` and `Int3`. This file will be our "experimental laboratory" for the first part of today's exercise.

A. Addresses.

Our first task today is to determine the addresses of the memory locations in which the three variables of `driver1` are stored. This can be accomplished using the **address-of** operator (`&`). More precisely, the expression:

```
& Variable
```

produces the address of the memory location in which a variable named `Variable` is stored.

An address can be displayed using a normal output statement, just as you would an integer. Modify the `driver` source program so that the addresses of `Int1`, `Int2` and `Int3` are displayed on the screen (each on a separate line) and record those addresses below:

Find the answer to this question: Is a variable's address the same each execution of a program, or does it change from one execution to another? Cite evidence for your answer.

B. Memory Mapping.

In the space below, sketch a memory map of the memory allocated to the three variables:

Using the displayed addresses (and some hexadecimal arithmetic), determine how many bytes are used to store an integer on your particular machine, showing your work.

C++ provides another operator called the `sizeof` operator, that has two common forms:

        sizeof (*Type*)
or
        sizeof *Variable*

Each form is an expression that produces a value. The first produces as its value the number of bytes allocated for an object of type *Type*, while the second produces as its value the number of bytes allocated for an object named *Variable*. Using either of these forms, verify the correctness of your answer to the last question. In the space below, show the expression used:

C. Pointer Variables.

There are situations in which it is useful to define a variable whose purpose is to store an address. Such variables, whose values are memory addresses are called **pointer** variables, because their value leads (or *points*) to another address.

One of the uses of a pointer variable is to hold the address of another variable. Because variables can be of different types, and different types are of different sizes, a pointer variable must be declared as a pointer to a type. The general declaration notation:

        Type   * *PointerName*;

declares *PointerName* as a variable capable of hold the address of a variable of type *Type* . Note that the asterisk (* — sometimes called the star) operator is the only difference between a pointer variable declaration and the declaration of a normal variable.

In the space below and in `driver1`, declare an integer pointer variable named `IntPtr`. Assign this variable the address of `Int2`, and then display the value of `IntPtr`.

Is the value of `IntPtr` the same as the address of `Int2` that you recorded in part A?

D. Dereferencing Pointer Variables.

`IntPtr` now contains the address of `Int2`. One of the reasons pointer variables are useful is that they provide an alternative means of accessing the memory location whose address is their value. That is, we just saw that the value of the expression

        IntPtr

is the value of `IntPtr` (currently the address of `Int2`). In your output statement, replace this expression with the expression:

        *IntPtr

and then retranslate and execute `driver1`. What is displayed?

When applied to a pointer variable in an expression:

        *PointerName

the * operator accesses the value at the memory location whose address is the value of `PointerName`, instead of accessing the value of `PointerName`. That is, the expression

        cout << *IntPtr

causes the occurrence of two actions:

    1. The value of `IntPtr` is accessed which is an address (currently of `Int2`); and
    2. The memory location at that address (containing the value 22) is accessed.

In this case, the purpose of the access is to retrieve the value so that it can be displayed, but other accesses to that memory location are also permitted. Enter the statement:

        *IntPtr = 44;

and then display the value of `Int1`, `Int2` and `Int3`. What change has occurred?

In your own words, explain how the assignment accomplished this:

This operation of accessing a remote memory location indirectly via a pointer variable is called **dereferencing** the pointer. Intuitively, dereferencing a pointer causes an access to the memory location it points at, instead of an access to its own memory location.

Note that although the same symbol (*) is used to both declare and dereference pointer variables, the two operations are completely distinct, and should not be confused.

E. Pointer Arithmetic.

Another unusual thing about pointers is the way that addition and subtraction work. Enter an output statement to display the values (IntPtr-1), IntPtr, and (IntPtr+1). What values appear?

What relationship can you observe between these three values?

Next, modify your output statement to display the result of dereferencing these three values (i.e., *(IntPtr-1), *IntPtr, and *(IntPtr+1).) What values appear?

Explain what happened in the space below:

When an arithmetic operation like addition, subtraction, increment or decrement is applied to the value in a pointer variable, that value changes by a multiple of sizeof(Type), where Type is the type of value to which the pointer was defined to point. That is, if IntPtr is a pointer to an integer and integers are stored in four bytes, then the expression

        IntPtr++;

adds 4 to the value of IntPtr; and the expression

        IntPtr--;

subtracts 4 from the value of IntPtr. Choose one of statements these to try in driver1, and determine which variable IntPtr points to following the execution of that statement. Give your results in the space below:

In general, the expression

        Ptr += i

can be used to make Ptr point to the address adds i × sizeof Ptr past its original address.

Introduction to Part II. Pointers, Arrays, and Run-Time Allocation.

In reality, pointers are almost never used to store the addresses of variables that have names, because it is so much simpler to access the value of the variable using its name, rather than by storing the address of the variable in a pointer and then dereferencing it. Instead, pointers are more typically used to store the addresses of *nameless variables*.

How can a variable have no name? The key is that the memory associated with a normal variable is allocated at *compile-time*, when the compiler encounters a declaration naming that variable:

```
Type VariableName;
```

However, this is not the only way to allocate memory for a variable. In particular, C++ provides an operator named new that can be used to allocate memory at run-time. More precisely, the expression

```
new Type
```

allocates a block of memory big enough to hold an object of type *Type*. The *address* of this block of memory is the value produced by the new operator. Thus, if we write

```
IntPtr = new int;
```

then (1) a new block of (sizeof int) bytes is allocated; (2) the new operator produces the address of that block of memory as its value; and (3) that address is then assigned to IntPtr. Anything that can be done with a normal int variable can now be done with this int-sized block of memory (even though it has no name), thanks to our being able to dereference IntPtr. That is, if we then write

```
*IntPtr = 44;
```

then the value 44 is assigned to that memory location. If we write

```
cout << *IntPtr;
```

then the value stored in that block of memory appears on the screen.

Such blocks of memory are sometimes called **anonymous variables**, because the compiler cannot associate a name with them since they are allocated at run-time. In the absence of a name, a pointer to such a block of memory provides us with a means of accessing its value.

However, it should be apparent that anonymous integers, characters, and so on are far less convenient to deal with than named variables of those types. As a result, new is almost never used to allocate anonymous variables of one of the fundamental types. Instead, new is used in one of two ways:

1. To allocate anonymous arrays; or
2. To allocate anonymous class objects.

The remainder of this exercise examines using new to allocate arrays. The allocation of a class object is dealt with in Lab 16.

II. Run-Time Allocated Arrays.

As we have seen in the past, arrays are most conveniently dealt with as members of a class, since the class can be used to store their length, as well as operations on the array.

Part II of this exercise involves the construction of a `RealArray` class (our final version). We have provided a driver program (`driver2.cc`) to perform some simple tests of the class, as well as a partial definition of the class and some of its operations. Take a few minutes to look over the driver program, to see what it does. Then open the header and implementation files for class `RealArray` for editing.

A. Declaring a Pointer Member.

Since we will be using `new` to allocate the storage for an anonymous array of `double` elements, and `new` produces an address as its value, our class needs a data member in which to store this address. Since this address will be the address of the first element in the array (which is a `double` value), this data member should be defined as a pointer to a `double`. In the private portion of class `RealArray`, declare a data member named `ArrayPtr` capable of storing the address of a `double`.

B. The Class Constructor.

Before we can declare `RealArray` objects, we need a class constructor. As shown in the driver program, such a constructor should allow us to write

```
RealArray RArray(N);
```

which should define `RArray` as an array capable of storing N real values. However, where the past versions of `RealArray` have had compile-time allocated array members named `theArray`, this version has a pointer `ArrayPtr` in which must be stored the address of an anonymous array whose storage is allocated at run-time. Our constructor function must accomplish this.

Using `new` to allocate an array of objects is almost as easy as using it to allocate non-arrays. The expression:

```
new Type [ Size ]
```

allocates an array of *Size* elements, each capable of holding a value of type *Type*. The `new` operator then produces the base address of this array (i.e., the address of its first element) as its value. To illustrate, suppose that `ChPtr` is a character pointer variable, and we write:

```
ChPtr = new char[8];
```

Suppose that when this statement is executed, `new` produces the value 0x21. Then we can visualize our memory map as follows:

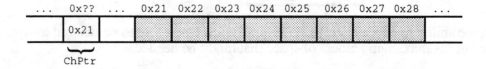

211

Complete the stub of the `RealArray` class constructor using the following algorithm:

1. Set `Length_` to *Size*.
2. If (`Length_` is greater than zero)
   a. Allocate a new array of `Length_` elements, each capable of storing a `double` value and store the address produced by `new` in `ArrayPtr`.
   b. Check that the value of `ArrayPtr` is not the NULL address (0).
   c. Set each element of the anonymous array to zero (using a for loop).
   Else
   Set `ArrayPtr` to the NULL address (0).
   End if.

To perform the subscript operation, it is helpful to understand that its general form is actually:

$$Address\ [\ Index\ ]$$

which is equivalent to

$$*(Address\ +\ Index)$$

That is, in a normal subscript operation `A[i]`, the `A` produces the base address of the array, to which index `i` is added, and the result is dereferenced. Similarly, if a pointer `APtr` contains the base address of an array, then `APtr[i]` accesses the element whose index is `i` in that array.

When you have defined this function, check that it is properly declared in class `RealArray`. Then translate and execute `driver2`, to test the correctness of your function.

It is important to understand the distinction between the object built by this constructor and the object built by previous versions of class `RealArray`. Previously, a `RealArray` declaration:

```
RealArray RArray(5);
```

would result in the construction of the following object:

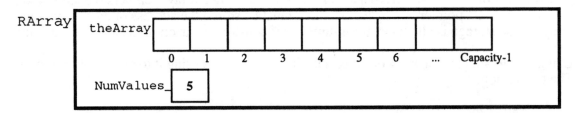

In such a declaration, `theArray` is an array of `Capacity` elements, of which only the first five are used — all the other elements are wasted space. By contrast, the same declaration in our new version of `RealArray` constructs a very different object:

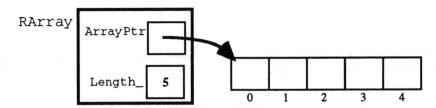

Thus, the ability to allocate arrays at run-time allows their size to be tailored to what is needed; instead of the maximum amount of space that might be needed.

Destructors and Memory Deallocation.

With the ability to allocate memory comes the responsibility to clean up after ourselves and deallocate whatever we allocate. In C++, this is done with the `delete` operation. When the object being deleted is an anonymous array, `delete` is invoked with the form:

    delete [] *PointerVariable*;

which deallocates the array whose address is stored in *PointerVariable*. The question is, how do we use `delete` if *PointerVariable* is a private data member like `ArrayPtr`?

We have seen that at the beginning of the lifetime of a C++ class object, a function called a constructor executes to initialize the object. When the lifetime of that object is over, its storage must be reclaimed. For objects of the classes we have built thus far, this storage reclamation occurs automatically, because all of their storage requirements are known at compile-time. However, the anonymous array in our new version of `RealArray` is allocated at run-time. To see why this is a problem, suppose that `RArray` is as follows:

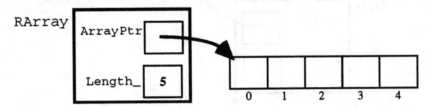

When the lifetime of `RArray` ends, its `ArrayPtr` and `Length_` members will automatically be reclaimed, since they were known at compile time; but since the anonymous array was allocated at *run-time* (i.e., after compile-time), it will not be automatically reclaimed:

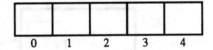

The result is a block of memory that is effectively "marooned." It is unreachable because with the reclamation of `ArrayPtr`, its base address has been lost.

To address this problem, C++ permits the designer of a class to supply a function called a **destructor** to reclaim storage allocated at run-time. Just as the compiler calls the class *constructor* when an object's lifetime *begins*, the compiler will call the *destructor* when an object's lifetime *ends*. By placing statements within the destructor to reclaim run-time allocated storage (i.e., `delete` operations), we can avoid "marooning" blocks of memory.

Just as the name of a constructor is always the name of the class, the name of a destructor function is always the name of the class preceded by the tilde (~) character. A destructor function is usually simple enough to define within the class, and so has the general form:

    ~*ClassName* () { *StatementList* }

Within class `RealArray`, define a `RealArray` destructor that uses `delete` to reclaim the anonymous array pointed to by `ArrayPtr`. (If you want to observe when the destructor is invoked, place an output statement within it, too.) Then recompile and execute your main program to verify the correctness of what you have written.

The Assignment Operator.

When one class object *Obj1* is assigned another class object *Obj2*:

```
Obj2 = Obj1;
```

the default action is for the data members of *Obj1* to be copied into *Obj2*. This works perfectly, so long as none of the data member are pointers to anonymous variables, but when this is the case, the pointer gets copied, rather than the anonymous variables. To see why this is a problem, consider what happens when *Obj1* and *Obj2* are `RealArray` objects:

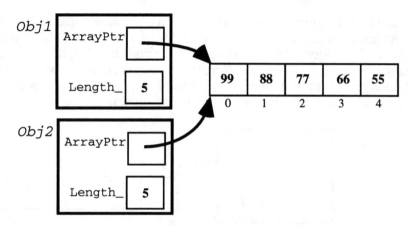

The result is that *Obj2* is not a distinct copy — any subsequent changes to the anonymous array of *Obj2* will also change the anonymous array of *Obj1*, because they are the same array, as illustrated by the assignment near the end of `driver2`. What is needed is for the assignment to produce a completely distinct object:

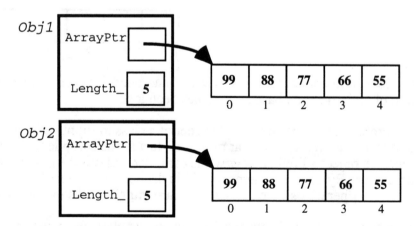

This can be accomplished by building a `RealArray` member function `operator=` that overloads the assignment operator with a definition that performs the copying correctly. This problem can be specified as follows:

Receive:	*Original*, a `RealArray` object.
	Copy, a `RealArray` object.
Return (parameters):	*Copy* as a completely distinct copy of *Original*.
Return(function):	(A reference to) *Copy*, to permit assignment chaining.

C++ requires that `operator=` be overloaded as a member function in a class, so we need not declare a parameter for the object *Copy*. A `RealArray` assignment statement:

```
RArray1 = RArray2;
```

will be treated by the compiler as

```
RArray1.operator=(RArray2);
```

and so the data members of the object on the left-hand side of the assignment can be referred to without qualification within the definition of `operator=`. Take a moment to examine the stub in the implementation file and compare it against this specification.

As we consider what actions must be taken, our function must accomplish the following:

- Make `ArrayPtr` point to a distinct copy of the anonymous array of `Original`.
- Make `Length_` a copy of the `Length_` member of `Original`.
- Return the `RealArray` containing this function.

To accomplish the first action, we must consider that `ArrayPtr` may already be pointing to an anonymous array. If its length is not the same as the length of `Original`'s array, then it must be deallocated. If the length of `Original`'s array exceeds zero, then a new array of the appropriate length must be allocated and the values from `Original`'s array copied; otherwise `ArrayPtr` should be set to the NULL address.

To accomplish the last action, we need a new piece of information: every member function has access to a predefined pointer variable named `this`, whose value is the address of the object containing the member function. That is, our function can return the object pointed to by `this`:

```
return *this;
```

This accomplishes the final action, because dereferencing `this` accesses the object it points to, which is the object we wish our function to return.

Organizing these actions gives us the following algorithm:

1. If `Length_` is not equal to `Original.Length_`:
   a. Set `Length_` to `Original.Length_`.
   b. Deallocate the array pointed to by `ArrayPtr`.
   c. If `Length_` is greater than zero:
      1) Allocate an array of `Length_` elements, store its address in `ArrayPtr`.
      2) Verify that `ArrayPtr` is not NULL.
      Else
         Set `ArrayPtr` to the NULL address.
      End if.
   End if.
2. Copy each value from `Original`'s array into the new array (using a for loop).
3. Return the object of which `operator=` is a member.

Using this algorithm, complete the stub of `operator=`. Then test what you have written using `driver2`, to verify that assignment creates a distinct `RealArray` object.

The Copy Constructor.

There are times a copy of an object is needed. Such times include when an object is passed to a function as a value parameter; and when a function produces an object as its return-value.

As with assignments, the default copying action simply copies the data members of an object. When those data members include a pointer to an anonymous variable, the resulting copy is not a distinct copy — the exact same problem we encountered with the assignment operation.

To allow the compiler to correctly copy such objects, the designer of a class can supply a special function called the **copy constructor**, whose declaration has the form:

```
ClassName (const ClassName& Original);
```

As with all constructors, the name of the function is the name of the class; the copy constructor is distinguished by a single parameter whose type is a *constant reference* to the class. The *StatementList* in its definition can take whatever actions are necessary to copy the object.

While their problems are similar, the copy constructor differs from assignment, in that it:

- builds a new object, and so no old anonymous variables exist requiring deallocation;
- returns no value, and so this need not be dereferenced.

These differences are illustrated by the different problem specification:

Precondition: A copy of a RealArray object is needed.
Receive: *Original*, the object to be copied.
Postcondition: A copy of *Original* has been constructed.

Thanks to these differences, the copy algorithm is somewhat simpler than that of assignment:

1. Set Length_ to the Length_ member of Original.
2. If Length_ is greater than zero
        a. Allocate an array of Length_ elements, store its address in ArrayPtr.
        b. Check that the value of ArrayPtr is not the NULL address (0).
        c. Copy each value from Original's array the new array (using a for loop).
    Else
        Set ArrayPtr to the NULL address (0).
    End if.

Declare a copy constructor in class RealArray whose parameter is named Original. Then define the copy constructor in the RealArray implementation file, so that its *StatementList* takes the actions specified in the preceding algorithm. To observe when this constructor is called, place a distinctive output statement in its *StatementList*. Then modify driver2 as necessary to find at least one circumstance in which the compiler needs a copy of an object.

This completes our renovation of class RealArray.

Phrases You Should Now Understand.

Address, Pointer, Pointer Dereferencing, Memory Allocation & Deallocation, Address-Of Operator, new Operator, delete Operator, Destructor, Copy Constructor.

Objective.

Practice using pointer variables and run-time memory allocation.

Projects.

15.1. A palindrome is a word that is spelled the same way forward and backward, such as *mom*, or *madam*. Write a program that given a character string, determines whether or not it is a palindrome. Have it do so using the following approach: (1) ask the user the number of letters in their word; (2) allocate an anonymous character array of that length; (3) fill the array with the input characters; (4) determine if the characters in the array comprise a palindrome, using a pointer to the first character, a pointer to the last character, and a loop that increments/decrements these pointers until the characters pointed at fail to match (indicating the string is not a palindrome) or the pointers "cross one another" (indicating the string is a palindrome).

15.2. Extend class `RealArray` with the following operations:

- A concatenate operation (either as a `Concatenate()` function or by overloading `operator&`) that, given two `RealArray` objects *R1* and *R2*, returns a `RealArray` consisting of the concatenation of *R1* and *R2*.
- A `Slice(i, j)` member function that, for valid indices `i` and `j`, returns a distinct `RealArray` of length `j-i+1` whose values are the values in indices `i` through `j`.
- A member `GrowBy(i)` that adds `i` new elements at the end of its array.
- A member `ShrinkBy(i)` that truncates the final `i` elements of its array.

Write a driver program that thoroughly tests your operations.

15.3. Proceed as in 15.2. Then update class `DataSet` so that it is derived from this latest version of class `RealArray`. In particular, `DataSet::Append()` should use `GrowBy()` to expand the capacity of the data set, and `DataSet::Delete()` should use `ShrinkBy()` to trim the size of the data set. Use this new version of `DataSet` to resolve Project 12 or 13.

15.4. An order-n polynomial is a function `f(X)` of the form:

$$f(X) = c_0 + c_1 X + c_2 X^2 + c_3 X^3 + \ldots + c_n X^n$$

where $c_0, c_1, \ldots, c_n$ are called its *coefficients*. Build a class `Polynomial`, such that

```
Polynomial  F(n);
```

constructs an order-n polynomial (using a run-time allocated array of n elements to store coefficients.) Supply the following operations: class and copy construction, input, output, retrieve the order of the polynomial, evaluate for a given x-value, access the coefficient for a given power of x, assignment, and destruction. Write a program that inputs a polynomial `P(x)`, a range of x-values `a` through `b`, and a delta-value `d`; and displays the values: `P(a)`, `P(a+d)`, `P(a+2d)`, ..., `P(b-d)`, `P(b)`.

<u>Extra credit</u>: Have the class constructor use the *ellipses mechanism* so that:

```
Polynomial G(n, c0, c1, c2, ..., cn);
```

constructs and correctly initializes `G` as an order-n polynomial with coefficients c_0 through c_n.

Project 15 Due Date _____

Turn in this grade sheet, attached to a hard copy of

a. All source code written for your project.
b. A sample execution of your program.

Name _____

Category	Points Possible	Points Received
Correctness and efficiency.	90	_____
Design and Structure.	40	_____
Style and Readability.	20	
Horizontal White Space.	5	_____
Vertical White Space.	5	_____
Meaningful Identifiers.	10	_____
Documentation.	50	
Opening Documentation.	15	_____
Specification(s).	35	_____
Total.	**200**	_____

Lab 16

Linked Objects

Note to the Instructor:

The main emphasis of this exercise is the implementation of a list consisting of a series of linked nodes. Because such nodes are defined recursively (i.e., the link's type is a pointer to a node), many of the node operations employ recursion, either direct or indirect. Accordingly, a thorough review of recursion may be useful before students begin the exercise.

While the exercise may appear to be quite lengthy, most of the space is consumed by drawings — the length of the exercise is actually somewhat shorter than most of the others.

Objectives.

1. Review the use of pointers.
2. Review the use of run-time allocation and deallocation.
3. Introduce self-referencing structures.

Prelab Questions:

1. If a pointer contains the address of a class object, then a member of that object can be accessed through the pointer using _____ notation.

2. A class *C* that is defined with a data member whose type is a pointer to a *C* is called a _____ structure.

3. In a linked list, the objects that are linked together are called _____.

4. The C++ _____ mechanism creates an alias or synonym for an existing type.

5. The action of examining each of the nodes in a linked list in performing some operation is called _____ the list.

Introduction.

We have seen that the array (allocated at either compile- or run-time) provides a means by which lists of data can be stored and processed. We have also seen that inserting or deleting values from such lists can involve extensive copying of values. For example, suppose that the following run-time allocated array contains a sorted list of values:

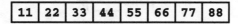

and we wish to append the value 99 to that list. Then we must
(1) allocate a new array that is 1 larger than the old array:

11	22	33	44	55	66	77	88

(2) copy the values from the old array into the new array:

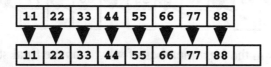

(3) insert the 99 into the last element:

11	22	33	44	55	66	77	88

11	22	33	44	55	66	77	88	99

and (4) deallocate the old array:

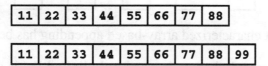

Deleting a value from such a list requires a similar sequence of steps. As a result, appending and deleting values are very time-expensive operations on an array-based list.

To reduce this expense, an alternative means of implementing lists has been devised that permits insertions and deletions without the extensive copying associated with arrays. This alternative approach is the subject of today's exercise.

Getting Started.

Create and change directory to labs/lab16. Copy and examine the files in the lab16 class directory, and begin editing the file LinkList.h.

Linked Lists.

The basic idea is to build a list of structures, each of which consists of

- a *Data* member, in which a data value is stored; and
- a *Next* member, in which the address of a structure can be stored.

These structures that contain both a value and a pointer are often called *nodes*. Given suitable declarations, we might visualize a node as follows:

A node's *Next* member makes it feasible to link nodes together into a list, by storing the address of a node containing the next list value. This ability to link values together solves our problem. To illustrate, if our original list of values is stored as follows:

then appending 99 consists of (1) allocating a new structure to hold the new value:

and (2) storing its address in the *Next* member of what was the final structure:

Note that the copying that characterized array-based appending has been eliminated!

Given the ability to construct linked nodes, a **simply linked list** is a structure that stores the address of the first node in the list, and perhaps the number of nodes (i.e., values) it contains:

This is one form of linked list, and simplicity is its primary advantage.

Another common form is the **circular linked list**, in which the list structure stores the address of the last node, and the last node's *Next* member contains the address of the first element, instead of the NULL address. This form also allows quick access to both the first and last nodes and is very space-efficient, since the list structure only has one pointer member.

A final common form is the **doubly-linked list**, in which each node has (in addition to its *Data* and *Next* members) a member *Prior* in which is stored the address of the previous node in the list. Unlike the other lists, this form allows movement within the list in both directions.

Design Issues.

Since a linked list is made up of nodes, we have two different objects to consider: `LinkedList` and `Node`. However, if we implement `Node` and `LinkedList` as two different classes, then the `LinkedList` operations will be unable to access the (private) members of struct `Node`.

The simplest way to circumvent this difficulty is to declare `Node` as a **struct** (which is exactly like a class, but its members are by default public, not private) *nested within* `LinkedList`:

```
class LinkedList
{
    struct Node
    {
        // members of struct Node...
    };
    // members of class LinkedList...
};
```

By doing so, members and friends of class `LinkedList` are able to access `Node` and its members because it is a part of class `LinkedList`. However, programs are unable to access `Node` or its members because it is declared within the class, and is thus private. This is as it should be, since a `Node` is really just a detail of our list's implementation.

Since a linked list consists of linked nodes, we will begin with struct `Node`.

The Data Members of Struct `Node`.

From the discussion above, it should be evident that struct `Node` needs two data members:

- `Data`, whose type is the type of value being stored in the list; and
- `Next`, whose type is a pointer to a `Node`.

In the context of our previous example, we can picture such an object as follows:

To define `Data`, an important question to be answered concerns the type of `Data`.

We could define `Data` to be of type `double`, as we have in the past. However, if we someday wish to store character strings in our list, then we would have to replace all occurrences of `double` with `String`, in our class definition and throughout its operations. This is clearly inconvenient, since it must be done every time we wish to store a different type of data in the list. One way to avoid this inconvenience is with the C++ `typedef` mechanism, which we describe next.

The `typedef` Mechanism.

To allow a programmer to rename existing types, C++ provides the `typedef` mechanism, whose general form is

```
typedef Type NewName ;
```

Such a statement declares *NewName* as a synonym, or alias for an existing type *Type*. For example, following the definition of struct `Node` is the line:

```
typedef Node* NodePtr;
```

This line defines the name `NodePtr` as a more readable alias for the type `Node*`, so that we can define variables of type `NodePtr` within the member functions of class `LinkedList`.

In the context of our problem with respect to the type of `Data`, if we write

```
typedef double DataType;
```

then the name `DataType` becomes an alias for the word `double` — the two can be used interchangeably. If we then define `Data` using the word `DataType` instead of `double` (and use `DataType` instead of `double` in all subsequent operations), then we will have a fully functional `Node` structure capable of storing `double` values. Moreover, if we someday wish to store character strings in our list, only 1 modification is required:

```
typedef String DataType;
```

By replacing the type `double` with the type `String`, the name `DataType` becomes an alias for `String` rather than `double`. When struct `Node` is recompiled, each use of the word `DataType` (that did refer to `double`) now refers to `String`. The type of value being stored in the list can thus be changed with a single edit, by changing the type for which `DataType` is an alias.

Defining the `Next` member of struct `Node` is straightforward (review Lab 15, if you've forgotten), so within the stub of struct `Node`, define data members: `Data`, whose type is `DataType`; and `Next`, whose type is a pointer to a `Node` (note that our alias `NodePtr` cannot be used to declare `Next`, since the definition of `Next` precedes the definition of `NodePtr`.) Then before the definition of struct `Node`, place a `typedef` statement to make the name `DataType` an alias for the type `double`.

To check the syntax of what you have written, compile the `LinkList` implementation file (which includes `LinkList.h`.) Continue when what you have written is syntactically correct.

The Data Members of Class `LinkedList`.

As described previously, our simple implementation of a linked list has two data members:

- *First*, a pointer to a `Node`, and
- *NumNodes*, an integer.

Within class `LinkedList`, define `protected:` data members for these two attributes.

The LinkedList Operations.

A linked list consists of a series of linked nodes. Because of this, some of the LinkedList operations will require us to implement Node operations. It is, however, difficult to anticipate in advance what Node operations will be needed. For this reason, we will work on LinkedList operations until the need for a particular Node operation becomes apparent, at which point we will implement the needed operation.

There are many LinkedList operations we could implement, from which we have chosen a few. The operations below were each chosen either out of necessity, or to illustrate something different about the way LinkedList operations can be implemented:

- A class constructor, so that empty LinkedList objects can be declared and initialized.
- An output operation, so that the contents of a LinkedList can be viewed.
- An Insert(v, i) operation, to insert a value v into a LinkedList at position i.
- A destructor, so that the run-time storage of LinkedList objects can be reclaimed.
- A · copy constructor, so that LinkedList objects can be copied when needed.

The LinkedList Class Constructor.

This is the simplest of our operations to build. The problem is specified as follows:

Precondition: A LinkedList object has been declared.
Postcondition: Its data members have been initialized appropriately for an empty list.

To accomplish this, our constructor must (1) set the First member to the NULL address (0); and (2) set the NumNodes member to 0.

These actions are simple enough to define the class constructor within class LinkedList. Do so in the public section of class LinkedList. Then use your driver program to test what you have written, by declaring a LinkedList object. Continue when testing is completed.

Displaying a LinkedList.

As usual, it is a good idea to build an output function early in our implementation, since the ability to display a LinkedList will prove useful in testing the subsequent operations. The specification for the problem to be solved should be familiar by now:

Receive:	*Out*, an ostream object;
	LList, a LinkedList object.
Output:	The values in *LList*, onto *Out*.
Return(parameters):	*Out*, containing the values of *LList*.
Return(function):	*Out* (to permit chaining).

Use this specification to declare operator<< as a (public) friend of class LinkedList.

To solve this problem, we must (beginning with the first node) visit every node in the list and display the value of its Data member. If we do this using a loop (as opposed to recursion), the possibility of the list being empty implies that the loop should be a pretest loop. Finally, our function must return *Out* to permit chaining of output operators.

We might combine these observations into the following algorithm:

> Set a `NodePtr` named *NPtr* to `LList.First`.
> While (*NPtr* ≠ the NULL address)
> > a. Using `Out`, display the `Data` value of the `Node` pointed to by *NPtr* .
> > b. Make *NPtr* point to the next `Node` in the list .
> End while.
> Return `Out`.

To encode this algorithm, there are a number of issues to be resolved. The first is that in order for a friend function to use a type name declared within a class, the type name must be qualified with the name of the class and the **scoping operator** (`::`). That is, `operator<<` must use the name `LinkedList::NodePtr` as the type for *NPtr*, rather than just `NodePtr`.

The second issue is how to access the data member of a class object through a pointer. If `Ptr` is a pointer to a class or structure containing a data member named *DataMem*, then we could write the expression:

```
(*Ptr).DataMem
```

which dereferences `Ptr` and then accesses `DataMem` within the dereferenced object. However, this approach is so clumsy and such accesses are needed so frequently that C++ supports the equivalent, but more readable expression:

```
Ptr->DataMem
```

Think of `->` as an arrow from a pointer variable to a data member in the object to which it points. This **arrow notation** is the standard means of accessing data members via pointers.

Finally, if *NPtr* contains the address of a node, how can we make *NPtr* point to the next node in the list? Since a node's Next member contains the address of its successor, we can write:

```
NPtr = NPtr->Next;
```

which changes the address in *NPtr* to that of the node after the one to which it was pointing.

We can combine these observations into the following while-loop version of `operator<<`:

```
LinkedList::NodePtr
   NPtr = First;

while (NPtr != 0)
{
   Out << NPtr->Data << ' ';
   NPtr = NPtr->Next;
}

return Out;
```

Define `operator<<` in the `LinkList` implementation file. Then test the syntax and correctness of your definition by using your driver program to display an empty linked list.

Inserting a Value into a `LinkedList`.

In designing an insertion operation, one issue that must be resolved is where the operation allows a value to be inserted. Some of the possibilities are (1) to always insert at the list's beginning; (2) always insert at its end; or (3) allow the caller to specify the insertion point.

The last choice is the most general, but requires that we provide some means of indicating the insertion point. One way to do so is to number each value in the list with an *index*, as is done with arrays. We will adopt the C++ array convention of numbering the first value in the list with the index 0, the second value in the list with the index 1, and so on.

Assuming this convention, we can specify our problem as follows:

> Receive: A `LinkedList` object of *N* nodes;
> *DataVal*, a `DataType` value;
> *Index*, an integer (default value, 0).
> Return: A `LinkedList` object of *N+1* nodes, such that:
> the values of nodes 0 through *Index-1* are the same as those received,
> the value of node *Index* is *DataVal*, and
> the values of nodes *Index+1* through *N+1* are those that were *Index* through *N*.

In the public section of class `LinkedList`, use this specification to declare `Insert()` as a member function of class `LinkedList` (and thus eliminate the `LinkedList` parameter.)

A Digression: The `Node` Constructor.

In order to insert a value, it must first be housed within a `Node`, and so `Insert()` must allocate a `Node` to house *DataVal* (using the `new` operation.) It would be convenient if we could write:

```
NodePtr NPtr = new Node(DataVal);
```

and have the `Node` constructor initialize the `Data` member of the `Node` to `DataVal` and the `Next` member to the NULL address. For example, if `DataVal` were 11, then this statement should result in the following scenario:

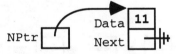

Accomplishing this requires that we go back to struct `Node` and write a constructor to solve the following problem:

> Precondition: A `Node` has been declared.
> Receive: *DataValue*, a `DataType` value;
> *NextValue*, the address of a `Node` (default NULL).
> Postcondition: The `Data` member has been set to *DataValue*,
> and the `Next` member set to *NextValue*.

Since this can be accomplished with two assignments, this function is simple enough to define within struct `Node`. Build a public function definition within struct `Node` that behaves as specified. Then check the syntax of what you have written, by using it to allocate a new `Node` in the `LinkedList::Insert()` operation, as described previously.

Back To Insertion.

Now that we can construct a new Node in which *DataVal* is stored, we are ready to actually insert the new node into the appropriate place within the linked list. It is usually helpful to draw a picture to determine what must be done. If we think about our problem, we can identify three distinct cases, each of which requires a different set of actions.

<u>Case 1</u>: *DataVal* is to be inserted at the beginning of the list (i.e., *Index* = 0).

The situation is as follows:

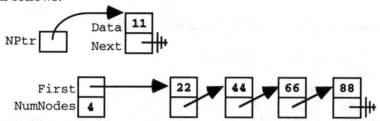

and we wish to change the situation as follows:

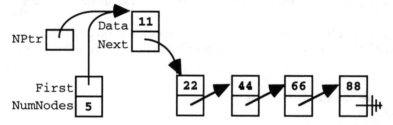

To do so, we (1) set NPtr->Next to First; (2) set First to NPtr; and (3) update NumNodes.

<u>Case 2</u>: *DataVal* is to be inserted at the end of the list (i.e., *Index* ≥ NumNodes).

The situation is as follows:

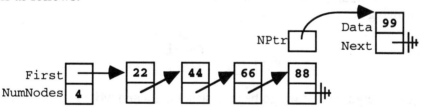

and we want to change the situation as follows:

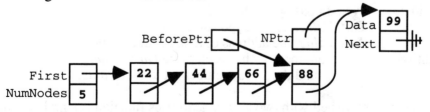

To do so, we (1) traverse the list, to position a new NodePtr named BeforePtr to point at the last node in the list; and (2) set BeforePtr->Next to NPtr; and (3) update NumNodes

<u>Case 3</u>: *DataVal* is to be inserted somewhere within the list.

The situation is as follows:

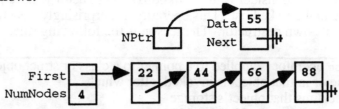

and we want to change the situation as follows:

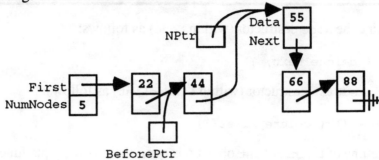

To accomplish this, we (1) loop through the list's nodes, until we have positioned `BeforePtr` to the node at position `Index-1`; (2) set `NPtr->Next` to `BeforePtr->Next`; (3) set `Before->Next` to `NPtr`; and (4) update `NumNodes`.

We can organize these three cases into the following algorithm:

1. Construct a new `Node` whose `Data` value is `DataVal` and whose `Next` value is `NextVal`, storing its address in a `NodePtr` named `NPtr`;
2. Declare another `NodePtr` object: `BeforePtr`;
3. If `Index` is zero,
   a. Set `NPtr->Next` to `First`.
   b. Set `First` to `NPtr`.
   Else if `Index` is greater than or equal to `NumNodes`,
   a. Traverse the list using `BeforePtr`, until it contains the address of the last node.
   b. Set `BeforePtr->Next` to `NPtr`.
   Else
   a. Set `BeforePtr` to `First`, `AfterPtr` to `First->Next`.
   b. For each integer `i` in the range 1 though `Index-1`:
         aSet `BeforePtr` to `BeforePtr->Next`.
      End for.
   c. Set `NPtr->Next` to `BeforePtr->Next`.
   d. Set `BeforePtr->Next` to `NPtr`.
   End if.
4. Increment `NumNodes`.

Using this algorithm, define `Insert()` as a member of class `LinkedList`. Then test its correctness by using your driver program to repeatedly insert a value and display the list following each insertion. Continue when `Insert()` has been thoroughly tested.

The **LinkedList** Destructor.

The next operation we will consider is the LinkedList destructor, whose purpose is to deallocate each node in the linked list. This operation is surprisingly easy to implement, if struct Node provides its own destructor. The reason is the following rule:

When the delete operator is applied to a pointer to a class or struct object:
   1. the destructor in that object is invoked, after which
   2. delete reclaims that object's storage
unless the pointer contains the NULL address,
   in which case delete does nothing.

That is, if we define the Node destructor (within Node) as follows:

```
~Node() { delete Next; }
```

and define our LinkedList destructor (within LinkedList) as follows:

```
~LinkedList() { delete First; }
```

then when the lifetime of a LinkedList object L is over, these two simple functions will reclaim all of the storage of L. To see how, suppose that L is the following list of N+1 nodes:

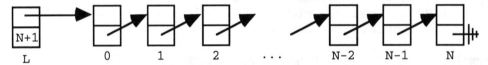

When the lifetime of L is over, ~LinkedList() is invoked, which executes

```
delete First;
```

According to the preceding rule, this invokes ~Node() in node 0 (we will use shading to indicate the particular node whose destructor is executing):

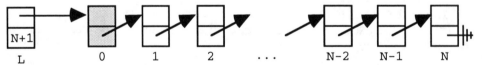

This destructor immediately executes

```
delete Next;
```

which, according to the preceding rule, invokes ~Node() in node 1:

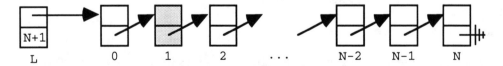

That destructor immediately executes

```
delete Next;
```

According to the preceding rule, this invokes ~Node() in node 2:

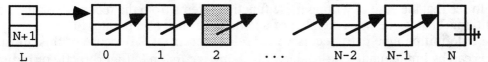

This *indirect recursion* continues until ~Node() is invoked in node N:

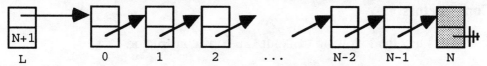

which executes

```
delete Next;
```

Since the value of the Next member of this node is the NULL address, this invocation of delete does nothing (see the preceding rule), which halts the indirect recursion.

The recursion then begins to "unwind." Control returns to the delete call in the destructor of node N-1 which reclaims the storage of node N:

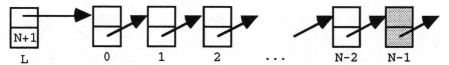

That ends the execution of the destructor in the last node, and so control returns to the delete call in the destructor of its predecessor, which reclaims the storage of the next-to-last node:

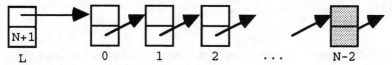

This pattern continues until the ~Node() delete call in node 0 reclaims the storage of node 1:

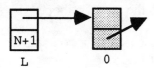

Control then returns to delete in ~LinkedList(), which reclaims the storage of node 0:

That ends the execution of the LinkedList destructor, and so the compile-time allocated storage of L is then reclaimed in the same way as that of any automatic object.

In classes Node and LinkedList, define these destructors, and then use the compiler to check the syntax of what you have written.

Self-Reference and Recursion.

It is important to see that the ease of writing these functions stems from the recursive nature of the Node definition. That is, the Next member of a Node is defined as a pointer to a Node, making a Node's definition inherently recursive (or **self-referential**). Because of this, most Node operations can be implemented quite elegantly using recursion (either directly or indirectly).

The Copy Constructors.

Take a few minutes to study the following LinkedList copy constructor:

```
LinkedList::LinkedList(const LinkedList& OrigList)
{
   if (OrigList.First == 0)
      First = 0;
   else
      First = new Node(*OrigList.First);
}
```

This version of the LinkedList copy constructor is so simple because most of the work is done by a recursive Node copy constructor, defined as follows:

```
LinkedList::Node::Node(const Node& OrigNode)
{
   Data = OrigNode.Data;

   if (OrigNode.Next == 0)
      Next = 0;
   else
      Next = new Node(*OrigNode.Next);
}
```

This two-pronged approach in which an operation consists of a non-recursive LinkedList function that invokes a recursive Node function becomes quite intuitive with some practice. As mentioned above, virtually all of the LinkedList operations that involve traversing the list can be implemented in this manner (they can also be implemented through the use of a loop.)

Note that since Node is a type declared within class LinkedList, its use as a struct outside of the class must be qualified with LinkedList and the scoping operator.

Implement these copy constructors for classes Node and LinkedList. Then test their correctness by (1) implementing a simple function that displays a LinkedList it receives via a value parameter; and (2) passing this function a LinkedList argument containing four values. Building the parameter will use the copy constructor, allowing its correctness to be checked.

These examples were chosen to provide an introduction to the implementation of LinkedList operations. The exercises will provide you with the chance to practice on your own.

Phrases You Should Now Understand.

Linked List, Node, Link, Arrow Notation, Self-Referential Structure, List Traversal, Scope Operator, typedef.

Objectives.

1. Practice using pointers and run-time memory management.
2. Practice building operations on linked lists.
3. Use linked lists in problem solving.

Introduction.

Part 1 of this week's project consists of a two-person group project. Each person should take responsibility for one of the two groups of operations below:

Group A:
- Linked list assignment (by overloading `operator=`.)
- Determine whether or not a linked list contains a given value using linear search.
- Access the value at a given index (by overloading `operator[]`) for const linked lists.

Group B:
- Delete a specified value from a linked list.
- Input a list of values (terminated by a newline) into a linked list, from keyboard or file.
- Access the value at a given index (by overloading `operator[]`) for non-const linked lists.

Your instructor may then give you one of the following projects to complete using your class:

Projects.

16.1. Using inheritance, build a class `DeckOfCards` as a linked list of 52 `Card` objects. Supply operations to construct a new deck, shuffle the deck (using random number generation), draw a card, deal a hand of a given number of cards, and so on. Then write a program to play a simple card game, such as *Go Fish*, or *Crazy Eights*.

16.2. Class `DataSet` (see Project 13) had several drawbacks, including: (1) it wasted memory for small data sets; and (2) it was too small to hold large data sets. Re-implement class `DataSet` by deriving it from class `LinkedList`. Verify its correctness by using it to resolve your problem from Project 13.

16.3. A stack is a special list in which values are always inserted and deleted from the same end, resulting in a Last-In-First-Out (LIFO) retrieval pattern. A queue is a different list in which values are always inserted at one end and deleted at the other end, resulting in a First-In-First-Out (FIFO) retrieval pattern. Using inheritance, derive efficient `Stack` and `Queue` classes from class `LinkedList` (Hint: Add a `NodePtr` data member named `Last` to class `Queue`.) Then write a program that uses a stack and a queue to detect palindromes (see Project 15.1) by adding each character from a line of input to both a stack and a queue; and then removing characters from the stack and queue until a mismatch is detected (indicating the input was not a palindrome) or the structures are empty (indicating the input was a palindrome.)

16.4. Build a line-oriented text-editor that can be used to edit files. Represent the file as a linked list of lines, where each line is represented as a linked list of characters. Your editor should display 15 lines of the file at a time, and provide its user with a menu of operations including read from a file, write to a file, scroll down a line, scroll up a line, insert text, delete text, replace text.

Project 16 Due Date _____

Turn in this grade sheet, attached to a hard copy of

a. your program,
b. the header file for your unified class library,
c. the implementation file for your unified class library, and
d. an execution of your program illustrating its correctness.

(Functions written by one group member will only affect the grade of that group member)

Name _____

Functions for which I was responsible: _____

Category	Points Possible	Points Received
Correctness and efficiency	150	_____
Design and Structure	80	_____
Style and Readability	20	
Horizontal White Space	5	_____
Vertical White Space	5	_____
Meaningful Identifiers	10	_____
Documentation	50	
Opening Documentation	15	_____
Specification(s)	35	_____
Total	**300**	_____

Lab 17

Templates

Note to the Instructor:

This week's exercise deals with templates, the C++ mechanism for implementing polymorphic container classes. Templates allow classes (and functions) to be parameterized, so that the type of data being stored (or operated upon) is received via a parameter.

The primary point that should be emphasized to students is that the template provides a means of writing code that is more easily reused, since one template definition can be used to create multiple instances of the class, each storing a different type of data.

The exercise also introduces the stack as a LIFO structure, using this (relatively) simple structure to provide students with their first introduction to templates.

Objectives.

1. Introduce the implementation of polymorphic containers.
2. Introduce the C++ template mechanism.
3. Introduce stacks as special-purpose containers.

Prelab Questions:

1. A stack is a _____ container.

2. A queue is a _____ container.

3. A container that can have many different forms from a single definition is called a _____ container.

4. A class template differs from normal container classes because the type of data being stored in it must be _____ .

5. The construction of a class object from a template class is called an _____ of the template.

Introduction.

The past few exercises have developed *containers* of various kinds, including array-based lists and linked lists. In Lab 16, we saw that the C++ typedef mechanism provides one means of building a container that is largely independent of the type of value stored within that container. To review, the declaration

    typedef double DataType;

declares the name DataType as a synonym for type double, whereas the declaration

    typedef String DataType;

declares the name DataType as a synonym for type String. By defining the data-storing member of a container class to be of type DataType (instead of using double or String explicitly), the type of value that can be stored in the container can be changed, simply by modifying the typedef statement. A single modification is thus all that is required for the same class definition to be used to provide a container for double values in one program and a container for String (or any other type) values in another program.

While typedef makes it much easier to modify a container class in order to store a different type of value, it is a far from perfect mechanism. To see why, suppose that the same program needs two containers, one for double and the other for String values. In such a situation, the typedef mechanism is of no avail, because *it does not allow us to define two differently-typed instances of the same container at the same time*. That is, DataType cannot be both double and String at the same time, and since a LinkedList is a container for DataType values, it can be one or the other but not both.

Beyond this problem, typedef is somewhat inelegant as a mechanism for creating type-independent container classes. Its requirement that we edit the header file every time we wish to change the type of data stored in the container is a further inconvenience, since any program using the class must then be recompiled.

What is needed is a means of creating a container class that is truly type-independent. One way that this can be accomplished is to define a container class that receives the type of its data via a *parameter*. As an analogy, the function:

    void Swap(int& A, int& B)
    {
        int T = A; A = B; B = T;
    }

can be used to exchange the values of any two integers, because it receives the *variables* to be exchanged via parameters, upon which it operates. What we need is for a class to be able to receive a *type* via a parameter, which it can then use to define its data members. In general, such containers are called *polymorphic containers*, since they can take many different forms. C++ provides polymorphic containers through its **class template** mechanism.

Stacks as Containers.

A stack is essentially a list in which values are always inserted and removed from the same end of the list, which is called the *top* of the stack. Inserting and removing from the same end of the list guarantees that when a value is removed, the removed value will be the value that was inserted most recently. To illustrate, suppose that the characters A, B, and C are inserted onto a stack one at a time. The stack changes as follows:

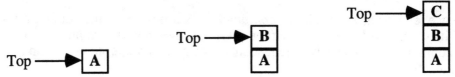

If those characters are subsequently retrieved from the stack:

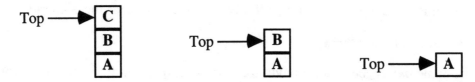

the C is retrieved first, then the B, and finally the A — the order in which the values are extracted is the reverse of the order in which they were inserted! For this reason, a stack is described as Last-In-First-Out (or LIFO) container, since the last (or most recently added) value on the stack is be the first value removed.

Since stacks "grow" and "shrink" as values are inserted into them, a memory-efficient way to implement them is as a list of linked nodes, similar to our linked list implementation in Lab 16. Unlike linked lists, the number of standard stack operations is restricted to four:

- `Push(v)`, which inserts a value *v* at the top of the stack;
- `Pop(v)`, which removes and returns the value *v* from the top of the stack;
- `Empty()`, a function that returns True if and only if there are no values in the stack; and
- `Full()`, a function that returns True if and only if no values can be added to the stack.

In addition to these standard operations, the implementation of a C++ `Stack` class whose memory is allocated at run-time needs three additional operations:

- A class constructor so that `Stack` objects can be declared and initialized;
- A copy constructor so that temporary `Stack` objects can be constructed as needed; and
- A destructor to deallocate a `Stack`'s memory at the end of its lifetime.

Today's exercise is the implementation of a stack class template. By implementing our stack as a container that receives its value's types via a parameter, a programmer can write

```
Stack<int>     IntStack;     // stack of integers
Stack<char>    CharStack;    // stack of characters
Stack<double>  DoubleStack;  // stack of reals
```

and thus simultaneously define stacks of integers, characters, and reals from the same class. Such definitions, in which an object is created from a template is called an **instantiation** (the creation of an *instance*) of the template.

Getting Started.

Create and change directory to `labs/lab17` and copy the files from the `lab17` class directory. We will be implementing a *stack* container class today, so begin editing `Stack.h`.

We have provided a skeleton for class `Stack`, complete with a `Node` structure nested within it.

```
class Stack
{
    struct Node
    {
        DataType Data;
        Node *Next;
        // ... other Node members ...
    };
    // ... other Stack members ...
};
```

Note that the structure of a stack will be similar to the structure of class `LinkedList` in Lab 16. That is, a stack will consist of a series of nodes, each containing a `DataType` member to store a data value and a `Node*` member to store a link to the next node in the stack. However, unlike class `LinkedList`, we will not use `typedef` to declare the name `DataType` as a synonym type. Instead, we will make `DataType` the name of a *parameter*, via which class `Stack` will receive the type of the `Data` member.

A container class named *SomeClass* can be given a type parameter as follows:

```
template <class ParameterName>
class SomeClass
{
    // ... members of SomeClass ...
};
```

The `template` tells the C++ compiler that what follows is a *pattern* for a class, as opposed to an actual class. The `class` in `<class ParameterName>` declares *ParameterName* as a type parameter, as opposed to a normal (data) parameter.

Thus, by prefacing our `Stack` definition with

```
template <class DataType>
```

our class becomes a *parameterized class* — a class to which a type argument must be passed when a class object is constructed. For example, in the `reverse` source file, we see:

```
Stack<char> CharStack;
```

This statement defines the object `CharStack` as a stack of characters by passing the argument `char` to the `Stack` template. `CharStack` is thus an *instantiation* of `Stack` in which the parameter `DataType` has the value `char`.

In `Stack.h`, make `Stack` a parameterized class having a type parameter named `DataType`. When you have done so, continue to the next page where we begin the implementation of `Stack` operations.

The `stack` Class Constructor.

Given the definition of a `Stack` object:

```
Stack<char> CharStack;
```

the role of the `Stack` constructor is to initialize that object's data members appropriately as an empty stack. We can specify this operation as follows:

Precondition: A `Stack` object has been instantiated.
Postcondition: The `Stack` object's members have been initialized as an empty stack.

Accomplishing this is quite easy, by setting the `Stack` object's `Top` member to the NULL address. The resulting operation is simple enough to encode within class `Stack`. Take a few moments to encode the `Stack` class constructor within the public section of class `Stack`. Then test what you have written by compiling the `reverse` source program, continuing when it is free of syntax errors.

The `stack` Destructor.

As with any other object that uses run-time allocation (e.g., a `LinkedList`), the task of the `Stack` destructor can be specified as follows:

Precondition: The lifetime of a `Stack` object is over.
Postcondition: The run-time allocated storage of that `Stack` object has been reclaimed.

That is, the node pointed to by `Top` must be deallocated, as well as the node pointed to by `Top->Next`, the node pointed to by `Top->Next->Next`, and so on.

To solve this problem, we could use a loop to traverse the stack from `Top` downwards, using `delete` to deallocate each of its nodes in turn. However, if you examine the `Node` structure nested within class `Stack`, you will note that we have provided a `Node` destructor:

```
~Node() { delete Next; }
```

As we saw in Lab 16, this function uses indirect recursion to deallocate the node pointed to by `Next`, as well as each of the nodes following that node. This greatly simplifies our `Stack` destructor, since it can simply execute the statement:

```
delete Top;
```

Doing so invokes `~Node()` in the `Node` pointed to by `Top`, which recursively deallocates all of the nodes that follow it. When `~Node()` terminates, control will return to the `delete` call in `~Stack()` which deallocates the storage of the `Node` pointed to by `Top`.

This operation is simple enough to encode within class `Stack`. Take a few moments to do so. If you want to check its execution, add an output statement to `~Stack()` and then compile and execute the `reverse` source program. Continue when what you have written has been tested.

The `Stack` Copy Constructor.

The task of the `Stack` copy constructor can be specified as follows:

> Precondition: A copy of a `Stack` object is needed.
> Receive: *OrigStack*, the `Stack` of which a copy is needed.
> Postcondition: A copy of *OrigStack* has been made.

As we saw in Lab 16, there are two cases to be considered: (1) If *OrigStack* is empty, then our function can simply set `Top` to the NULL address and the resulting `Stack` will be a perfect copy of *OrigStack*; and (2) If *OrigStack* is empty, then our function can simply pass the top node of *OrigStack* to a recursive `Node` copy constructor that copies that node and all of those beneath it. If we set `Top` to the address of that copy, then the resulting `Stack` will be a perfect copy of *OrigStack*.

This logic can be encoded as follows:

```
if (Orig.Top == 0)
   Top = 0;
else
   Top = new Node(*OrigStack.Top);
```

While this isn't too complicated a function, let's define it outside of class `Stack` to illustrate the definition of a template's member functions. The first thing to keep in mind is

> Member functions of a template class that are defined outside of their class should be *defined in the class header file*, not in a separately-compiled implementation file.

A second complication is that an externally-defined template class operation (member or friend) must be encoded as a **template function**, meaning that it must also be parameterized:

```
template<class DataType>
FunctionDefinition
```

The final complication can be summarized with the following rule:

> If the name of a template class is used *as a type* outside of the class,
>   then its name must be parameterized with the names of its parameter(s).

That is, our copy-constructor's definition must take the following form:

```
template<class DataType>
Stack<DataType>::Stack(const Stack<DataType>& OrigStack)
{
   StatementList
}
```

As described above, each use of `Stack` as a type must be parameterized. Note that the name of the constructor function is not a use of the class name as a type, and is thus not parameterized.

Define this `Stack` copy constructor in `Stack.h`, as described above. Then compile the reverse source program to check the syntax of what you have written, continuing when it is correct.

The `Empty()` and `Full()` Operations.

The `Empty()` and `Full()` stack operations enable a user of a program to check the status of the stack. More precisely, if a stack is empty, then the stack should not be popped; and if a stack is full, then values should not be pushed onto the stack. The `Empty()` and `Full()` operations are thus boolean functions that indicate the status of the stack.

The `Empty()` Operation.

We can specify the behavior of the `Empty()` operation as follows:

> Receive: A `Stack`.
> Return: True, if there are no values in the `Stack`; False, otherwise.

It is natural to implement this operation as a member of class `Stack`, since that allows us to avoid having to declare a `Stack` parameter. However, since its behavior does not require the modification of any `Stack` members, `Empty()` should be defined as a constant function.

Recall that our class constructor initializes a `Stack` as empty by setting its `Top` member to the NULL address. We can thus compare `Top` and the NULL address — if they are equal, then the `Stack` is empty; otherwise the `Stack` is not empty.

The resulting function is simple enough to define within class `Stack`. Take a few moments to do so, and then test the syntax of what you have written. Continue when it is correct.

The `Full()` Operation.

We can specify the behavior of the `Full()` operation as follows:

> Receive: A `Stack`.
> Return: True, if the `Stack` has been filled; False, otherwise.

As with `Empty()`, it is natural to implement `Full()` as a member of class `Stack`, since that allows us to avoid having to declare a `Stack` parameter, and `Full()` should be defined as a constant function, since its behavior does not modify any of the `Stack` members.

`Full()` differs from `Empty()` in that while a linked stack can easily be empty, a linked stack can only be full if the free store of available memory has been exhausted. The `new` operation can be thought of as a request for more memory. If the free store contains insufficient memory to fulfill that request, `new` returns the NULL address. `Full()` can thus behave as follows:

1. Using `new`, try to allocate a new `Node` storing its address in a `NodePtr` named *NPtr*;
2. If *NPtr* is equal to the NULL address,
> > return True;
> Else
> > a. Using `delete`, deallocate the `Node` pointed to by *NPtr*;
> > b. return False.

The resulting function is complicated enough to be define outside of class `Stack`. Take a few moments to do so, and continue when the syntax of your function is correct.

The `Push()` Operation.

The `Push()` operation is the means by which values are inserted into a `Stack`. Note that since `Stack` values are stored in `Node` objects, this implies that `Push()` must allocate a new `Node` to hold the value being pushed. We can thus specify the behavior of `Push()` as follows:

> Receive: A `Stack` object and a `DataType` value named *DataVal*.
> Return: The `Stack` object with a new top `Node` containing *DataVal*.

As usual, it is natural to implement this operation as a member of class `Stack`, and thus avoid the need for a parameter to hold the `Stack` being received.

We can implement `Push()` using the following logic:

> 1. Using `new`, allocate a new `Node`, such that
>   a. its `Data` member is *DataVal*, and
>   b. its `Next` member is the address of the top `Node` on the `Stack`,
>   storing its address in a `NodePtr` named *NPtr*.
> 2. Verify that *NPtr* does not contain the NULL address.
> 3. Set `Top` to *NPtr*.

That is, suppose we have an empty stack of characters:

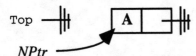

onto which we want to push the character **A**. We (1) allocate a new `Node` whose `Data` member is **A** and whose `Next` member is `Top`:

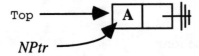

Note that by setting the `Next` member of the new `Node` to the address in `Top`, it gets set to the NULL address, which is appropriate for the "bottom" `Node` in a `Stack`.

We then continue and (2) verify that *NPtr* is non-NULL; and (3) set `Top` to *NPtr*:

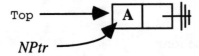

If we then want to push the character **B** onto the stack, we (1) (1) allocate a new `Node` whose `Data` member is **B** and whose `Next` member is `Top` (a pointer to the `Node` containing **A**):

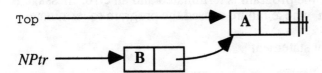

Note that by setting the `Next` member of the new `Node` to the address in `Top`, it is set to the `Node` containing **A** — the "old top" `Node`, rather than the NULL address.

We then continue and (2) verify that *NPtr* is non-NULL; and (3) set Top to *NPtr*:

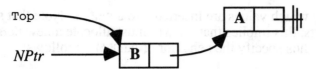

If we then want to push the character **C** onto the stack, we (1) (1) allocate a new Node whose Data member is **C** and whose Next member is Top (a pointer to the Node containing **B**):

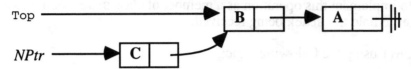

Note that by setting the Next member of the new Node to the address in Top, it is again set to the Node containing **B** — the "old top" Node, rather than the NULL address.

We then continue and (2) verify that *NPtr* is non-NULL; and (3) set Top to *NPtr*:

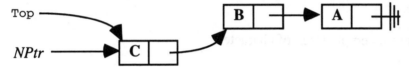

This pattern continues with each new value being stored in a Node pointed to by Top, and the Next member of that Node being used to store the address of the Node "under" it on the Stack.

How do we encode these steps?

1. Thanks to the second Node constructor, step (1) is easy:

```
NodePtr NPtr = new Node(DataVal, Top);
```

When executed, this statement constructs a new Node whose Data value is DataVal, and whose Next member is Top, and stores the address of the new Node in NPtr.

2. To verify that NPtr is non-NULL, we can use the convenient C++ assert() operation:

```
assert(NPtr != 0);
```

Provided in <assert.h>, the assert() operation has the form:

```
assert( Condition );
```

When executed, *Condition* is tested. If it is True, then execution proceeds as normal. However should *Condition* be False, the program is terminated and an error message is displayed that indicates the *Condition* whose failure caused the program to terminate.

3. The last step is a simple assignment statement.

These three steps are simple enough to define the function within class Stack. Do so, and continue when you have tested the correctness of what you have written.

The Pop() Operation.

Just as Push() is used to insert a value into the top position on a stack, Pop() is used to remove the top value from a stack. We can specify its behavior as follows:

Receive: A Stack; and a (reference to a) DataType variable *DataVal*;
Return: The Stack minus its top Node; and *DataVal* containing the (former) top value.

As usual, it is natural to define Pop() as a member of class Stack, to avoid having to declare a Stack parameter.

In considering what might go wrong, the stack being popped could be empty, and so we should check that Top does not contain the NULL address, before doing anything else. If the stack is not empty, then we can set *DataVal* to the Data member of the Top node; and then update Top and reclaim the storage of what was the top node.

However these last two actions are a problem: To see why, return to our previous Stack:

If we first update Top:

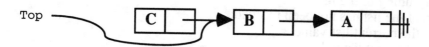

then we are unable to reclaim the storage of the node containing **C** because we no longer have its address anywhere. Moreover, if we first reclaim the storage of the node containing **C**, then we lose its Next member which is our only means of accessing the nodes "beneath" it. What is needed is a separate NodePtr in which the address of the top node can be stored while Top is updated. Once that is done, we can then reclaim its storage.

We can organize these observations into the following algorithm:

1. Using assert(), check that Top is not NULL.
2. Set *DataVal* to the Data member of the top node.
3. Store the address of the top node in a NodePtr named *NPtr*.
4. Set Top to the Next member of the top node.
5. Use delete to reclaim the storage of the node whose address is in *NPtr*.

Note that step (4) serves a dual purpose. When a stack containing one value is being popped, step (4) will reset Top to the NULL address, which is appropriate for an empty stack. When the stack being popped contains multiple values, step (4) will reset Top to the address of the new top node, again as appropriate for a non-empty stack.

The combination of these steps is sufficiently complicated to define Pop() outside of class Stack. Do so and then use the compiler to check the syntax of what you have written.

At this point, all of the Stack operations needed by reverse have been completed. Use reverse to check the correctness of your class, continuing when it has been thoroughly tested.

Output.

Our final `Stack` operation will·be an output operation. While displaying a stack is not a standard stack operation, it is useful for debugging purposes, and will serve to illustrate the implementation of functions that are *friends* of a template class.

The output operation can be specified as follows:

> Receive: *Out*, an `ostream`; and *theStack*, a `Stack`.
> Output: The values in *theStack* onto *Out*.
> Return (parameters): *Out* containing the output values.
> Return(function): *Out*, for chaining.

In class `Stack`, declare `operator<<` as a friend function. Note that when declaring parameter *theStack*, its type is a use of the name `Stack` as a type, and so must be parameterized:

```
friend ostream& operator<<(ostream& Out, const Stack<DataType>& aStack);
```

We could define this operation by a `Node` version of `operator<<` that displays the value in a node and then recursively displays the values of the nodes beneath it. For variety, let's instead use a loop to traverse the stack, displaying each value from top to bottom. This can be done using a loop that uses the standard list-traversal pattern:

1. Start at the beginning of the list.
2. While the end of the list has not been reached:
   a. Process the current list value.
   b. Move to the next list value.
   End while.

Since the `Stack` could be initially empty, a pretest loop should be used. We can organize all of these observations into the following algorithm:

1. Set *NPtr* to the address of the top node;
2. While *NPtr* is not the NULL address:
   a. Using *Out*, display the value in the node pointed to by *NPtr*.
   b. Set *NPtr* to the address of the node beneath the one to which it currently points.
   End while.
3. Return *Out*

This operation is complicated enough to warrant defining `operator<<` outside of class `Stack`. To do so, recall that an externally-defined template class operation (member or friend) must be encoded as a **template function**, meaning that the function must also be parameterized:

```
template<class DataType>
ostream& operator<<(ostream& Out, const Stack<DataType>& aStack)
{
    // ...
}
```

Enter and complete this stub in `Stack.h`. Then use `reverse` to test its correctness by using `operator<<` to display `CharStack` following each call to `Push()` and `Pop()`.

This completes our implementation of class `Stack` and our introduction to templates.

Objectives.

1. Practice the design of polymorphic containers.
2. Practice building template classes.

Introduction.

Many of the container classes we have implemented thus far are more useful if implemented as polymorphic containers (i.e., class templates). The following exercises provide practice in the construction of such containers.

Projects.

17.1. Rewrite class `RealArray` from Lab 15 as a template class named `Array`. Then redo project 15, replacing `RealArray` with this polymorphic container.

17.2. Just as a stack is a LIFO (Last-In-First-Out) container, a queue is a FIFO (First-In-First-Out) container. Build a `Queue` class template from start to finish, as a sequence of linked nodes. Your class should have two data members: *First* and *Last*, each pointers to nodes, storing the addresses of the first and last nodes in the sequence, respectively. Provide the following `Queue` operations: `Queue()` that constructs an empty queue, `Queue(const Queue&)` that constructs a copy of a queue, `~Queue()` that reclaims the storage of a queue, `operator<<` that displays the values in a queue, `Empty()` that returns True if and only if a queue is empty, `Full()` that returns True if and only if memory is exhausted, `Insert(const DataType&)` that places a `DataType` value at the last position in the queue, and `Remove(DataType&)` that removes and returns the value at the first position in the queue.

Write a program that detects palindromes (see Project 15.1) by adding each character from a line of input (converting upper- to lower-case and ignoring punctuation) to both a stack and a queue; and then removing characters from the stack and queue until a mismatch is detected (the input was not a palindrome) or the structures are empty (the input was a palindrome.)

17.3. Implement the `Queue` template described in the first part of 17.2. Then build a *post-fix calculator*, that reads a postfix expression (a sequence of operands and operators) from the keyboard, pushing operands onto a numeric stack and inserting the operators into a character queue. The calculator should then repeatedly pop two operands from the stack, remove an operator from the queue, apply the operator to the two operands, and push the result back on the stack so long as the queue is non-empty. When the queue is empty, the value at the top of the stack is the evaluation of the expression. For example, to evaluate the postfix expression

    4 2 1 + -

push the 4, the 2 and the 1 onto the stack, insert the + and - into the queue; and then iterate twice to produce the value 1 by (a) replacing the 2 and the 1 with 2+1 = 3; and (b) replacing the 4 and the 3 with 4-3 = 1.

17.4. Rewrite class `LinkedList` from Lab 16 as a class template. Then derive the `Queue` class template described in 17.2 from class `LinkedList`, so that `Queue` inherits its `First` data member and the other members of class `LinkedList`. Then use this class and your `Stack` class to implement the postfix calculator described in 17.3.

Project 17 Due Date _____

Turn in this grade sheet, attached to a hard copy of

a. your source program;
b. the header file of each class (there are no implementation files); and
c. a sample execution of your program.

Name _____

Category	Points Possible	Points Received
Correctness and efficiency	100	_____
Design and Structure	80	_____
Style and Readability	20	
Horizontal White Space	5	_____
Vertical White Space	5	_____
Meaningful Identifiers	10	_____
Documentation	100	
Opening Documentation	15	_____
Specification(s)	85	_____
Total	**300**	_____

UNIX Commands Quick Reference

This page lists some frequently used UNIX commands. The symbols *DName* and *FName* stand for arbitrary directory and file names, respectively.

Desired Action:	UNIX Command:
Get information about a UNIX command	`man Command`
Create a directory	`mkdir DName`
Change (to arbitrary) directory	`cd DName`
List contents of working directory	`ls`
List contents of arbitrary directory	`ls DName`
List contents of directory in detail	`ls -l DName`
List all (hidden) files in directory	`ls -a DName`
Remove an empty directory	`rmdir DName`
Remove a non-empty directory	`rm -r DName`
Remove a file	`rm FName`
Rename a file or directory	`mv OldName NewName`
Move a file into a different directory	`mv FName DName`
Copy a file	`cp OriginalFName CopyFName`
Copy a directory and all its subdirectories	`cp -r OriginalDName CopyDName`

Clear the screen/window	`clear`
Record what appears on the screen/window	`script`

Edit a file	`emacs FName`
Translate a self-contained C++ program	`g++ SourceFName -o ExecFName`
(Separately) compile C++ program	`g++ -c SourceFName`
Link C++ object files	`g++ FName$_1$.o ... FName$_N$.o -o ExecFName`

Emacs Commands Quick Reference

This page lists some frequently used emacs commands. `C-x` means press the `Cntl` and `x` keys simultaneously, and `M-x` means press the `Meta` (or `ESC`) and `x` keys simultaneously.

─── Emacs Control ───

invoke emacs	`emacs FileName`	quit emacs	`C-x C-c`
suspend emacs	`C-z`	resume emacs	`fg` or `%emacs`
quit current command	`C-g`	undo last command	`C-x u`

─── Cursor Movement ───

next char (forward)	`C-f`	previous char (back)	`C-b`
next word	`M-f`	previous word	`M-b`
beginning of line	`C-a`	end of line	`C-e`
next line	`C-n`	previous line	`C-p`
next page	`C-v`	previous page	`M-v`
first page	`M-<`	last page	`M->`

─── Erasing Chars ───

delete right	`C-d`	delete left	`DEL`

─── Cut and Paste ───

cut line right (kill)	`C-k`	paste (yank)	`C-y`

─── Buffers & Files ───

read file into buffer	`C-x C-f`	kill buffer	`C-x k`
write buffer as new file	`C-x C-w`	save all buffers	`C-x s`
split screen (horiz.)	`C-x 2`	split screen (vert.)	`C-x 3`
combine screens	`C-x 1`	redraw screen	`C-1`
move to other buffer	`C-x o`	move to buffer	`C-x b`
view list of buffers	`C-x C-b`		

─── Search/Replace ───

global-replace string	`M-x replace string`	query-replace string	`M-x query replace`

─── Compilation ───

compile	`M-x compile`	move to next error	`C-x`

─── Debugging ───

invoke gdb	`M-x gdb`	quit gdb	`q`
set breakpoint	`C-x SPC`	print value of expr	`p Expression`
run program	`r`	continue program	`c`
next statement	`n`	step into function	`s`

─── On-line Help ───

help about *Subject*	`C-h a Subject`	describe all bindings	`C-h b`
Command binding	`C-h w Command`	*Key* binding	`C-h c Key`
run emacs on-line info	`C-h i`	run emacs tutorial	`C-h t`